REA

Eighteenth Edition

Rugg's

Recommendations

on the

Colleges

*Compiled and Edited by the College Staff of
Rugg's Recommendations*

by Frederick E. Rugg

Rugg's Recommendations • Fallbrook, California

To
Barbara, Betsie, and Sue

TABLE OF CONTENTS

SOME NOTES FROM THE AUTHOR

WHY THIS BOOK?

As a secondary school college counselor, I heard the following question from a student or parent almost daily: "Can you please give us a list of quality colleges where one can major in psychology (or engineering or business or whatever)?"

For many years I pulled out the college handbooks and came up with a list of hundreds of colleges for each category and spent too much time with the student sifting through the multitude of schools, trying to narrow down the huge list.

I thought about a way out of this dilemma for a long time. People from Harvard would find an easy solution. They might tell the parents and student not to worry about a college major—just go to a fine liberal arts college (like Harvard) and everything will fall into place. After all, it's not the major and professors that count, it's the wonderful student body that makes a great college great. Right?

Well...over the years, I had trouble convincing parents of the merits of that argument. I guess they realize that all good universities are not good in every field.

Today, there's just so much pressure on young people to line up their careers and pick their occupations in life early. Career education seems to start in kindergarten these days. I've noticed that many parents pick right up on it and give Johnny the business if he hasn't chosen his career by the sophomore year of high school or earlier. No matter what I told Johnny and his parents, they still wanted a list of "the quality colleges with a good psychology (or whatever) department."

This book lists the quality departments at quality colleges and it will make the school counselor's job easier. For example, a public school counselor can use it constantly in January when juniors (and sometimes sophomores) line up outside his/her office, asking for a list of colleges to "go with" their PSAT scores. Probably a prep school counselor, a junior and community college transfer counselor, or a librarian might even find more use of this guide for college majors. Since this book is for the aid of the counselor, it is, then, also a guide for students and their parents in the college admissions process.

WHY THESE 900 COLLEGES?

From our experience in the college admissions process, we have chosen 900 quality four-year colleges (out of over 2000 that offer bachelor degrees) to study. We began with the 272 colleges that have survived the careful screening process involved in the granting of a Phi Beta Kappa chapter. The Phi Beta Kappa schools are listed in Appendix A. These colleges received chapters for superior undergraduate performance in the liberal arts and sciences.

To this list were added almost 640 colleges—schools that our staff felt are as good (or better) as several of the Phi Beta Kappa colleges or have excellent specialized programs. We should also note that, in general, the more well-respected the college, the more departments and majors were included. Berkeley is listed under 25 departments while some others only under one. The typical school in the study was noted with 6.0 departments. A departmental page averages 118 recommended colleges.

HOW IT'S DONE

Over the years, college students have been surveyed - the number well into five figures. If you want a straight answer, the young folks seldom waiver. We also receive monthly evaluations from secondary school counselors around the country. Some colleges submit to us departments at their schools that they consider "hidden gems". They also send us departments they consider their "strongholds". Weekly, a variety of college personnel lobby for a certain program at their university. Also, almost every week we get "tipped off" on a great department at a college at workshops I present around the U.S.A. on the college admissions process. Almost every year since 1977 I've added 300 departments to my list. This year the number is over 600.

What can eliminate a department or stop its consideration? No balance. For example, too many professors from the same alma mater in a department, or too many professors in a department graduating from that very college. If the average college in America gives out 10% of it's degrees in, say, the field of Psychology, and the department in question is at a 5% level, this sets up a "red flag", too.

HOW DO YOU USE THIS BOOK?

If you know what you want to major in at college—great!—just look it up. In most cases, you will find each departmental section organized into three groups of colleges:

Group I—Most Selective Colleges

Colleges here are among the 100 most selective colleges in America. They accept very few students with high school averages below 80 (top prep schools can, of course, lower this figure significantly) and College Board scores below (recentered)1200 (SAT-1 combined) and 27 (on the American College Test).

Group II—Very Selective Colleges

Many of the students at these colleges have "B" averages (80-90), and College Board scores between 1100 and 1200 (SAT-1 total) and ACTs between 24 and 26.

Group III—Selective Colleges

Although these colleges are, in general, easier to get into than Group I and II colleges, please keep in mind that they are, in our opinion at least, among the top 850 colleges in the country. Many students at these colleges have College Board scores just under 1100 (SAT-1 total), or just under 24 on the ACTs.

Now that we have an idea of the group breakdown, a student may need help deciding from which group(s) to select his/her colleges. The guidance counselor can help here—having knowledge of colleges and a student's grade point average, class rank, board scores, etc. Most students will want to start with a group of 8 to 10 colleges from the departmental major page. This "major page" is a starting point. Schools can be added to the student's list by his/her counselor—from the counselor's own knowledge of the student, and knowledge of other colleges that might "fit" the student. Schools can be eliminated from a student's list after reviewing the college catalogs (see Appendix F—The Get Going Form), checking out undesirable features (city vs. rural setting, etc.), visiting the colleges, and other personal preferences. If the student does *not* have a major in mind, he or she should go to a typical liberal arts (e.g., English or Math) page to get started. I've also included a letter code system for the college's enrollment figure. The enrollment letter appears beside each college name with the following code:

XL = Extra Large Enrollment (over 20,000 students)
L = Large Enrollment (from 8,000 to 20,000 students)
M = Medium Enrollment (from 3,000 to 8,000 students)
R = Moderate Enrollment (from 1,000 to 3,000 students)
S = Small Enrollment (under 1,000 students)

SOME PARTING SHOTS

I don't care to go into the argument of "Picking a college because it has a great Mathematics Department" vs. "Picking a school because the school overall is great (Yeah Harvard!) and you'll probably change your major anyway." The fact of the matter is that parents, career educators, and other educators are telling 16-year-olds (and younger) to have a career and a major all mapped out and I bet will continue to do so. I'm sure high school counselors will continue to be asked to help

Suzy find a list of quality schools with "excellent majors in mathematics." Personally, I see nothing wrong with a high school senior, who loves mathematics, trying to pick a quality school where the math department at that institution is ranked by its students as one of the top majors at that school and is generally recognized as being top notch by college counselors. If Suzy changes her mind after a year or two, she's at least given it a good shot with a premier math department. And chances are excellent that if she changes her major, it was because another outstanding department at that school helped her grow and reassess her career goals. She'll probably stay with that department for her new major. No harm done.

A few other comments on this book and some random thoughts...

1. Some state universities, like Penn State, are very competitive for out-of-staters. A university such as this may be in Group II for in-staters, but, in reality, is a Group I school for "outsiders."

2. In general, a college that is competitive is that way for all majors—but there are some departments that are exceptions. For example, engineering is a tough major and must be considered "Group II" at a "Group III" school.

3. A knowledgeable observer of the college scene will note that some competitive "alternative" colleges do not appear in this work, e.g., Hampshire College (MA), St. John's (MD). The jury is not unanimous on these progressive schools, and they are not included in this book except under "Miscellaneous Majors Pages."

4. A few majors in this book, such as engineering, have *not* been broken down into subdivisions (Civil, Electrical, Mechanical, etc.). Students will have to research these majors more fully. Well, what's wrong with that? Good to have the youngsters doing some hard work and research on the college admissions process. Foreign Languages, however, is broken down.

5. Every year a few more colleges close their doors. Today, colleges are under pressure to compete and "Be Hot." We need a college guide to weed things out a bit, a consumer-oriented handbook. We hope this helps.

6. Don't overlook the *good* small liberal arts college. Too many large universities are too impersonal. But some kids love a big school. Some thrive in the anonymity of a huge lecture hall.

7. Keep in mind that weak departments at Harvard, Yale, Stanford, Princeton, etc. might be equal to or better than the strongest departments at many colleges and universities.

8. This book is an aid for counselors, parents, and kids—nothing more. It is not a guide for the colleges to compare themselves one with the other.

9. Do not be surprised if you discover that the best of the more expensive schools are actually least expensive—because they have financial aid, the part-time jobs, etc. They're able to meet a student's financial need in many cases.

10. Students should discuss with their counselors the socioeconomic factors of the colleges they are considering. Will the college of your choice have several students enrolled with your socioeconomic background?

11. When you visit a college, seek out the students who attend and ask them the following question: "When you sign up for classes, do you get 100% of your choices, or only 4 out of 10 courses, or...?" Also, does the faculty seem to be there, to like to talk to you, to meet and greet you? Or are they not to be found?

12. Most states have a "flagship" university, the leader of the system (e.g., The University of North Carolina at Chapel Hill). In this book it is listed as just "No. Carolina." The other members of the University system are listed as follows: No. Carolina (Asheville), No. Carolina (Charlotte), No. Carolina (Greensboro), No. Carolina (Wilmington).

13. Some colleges do a great job with private school youngsters, others do a fantastic job with public school youngsters. Some colleges are outstanding with both groups. A very fine college with an outstanding record with public school youngsters is Virginia's Roanoke College.

14. A tip for the high school senior: Don't ease up in your senior year. Take a tough course load with courses such as Physics. College admissions people aren't stupid. The first thing they look at when they review your high school record is the quality of your high school courses.

15. To parents and counselors: Hang tough. The pieces will finally fit.

16. If you review only one page in this book, make it the page near the front called "Fred Rugg's One Hundred Colleges...Just Darn Good Schools." This is probably the most used and Xeroxed page in the U.S.A. on the colleges.

17. Keep in mind that a starter list of colleges to consider for your daughter #1 may be a terrible list for your daughter #2.

18. I received a phone call from a community college instructor in the Mid-West. He also consults with companies recruiting college graduates, and has found my lists to be the best. He said to me on the phone, "The true test of any college guidebook or college list is, 'Does the information work?' So if the best information comes from college janitors, you go after college janitors."

19. I give an apology now to many of the top secondary prep schools in the country. Many of you may not be happy with my recent emphasis on adding departments to the Cal States, the Mass States, Connecticut States, etc. But the public school counselors and parents need these recommendations and they are over 90% of my customer base.

20. This book is not perfect. It has never claimed to be perfect. Our study is not scientific. It has never claimed to be. But it is a good place to start and represents tens of thousands of contacts. I'll repeat that. We have never claimed to be perfect. There is no expert in the field. There never will be. The field is too big. We've even moved to many parts of the country to try to put together "the big picture." We do our best.

Frederick E. Rugg

San Diego County, California
January, 2001 (18th Edition)

SOME NOTES ON THE EIGHTEENTH EDITION

The eighteenth edition contains over 1000 entry changes since the seventeenth edition. All 86 plus majors have been revised and changed. Art Therapy, Music Therapy and Forensic Science majors have been added.

The "Average SAT-1 Total/ACT Total/Recommended majors" pages are included mainly because of counselors' requests. School counselors wanted average score comparisons and an index of colleges showing recommended majors. In all cases, SAT-1 Total Scores are noted and the equivalent ACT score is now provided. These scores are the best estimate by our staff for the entering fall class of 2001. Especially young counselors tell us this section is a quick ready reference—a marker for them.

The eighteenth edition still contains "One Hundred Just Darn Good Schools"—found on the following page. I hear more nice things about these schools than any others. As in the past, when a state university is noted like Wisconsin, we mean the flagship at Madison, if no other city follows in parenthesis.

Frederick E. Rugg

San Diego County, California
January, 2001 (18th Edition)

ACKNOWLEDGMENTS

I would like to thank the following for their help in the preparation of this guidebook: Phi Beta Kappa Office, Bureau of Educational Statistics, our Research Aides, Officers of Institutional Research who returned our requests, and especially the great number of secondary counselors who've filled out questionnaires and tip me off on quality departments to look at. I am independent of the colleges and these people are, too.

A "Thank You" also goes to the counselors and students I've worked with who have contributed each in their own way. At last count, I've worked 25,000 hours in five secondary school guidance cubicles with 30 counselors, and conducted over 450 workshops with over 6000 counselors. Of course I've learned from them. Together we've probably done the college admissions process a million times. Also I thank the counselors and students and university officials in the United States and abroad for their help, suggestions, and, yes, their complaints. I appreciate, too, those departments who have sent us vitae on their professors. College PR officers who write always get a reading. And the same goes for anyone who e-mails me. Seventy-five percent of college personnel who write me and tip me off on a great major at their school find it in the next year's book!

I am also grateful to George Gibbs, Ed Wall, Reg Alexander, Arvin R. Anderson, Howard Ahlskog, Hy Kleinman, Michele M. Charles, Gary Metras, Edward Field, Betty Rossie, Horacio Rodriquez, A.P. Stevens, Madeline Field, Cyrus Benson, John Barker, Fred Ames, Matthew Jagielski, Gilbert Field, Jeff Sheehan, Charles Doebler, Joan Girard, Mrs. Fran Fisher, Ralph Strycharz, Dennis Gurn, John DeBonville, Sammy Edwards, Eric Goodhart, Kevin L. Miller, Gloria Broecker, Hoover Sutton, Francona, J.R., Rebecca Lou, Cousin Leonard, professional photographer Lynn C. Henkel of Bradenton, Florida, Dave Congalton, and to all the secretaries I've worked with over the years.

And finally, a special thanks to my wife, Barbara, for her patience and industry.

Inquiries and comments about this guide should be addressed to:

Rugg's Recommendations
P.O. Box 417
Fallbrook, CA 92088

FRED RUGG'S ONE HUNDRED COLLEGES...

Just Darn Good Schools

"I Hear More Nice Things About These Schools Than Any Others"

The most valuable list in this book. Places where students maximize their education.

Alfred (NY)
Allegheny (PA)
Auburn (AL)
Austin (TX)
Baldwin-Wallace (OH)
Barnard (NY)
Bates (ME)
Beloit (WI)
Bemidji State (MN)
Berry (GA)
Bethany (WV)
Biola (CA)
Bluffton (OH)
Bradley (IL)
Bryn Mawr (PA)
Butler (IN)
California, U. of (Davis)
California, U. of (Riverside)
Clemson (SC)
Coe (IA)
Creighton (NB)
Dayton (OH)
Delaware
Denison (OH)
DePaul (IL)
DePauw (IN)
Drake (IA)
Earlham (IN)
Edinboro (PA)
Elon (NC)
Evansville (IN)
Flagler (FL)
Franklin & Marshall (PA)
George Fox (OR)
George Washington (DC)
Georgia Institute of Technology
Grinnell (IA)
Hanover (IN)
Harvard (MA)
Haverford (PA)
Hawaii Pacific
Heidelberg (OH)
Hendrix (AR)
Hiram (OH)

Hollins (VA)
Humboldt (CA)
Idaho, U. of
Illinois Wesleyan
Iowa
Kansas State
Keene State (NH)
Kentucky, U. of
Knox (IL)
Kutztown (PA)
Lawrence (WI)
LeMoyne (NY)
Loyola Marymount (CA)
Macalester (MN)
Maine, U. of
Maine, U. of (Farmington)
Marquette (WI)
Mary Baldwin (VA)
Mary Washington (VA)
Michigan State
Michigan Tech
Minnesota (Morris)
Minnesota, U.of
Montana State
Moravian (PA)
Muhlenberg (PA)
Muskingum (OH)
Nazareth (NY)
Nevada, U. of (Reno)
North Carolina State
Northern Colorado
Northern Michigan
Ohio State University
Ohio Wesleyan
Oregon, U. of
Pacific Lutheran (WA)
Pittsburgh, U. of
Pitzer (CA)
Pt. Loma Nazarene (CA)
Portland, U. of (OR)
Regis (CO)
Rhodes (TN)
Ripon (WI)
Roanoke (VA)

Rochester Institute of Tech. (NY)
Rockhurst (MO)
St. Andrews (NC)
St. Anselm (NH)
St. Louis U. (MO)
St. Mary's (IN)
St. Norbert (WI)
St. Olaf (MN)
Salisbury (MD)
Santa Clara (CA)
Seton Hall (NJ)
Simmons (MA)
South Florida
South Oregon
South, U. of the (TN)
Southwestern (TX)
Spring Hill (AL)
Stanford (CA)
Stonehill (MA)
Susquehanna (PA)
Syracuse (NY)
Texas A&M
Ursinus (PA)
Valparaiso (IN)
Vanderbilt (TN)
Virginia Wesleyan
Wabash (IN)
Washington & Jefferson (PA)
Washington, U. of
Wells (NY)
Western Maryland
Western Michigan
Westminster (MO)
West Virginia Wesleyan
Wheaton (MA)
Williams (MA)
Wingate (NC)
Winona State (MN)
Wisconsin, U. of
Wittenberg (OH)
Wofford (SC)
Wooster (OH)
Wyoming, U. of

1055 Secondary School Counselors responded to the question, "What colleges do you believe offer students the best opportunity to maximize their education?" The list is above. Please don't count the colleges in this list. There's actually a little over 100. I just couldn't get it down to the magic number.

Rugg's Recommendations • Fallbrook, California • 760-728-4558

SECTION ONE

RECOMMENDED
UNDERGRADUATE PROGRAMS

AGRICULTURE

Author's Note: *Students in the schools of Agriculture, in general, tend to have median college test scores below the University's overall median.*

GROUP I
Most Selective

Cornell (NY)	L	Iowa State	XL
Florida, U. of	XL	Pennsylvania State	XL
Illinois, U. of (Urbana-Champaign)	XL	Rutgers (NJ)	L

GROUP II
Very Selective

Auburn (AL)	L	Michigan State	XL
California, U. of (Davis)	L	Minnesota, U. of	XL
California, U. of (Riverside)	M	Missouri, U. of	XL
Cal. Poly. State U. (San Luis Obispo)	L	New Hampshire, U. of	L
Clemson (SC)	L	North Carolina State	L
Connecticut, U. of	L	Purdue (IN)	XL
Hawaii, U. of	L	Texas A&M	XL
Kansas State	L	Vermont, U. of	M
Maine, U. of	M	Virginia Poly. Inst.	L
Maryland, U. of	XL	Wisconsin, U. of	XL

GROUP III
Selective

Arizona, U. of	XL	Nevada, U. of (Reno)	M
Arkansas, U. of	L	New Mexico State U.	L
Berea (KY)	R	North Dakota State	L
Cal. Poly. State U. (Pomona)	L	Ohio State	XL
California State U. (Fresno)	L	Oklahoma State	L
Colorado State	L	Oregon State	L
Delaware Valley (PA)	R	Ozarks, College of the (MO)	R
Dordt (IA)	S	Tennessee, U. of	XL
Georgia, U. of	XL	Texas Tech U.	L
Idaho, U. of	M	Tuskegee University (AL)	M
Kentucky, U. of	L	Utah State	L
Louisiana State	XL	Washington State	L
Mississippi State	L	Wilmington (OH)	S
Montana State	L	Wisconsin, U. of (Platteville)	M
Nebraska, U. of	L	Wyoming, U. of	L

Enrollment Code		
■ **Men Only**	**S = Small** (less than 1000 students) **R = Moderate** (1000-3000 students)	**M = Medium** (3000-8000 students)
▲ **Women Only**	**L = Large** (8000-20,000 students)	**XL = Extra Large** (over 20,000 students)

AMERICAN STUDIES

GROUP I
Most Selective

American U. (DC) .... M	Pomona (CA) .... R
Amherst (MA) .... R	Sarah Lawrence (NY) .... S
Buffalo (SUNY) (NY) L	▲ Smith (MA) .... R
California, U. of (San Diego) L	St. Olaf (MN) .... R
Franklin & Marshall (PA) .... R	South, U. of the (TN) .... R
George Washington (DC) .... M	Stanford (CA) .... M
Georgetown (DC) .... M	Tulane (LA) .... M
Harvard (MA) .... M	Virginia, U. of L
Kalamazoo (MI) .... R	Wake Forest (NC) .... M
Michigan, U. of XL	Wesleyan (CT) .... R
North Carolina, U. of L	William & Mary (VA) .... R
Northwestern (IL) .... M	Williams (MA) .... R
Pennsylvania, U. of............................ L	Yale (CT) .... M

GROUP II
Very Selective

Arizona, U. of XL	Skidmore (NY) .... R
California, U. of (Santa Cruz) .... M	South Florida, U. of L
George Mason (VA) L	Texas, U. of XL
Hawaii, U. of L	Wagner (NY).. R
Hobart & Wm. Smith (NY)................. R	Washington College (MD) .... S
▲ Hollins (VA) .... S	▲ Wells (NY) .... S
Mary Washington (VA) .... R	▲ Wesleyan College (GA) .... S
Minnesota, U. of XL	Wyoming, U. of L
▲ Pine Manor (MA) .... S	

ANTHROPOLOGY

GROUP I
Most Selective

Albany (SUNY) (NY) L	Lafayette (PA) .... R
▲ Barnard (NY) .... R	Macalester (MN) .... R
Brandeis (MA) .... R	Michigan, U. of XL
▲ Bryn Mawr (PA) ....S	New College (FL) ....S
Buffalo (SUNY) (NY) L	Northwestern (IL) .... M
California, U. of (Berkeley) XL	Pennsylvania, U. of L
California, U. of (Los Angeles) XL	Pitzer (CA) ....S
Case Western Reserve (OH) .... R	Pomona (CA) .... R
Chicago, U. of (IL) .... M	Rice (TX) .... R
Colorado College............................... R	Skidmore (NY) .... R
Columbia (NY) .... M	▲ Smith (MA) .... R
Dartmouth (NH) .... M	South, U. of the (TN) .... R
Duke (NC) .... M	Stanford (CA) .... M
Florida, U. of XL	Vanderbilt (TN) .... M
Grinnell (IA) .... R	Washington U. (MO) .... M
Harvard (MA) .... M	Yale (CT) .... M
Illinois, U. of (Urbana-Champaign) XL	

GROUP II
Very Selective

Arizona, U. of XL	Oregon, U. of L
Beloit (WI) .... R	Pittsburgh, U. of (PA) L
California, U. of (Santa Cruz) .... M	Rhode Island, U. of............................. L
California, U. of (Davis) L	St. Mary's College of Maryland .... R
Colorado, U. of................................... L	Tulsa, U. of (OK) .... M
Earlham (IN).. R	Washington State L
Hamline (MN) .... R	Washington, U. of XL
Hofstra (NY) .... M	Wisconsin, U. of XL
Kansas, U. of L	Wisconsin, U. of (Milwaukee) L
Maryland, U. of XL	

GROUP III
Selective

California State U. (Fullerton).............. L	New Mexico, U. of .... M
California State U. (Sacramento) .... M	Queens (CUNY) (NY)........................... L
Hawaii, U. of L	Tennessee, U. of XL
New Mexico State U. L	

Enrollment Code		
■ Men Only	S = Small (less than 1000 students) R = Moderate (1000-3000 students) M = Medium (3000-8000 students)	
▲ Women Only	L = Large (8000-20,000 students) XL = Extra Large (over 20,000 students)	

ARCHITECTURE

GROUP I
Most Selective

▲ Barnard (NY) .... R	Miami U. (OH) L
Buffalo (SUNY) (NY) L	Michigan, U. of XL
California, U. of (Berkeley) XL	MIT (MA) .... M
Carnegie Mellon (PA) .... M	Notre Dame (IN) .... M
Columbia (NY) .... M	Princeton (NJ) .... M
Cooper Union (NY) .... S	Rensselaer (NY) .... M
Cornell (NY) L	Rice (TX) .... R
Florida, U. of XL	Tulane (LA) .... M
Georgia Inst. of Tech. L	Virginia, U. of L
Illinois Inst. of Tech. .... R	Washington U. (MO) .... M
Illinois, U. of (Urbana-Champaign) XL	Yale (CT) .... M
Maryland, U. of XL	

GROUP II
Very Selective

Arizona State XL	Milwaukee Sch. of Engineering (WI) ... R
Arizona, U. of XL	Montana State L
Auburn (AL) L	Nebraska, U. of L
Cal. Poly. State U. (San Luis Obispo) .. L	North Carolina State L
Catholic U. (DC) .... M	Oklahoma, U. of L
Cincinnati, U. of (OH) L	Oregon, U. of L
Clemson (SC) L	Pennsylvania State XL
Detroit Mercy, U. of (MI) .... M	Rhode Island School of Design (RI) .... R
Drury (MO) .... S	Southern California, U. of L
Houston, U. of (TX) L	Syracuse (NY) L
Illinois, U. of (Chicago) L	Texas A&M XL
Kansas State L	Texas, U. of (Austin) XL
Kansas, U. of L	Virginia Poly. Inst. L
Miami, U. of (FL) L	Washington, U. of XL

GROUP III
Selective

Arkansas, U. of L	Ohio State XL
Cal. Poly. State U. (Pomona) L	Pratt Inst. (NY) .... R
City College (CUNY) (NY) L	Roger Williams (RI) .... R
Idaho, U. of .... M	Texas, U. of (Arlington) L
Kent State (OH) L	Tuskegee University (AL) .... M
Louisiana State XL	Woodbury (CA) .... S
Nevada, U. of (Las Vegas) .... M	

Enrollment Code

■ Men Only | S = Small (less than 1000 students) | R = Moderate (1000-3000 students) | M = Medium (3000-8000 students)
▲ Women Only | L = Large (8000-20,000 students) | XL = Extra Large (over 20,000 students)

ART (STUDIO)

GROUP I
Most Selective

Bard (NY)	R	New Jersey, College of	M
Bates (ME)	R	New York U.	L
Boston U. (MA)	L	Pennsylvania, U. of	L
Brown (RI)	M	R.I. School of Design	R
▲ Bryn Mawr (PA)	S	Rochester, U. of (NY)	M
Carnegie Mellon (PA)	M	▲ Scripps (CA)	S
Centre (IA)	R	Skidmore (NY)	R
Cooper Union (NY)	S	▲ Smith (MA)	R
Cornell (NY)	L	Southwestern (TX)	R
Cornish (WA)	S	St. Olaf (MN)	R
Dallas, U. of (TX)	R	Trinity (TX)	R
Dartmouth (NH)	M	Tulane (LA)	M
Drew (NJ)	R	Virginia, U. of	L
Florida, U. of	XL	Washington U. (MO)	M
Furman (SC)	R	▲ Wellesley (MA)	R
Harvard (MA)	M	Wesleyan (CT)	R
Lafayette (PA)	R	Wheaton (IL)	R
Macalester (MN)	R	Williams (MA)	R
Michigan, U. of	XL	Wisconsin, U. of (Madison)	XL
Middlebury (VT)	R	Yale (CT)	M

GROUP II
Very Selective

▲ Agnes Scott (GA)	S	Hamline (MN)	R
Alabama, U. of	L	Hofstra (NY)	M
Alaska, U. of (Anchorage)	M	▲ Hollins (VA)	S
Alfred (NY)	R	Houghton (NY)	S
Alma (MI)	R	Houston, U. of (TX)	L
Arizona, U. of	XL	Hunter (CUNY) (NY)	L
Art Center College of Design (CA)	R	Illinois, U. of (Chicago)	L
Art Institute of Chicago (IL)	R	James Madison (VA)	R
Auburn (AL)	L	Juniata (PA)	R
Augustana (IL)	R	Kansas, U. of	L
Beaver (PA)	R	Knox (IL)	R
Birmingham-Southern (AL)	R	Lake Forest (IL)	S
Bowling Green (OH)	L	Loras (IA)	R
Bradley (IL)	M	Loyola Marymount (CA)	M
Brigham Young (UT)	XL	Manhattanville (NY)	S
California Institute of the Arts	S	Marietta (OH)	R
California, U. of (Irvine)	L	Maryland Institute–College of Art	S
California, U. of (Santa Barbara)	L	Mass. College of Art	R
Clarke (IA)	S	Messiah (PA)	R
Colorado State	L	▲ Mills (CA)	S
Connecticut, U. of	L	Missouri, U. of (Kansas City)	M
▲ Converse (SC)	S	Montana State	L
Delaware, U. of	L	Moore College of Art (PA)	S
Drake (IA)	M	Moravian (PA)	R
East Carolina (NC)	L	Muhlenberg (PA)	R
Florida State	L	North Dakota, U. of	M
Gordon (MA)	R	Ohio State	XL
Guilford (NC)	R		

GROUP II continues next page

ART (STUDIO), *continued*

GROUP II, continued

Ohio U.	L	Southern Methodist (TX)	M
Otis Art Institute (CA)	S	Syracuse (NY)	L
Pacific, U. of the (CA)	M	Temple (PA)	L
Parsons School of Design (NY)	R	Tennessee, U. of	XL
Principia (IL)	S	Washington & Jefferson (PA)	R
▲ Randolph-Macon Woman's Col. (VA)	S	Washington, U. of	XL
Redlands, U. of (CA)	R	▲ Wesleyan Col. (GA)	S
▲ Rosemont (PA)	R	Western Washington U. (WA)	L
▲ St. Mary's College (IN)	R	West Virginia, U. of	L
St. Rose (NY)	R	Wheaton (MA)	R
San Diego State (CA)	XL	Whitworth (WA)	R
Sch. of the Art Institute of Chicago	S	Wisconsin, U. of (Steven's Point)	L
Shepherd (WV)	R	Wittenberg (OH)	R

GROUP III
Selective

Anna Maria (MA)	S	Maryville (St. Louis) (MO)	R
Arizona State	XL	Massachusetts, U. of (Dartmouth)	M
Arts, U. of the (PA)	R	Mercyhurst (PA)	R
Ball State (IN)	L	Millikin (IL)	R
Belhaven (MS)	R	Monmouth (NJ)	R
Bloomsburg (PA)	M	Montana State (Billings)	R
Brescia (KY)	S	Montclair State (NJ)	M
California State U. (Fresno)	L	Montevallo (AL)	R
California State U. (Hayward)	M	Moorhead (MN)	M
California State U. (Long Beach)	L	Mount St. Joseph (OH)	R
California State U. (Monterey Bay)	R	Nevada, U. of (Las Vegas)	M
California State U. (San Bernardino)	M	New Mexico, U. of	L
California State U. (San Jose)	L	North Carolina (Greensboro)	M
▲ Chatham (PA)	S	Northern Iowa	L
Chowan (NC)	S	Old Dominion (VA)	L
Eastern Illinois	L	Philadelphia College of Art (PA)	S
Edinboro (PA)	M	Roanoke (VA)	R
Emmanuel (MA)	S	Rockford (IL)	S
Fairleigh Dickinson (NJ)	M	▲ Salem College (NC)	S
Fort Hays (KS)	M	Santa Fe, College of (NM)	S
Grand Valley (MI)	L	▲ Seton Hill (PA)	S
Hawaii, U. of	L	Siena Heights (MI)	S
Humboldt State (CA)	M	South Dakota, U. of	M
Indiana State	L	Southern Maine	M
Jacksonville (FL)	R	Texas Tech. U.	L
Keene State (NH)	R	Texas, U. of (San Antonio)	L
Kent State (OH)	L	Virginia Commonwealth U.	L
Kutztown (PA)	M	West Virginia Wesleyan	R
Long Island U. (Southampton)	R	Western Connecticut	M
Louisiana State	XL	Western Michigan	L
▲ Mary Baldwin (VA)	S		

ART HISTORY

GROUP I
Most Selective

▲ Barnard (NY) .... R
Bowdoin (ME) .... R
Brown (RI) .... M
▲ Bryn Mawr (PA) .... S
California, U. of (Los Angeles) XL
Case Western Reserve U. (OH) .... R
Chicago, U. of (IL) .... M
Columbia (NY) .... M
Harvard (MA) .... M
Johns Hopkins (MD) .... R
Michigan, U. of XL
▲ Mount Holyoke (MA) .... R
New York U. L
North Carolina, U. of L

Oberlin (OH) .... R
Pennsylvania, U. of L
Princeton (NJ) .... M
Rochester, U. of (NY) .... M
Skidmore (NY) .... R
▲ Smith (MA) .... R
Swarthmore (PA) .... R
Trinity (TX) .... R
Vassar (NY) .... R
Washington U. (MO) .... M
▲ Wellesley (MA) .... R
Willamette (OR) .... R
Williams (MA) .... R
Yale (CT) .... M

GROUP II
Very Selective

California, U. of (Riverside) .... M
California, U. of (Santa Barbara) L
Clarke (IA) .... S
Colorado State L
Delaware, U. of L
Edinboro (PA) .... M
Florida State L
▲ Hollins (VA) .... S
Hunter (CUNY) (NY) L
Kansas, U. of L
Lake Forest (IL) .... S

Manhattanville (NY) ....S
Minnesota, U. of XL
Missouri, U. of XL
Oregon, U. of L
▲ Pine Manor (MA) .... S
▲ Rosemont (PA) .... S
▲ Salem College (NC) ....S
Southern Methodist (TX) .... M
▲ Sweet Briar (VA) .... S
Wheaton (MA) .... R
Wooster (OH) .... R

Enrollment Code		
■ **Men Only**	**S = Small** (less than 1000 students)	**R = Moderate** (1000-3000 students)	**M = Medium** (3000-8000 students)
▲ **Women Only**	**L = Large** (8000-20,000 students)	**XL = Extra Large** (over 20,000 students)

ASTRONOMY

GROUP I
Most Selective

Boston U. L
Brigham Young (UT) XL
▲ Bryn Mawr (PA) .... S
California Inst. of Tech. .... S
Case Western Reserve U. (OH) .... R
Cornell (NY) L
Harvard (MA) .... M
Haverford (PA) .... S
Illinois, U. of (Urbana-Champaign) XL
Michigan, U. of XL
MIT (MA) .... M

Northwestern (IL) .... M
Pennsylvania, U. of L
Pennsylvania State XL
Vassar (NY) .... R
Villanova (PA) .... M
Virginia, U. of L
▲ Wellesley (MA) .... R
Wesleyan (CT) .... R
Whitman (WA) .... R
Williams (MA) .... R
Wisconsin, U. of XL

GROUP II
Very Selective

Arizona, U. of XL
Colorado, U. of.................................... L
Drake (IA) .... M
Earlham (IN) .... R
Florida Inst. of Tech. .... R
Florida, U. of XL
Georgia, U. of.....................................XL
Hawaii, U. of L
Indiana U. XL
Iowa, U. of..XL
Kansas, U. of L
Maryland, U. of XL

Massachusetts, U. of L
Minnesota, U. of XL
Ohio State U. XL
Oklahoma, U. of L
Pittsburgh, U. of (PA) L
San Diego State XL
San Francisco State U. L
Southern California L
Stony Brook (SUNY) (NY) L
Texas, U. of (Austin) XL
Washington, U. of...............................XL

GROUP III
Selective

Benedictine (KS) .... S
Louisiana State XL
Lycoming (PA) .... R
Montana, U. of .... M

Nebraska, U. of L
Northern Arizona XL
Wisconsin, U. of (La Crosse) L
Wyoming, U. of L

Enrollment Code		
■ Men Only	**S = Small** (less than 1000 students)	**R = Moderate** (1000-3000 students)	**M = Medium** (3000-8000 students)
▲ Women Only	**L = Large** (8000-20,000 students)	**XL = Extra Large** (over 20,000 students)

BIOCHEMISTRY (MOLECULAR BIOLOGY)

GROUP I
Most Selective

▲ Barnard (NY) .... R
Binghamton (SUNY) (NY) L
Bowdoin (ME) .... R
Brandeis (MA) .... R
Brown (RI) .... M
California, U. of (Berkeley) XL
California, U. of (Los Angeles) XL
California, U. of (San Diego) L
Columbia (NY) .... M
Cornell (NY) L
Dallas, U. of (TX) .... R
Geneseo (SUNY) (NY) .... M
Harvard (MA) .... M

Iowa, U. of...............................XL
Miami, U. of (FL) L
MIT (MA) .... M
▲ Mount Holyoke (MA) .... R
Pennsylvania, U. of L
Princeton (NJ) .... M
Rice (TX) .... R
Rutgers (NJ) L
Rochester, U. of (NY) .... M
Swarthmore (PA) .... R
Tulane (LA) .... M
Yale (CT) .... M

GROUP II
Very Selective

Albright (PA) .... R
Beloit (WI) .... R
California, U. of (Davis) L
California, U. of (Riverside) .... M
Colorado, U. of L
Denison (OH) .... R
Florida Inst. of Tech. .... R
Kansas State.............................. L
Lewis & Clark (OR) .... R
Louisiana State XL
Michigan State...........................XL
Muhlenberg (PA) .... R

Pennsylvania State XL
Pittsburgh, U. of (PA) L
Purdue (IN)...............................XL
Regis (CO) .... R
Ripon (WI) .... R
Skidmore (NY) .... R
St. Andrews Presbyterian (NC) .... S
Stony Brook (SUNY) (NY) L
Susquehanna (PA) .... R
Virginia Poly. Inst. L
Wisconsin, U. of XL

GROUP III
Selective

Misericordia, College (PA) .... S
Ohio Northern .... R
Oregon State L

Sacred Heart (CT) .... R
Temple (PA) L

Enrollment Code		
■ Men Only	**S = Small** (less than 1000 students)	**R = Moderate** (1000-3000 students)	**M = Medium** (3000-8000 students)
▲ Women Only	**L = Large** (8000-20,000 students)	**XL = Extra Large** (over 20,000 students)	

BIOLOGY

GROUP I
Most Selective

Albany (SUNY) (NY)	L	Middlebury (VT)	R
Amherst (MA)	R	Minnesota, U. of (Morris)	R
Bates (ME)	R	MIT (MA)	M
Bethany (WV)	S	▲ Mount Holyoke (MA)	R
Boston College (MA)	L	New College (FL)	S
Bowdoin (ME)	R	Occidental (CA)	R
Brandeis (MA)	R	Pitzer (CA)	S
Brown (RI)	M	Pomona (CA)	R
▲ Bryn Mawr (PA)	S	Princeton (NJ)	M
Bucknell (PA)	R	Reed (OR)	R
California Inst. of Tech.	S	Rhodes (TN)	R
California, U. of (Los Angeles)	XL	Rice (TX)	R
California, U. of (San Diego)	L	Rochester, U. of (NY)	M
Carleton (MN)	R	Rutgers (NJ)	L
Chicago, U. of (IL)	M	Skidmore (NY)	R
Claremont McKenna (CA)	R	▲ Smith (MA)	R
Colby (ME)	R	South, U. of the (TN)	R
Colgate (NY)	R	Southwestern (TX)	R
Colorado Col.	R	Stanford (CA)	M
Cornell (NY)	R	St. Mary's Col. of Maryland	R
Dallas, U. of (TX)	R	St. Olaf (MN)	R
Dartmouth (NH)	M	Swarthmore (PA)	R
Dickinson (PA)	R	Trinity (CT)	R
Duke (NC)	M	Tufts (MA)	M
Emory (GA)	R	Tulane (LA)	M
Franklin & Marshall (PA)	R	Union (NY)	R
Geneseo (SUNY) (NY)	M	Ursinus (PA)	R
Georgetown (DC)	M	Vanderbilt (TN)	M
Gettysburg (PA)	R	Vassar (NY)	R
Grinnell (IA)	R	Vermont, U. of	L
Hamilton (NY)	R	Villanova (PA)	M
Harvard (MA)	M	Virginia, U. of	L
Harvey Mudd (CA)	S	■ Wabash (IN)	S
Haverford (PA)	S	Wake Forest (NC)	M
Holy Cross (MA)	R	Washington U. (MO)	M
Illinois Wesleyan	R	▲ Wellesley (MA)	R
Iowa State	XL	Wesleyan (CT)	R
Johns Hopkins (MD)	R	Wheaton (IL)	R
Kalamazoo (MI)	R	Whitman (WA)	R
Kenyon (OH)	R	Willamette (OR)	R
Lafayette (PA)	R	William & Mary (VA)	M
Lawrence (WI)	R	Williams (MA)	R
Macalester (MN)	R	Yale (CT)	M
Miami, U. of (FL)	L	Yeshiva (NY)	R

BIOLOGY continues next page

BIOLOGY, *continued*

GROUP II
Very Selective

▲ Agnes Scott (GA) .... S
Albertson (ID) .... S
Albright (PA) .... R
Allegheny (PA) .... R
Alma (MI) .... R
Augustana (SD) .... R
Benedictine (IL) .... R
Berry (GA) .... R
Birmingham-Southern (AL) .... R
California, U. of (Davis) L
California, U. of (Irvine) L
California, U. of (Riverside) .... M
California, U. of (Santa Cruz) .... M
Canisius (NY) .... M
Clarke (IA) .... S
Columbia College (SC) .... R
Concordia (MN) .... R
Connecticut, U. of................................ L
Cornell Col. (IA) .... R
Creighton (NE) .... R
Delaware, U. of L
Denison (OH) .... R
Denver, U. of (CO) .... M
Duquesne (PA)...................................... M
Earlham (IN) .... R
Eckerd (FL) .... R
Erskine (SC) .... S
Fairfield (CT) .... M
Georgia, U. of......................................XL
Grove City (PA) .... R
Guilford (NC) .... R
Hamline (MN) .... R
■ Hampden-Sydney (VA) .... S
Hendrix (AR) .... R
Hiram (OH) .... R
Hobart & William Smith (NY) .... R
▲ Hood (MD) .... S
Hope (MI) .... R
Houghton (NY) .... S
Illinois College .... S
Illinois, U. of (Chicago) L
Indiana U. XL

Juniata (PA) .... R
Kansas State L
Kentucky, U.of...................................... L
Lake Forest (IL) .... S
Lewis & Clark (OR) .... R
Linfield (OR) .... R
Loras (IA) .... R
Loyola (IL) .... M
Loyola (LA) .... R
Loyola (MD) .... R
Marist (NY) .... M
Marquette (WI) .... M
Mary Washington (VA) .... R
Michigan State.....................................XL
Millersville (PA) .... M
Millsaps (MS).. S
Minnesota, U. of (Duluth) .... M
Morningside (IA) .... S
Muhlenberg (PA) .... R
Nazareth (NY) .... R
Nebraska Wesleyan .... R
New Hampshire, U. of L
North Central (IL) .... R
Ohio Northern .... R
Ohio Wesleyan .... R
Oklahoma City U. .... R
Oklahoma, U. of L
Presbyterian (SC) .... S
Puget Sound (WA) .... R
Randolph-Macon (VA) .... R
▲ Randolph-Macon Woman's Col. (VA) ..S
Ripon (WI) .... R
Roanoke (VA) .... R
Scranton, U. of (PA) .... M
▲ Scripps (CA) .... S
Spring Hill (AL) .... R
St. John's (MN) .... R
St. Louis (MO) .... M
Stony Brook (SUNY) (NY) L
Truman State (MO).............................. M
Washington & Jefferson (PA) .... R

GROUP II continues next page

Enrollment Code

■ **Men Only**　　**S = Small** (less than 1000 students)　　**R = Moderate** (1000-3000 students)　　**M = Medium** (3000-8000 students)
▲ **Women Only**　　　　**L = Large** (8000-20,000 students)　　**XL = Extra Large** (over 20,000 students)

BIOLOGY, *continued*

GROUP II, continued

Washington College (MD) .... S
Western Maryland .... R
Westminster (PA) .... R
Wheaton (MA) .... R
Winona State U. (MN) .... M

Wisconsin, U. of (Stevens Point) .... M
Wittenberg (OH) .... R
Wofford (SC) .... R
Wooster (OH) .... R

GROUP III
Selective

Blackburn (IL) .... S
California State U. (Monterey Bay) ..... R
Carroll (MT) .... R
College of Charleston (SC) L
Delaware Valley (PA) .... R
East Stroudsburg (PA) .... M
Eastern Connecticut.......................... M
Eastern Oregon .... R
Emmanual (MA) .... S
Fort Lewis (CO) .... M
Framingham (MA)............................. M
Houston Baptist (TX) .... R
Jacksonville (FL) .... R
Kentucky Wesleyan........................... S
Long Island U. (Southampton Col.)(NY) R
Lynchburg (VA)................................ R
Maryville (TN)................................. S
▲ Meredith (NC)................................ R
Misericordia, College (PA) .... S
Mount St. Mary's (CA) .... R

Northland (WI) .... S
Northwestern (IA) .... S
▲ Pine Manor (MA) .... S
Puerto Rico (Cayey), U. of .... M
Reinhardt (GA) .... S
▲ Spelman (GA) .... R
St. Vincent (PA) .... R
Temple (PA) L
Texas Lutheran .... S
Texas, U. of (San Antonio).................. L
Thomas More (KY) .... S
Tougaloo (MS)................................. S
Virginia Wesleyan .... R
Wartburg (IA)................................. R
Wheeling Jesuit (WV) .... R
Wilkes (PA) .... R
Wisconsin, U. of (Eau Claire) L
Wyoming, U. of L
Xavier University of Louisiana .... R

Enrollment Code

■ Men Only
▲ Women Only

S = Small (less than 1000 students)   R = Moderate (1000-3000 students)   M = Medium (3000-8000 students)
L = Large (8000-20,000 students)   XL = Extra Large (over 20,000 students)

BOTANY

GROUP I
Most Selective

California, U. of (Berkeley) XL
Connecticut College.......................... R
Cornell (NY) L
Duke (NC) .... M

Florida, U. of XL
Miami U. (OH) L
Michigan, U. of XL

GROUP II
Very Selective

California, U. of (Davis) L
California, U. of (Riverside) .... M
Connecticut, U. of.............................. L
Delaware, U. of L
Maine, U. of.. M
Maryland, U. of L
Michigan State...................................XL
Montana, U. of .... M
North Carolina State L

Ohio U. L
Ohio Wesleyan .... R
Pennsylvania State XL
Purdue (IN)...XL
Tennessee, U. of L
Texas, U. of (Austin) XL
Vermont, U. of.................................... L
Washington, U. of XL
Wisconsin, U. of XL

GROUP III
Selective

Alabama, U. of L
Colorado State L
Eastern Illinois L
Hawaii, U. of L
Humboldt State (CA) .... M

Louisiana State...................................XL
Northern Arizona XL
Oregon State L
Southern Illinois U. (Carbondale) L
Wyoming, U. of L

BUSINESS ADMINISTRATION

GROUP I
Most Selective

Albany (SUNY) (NY)	L	Miami U. (OH)	L
American (DC)	M	Michigan, U. of	XL
Babson (MA)	R	Missouri, U. of	XL
Binghamton (SUNY) (NY)	L	MIT (MA)	M
Boston College (MA)	L	Muhlenberg (PA)	R
Boston U. (MA)	L	New York U.	L
Bucknell (PA)	R	North Carolina, U. of	L
Buffalo (SUNY) (NY)	L	Notre Dame (IN)	M
California, U. of (Berkeley)	XL	Pennsylvania, U. of	L
Carnegie Mellon (PA)	M	Rensselaer (NY)	M
Case Western Reserve U. (OH)	R	Rhodes (TN)	R
Claremont McKenna (CA)	R	Richmond, U. of (VA)	R
Clarkson (NY)	M	Southwestern (TX)	R
➤ Colby (ME)	R	Syracuse (NY)	L
DePauw (IN)	R	Trinity (TX)	R
Emory (GA)	R	Tulane (LA)	M
Fairfield (CT)	R	U.S. Air Force Academy (CO)	M
Florida, U. of	XL	Vermont, U. of	L
Florida State	L	Villanova (PA)	M
Franklin & Marshall (PA)	R	Virginia Poly. Institute	L
Geneseo (SUNY) (NY)	M	Virginia, U. of	L
Georgetown (DC)	M	Wake Forest (NC)	M
Gettysburg (PA)	R	Washington U. (MO)	M
Gustavus Adolphus (MN)	R	Washington & Lee (VA)	M
Illinois, U. of (Urbana-Champaign)	XL	William & Mary (VA)	M
Indiana U.	XL	Wisconsin, U. of	XL
Lehigh (PA)	M	Yeshiva (NY)	R

➤ *Administrative Science*

GROUP II
Very Selective

Alabama, U. of	L	Auburn (AL)	L
Alaska Pacific	S	Augustana (IL)	R
Albertson (ID)	S	Austin (TX)	R
Albright (PA)	R	Baylor (TX)	M
Alfred (NY)	R	Bentley (MA)	M
Alma (MI)	R	Birmingham Southern (AL)	R
Arizona, U. of	XL	Bowling Green (OH)	L
Arizona State	XL	Bryant (RI)	R
Asbury (KY)	R		

GROUP II continues next page

Enrollment Code

■ Men Only   S = Small (less than 1000 students)   R = Moderate (1000-3000 students)   M = Medium (3000-8000 students)
▲ Women Only   L = Large (8000-20,000 students)   XL = Extra Large (over 20,000 students)

BUSINESS ADMINISTRATION, *continued*

GROUP II, *Continued*

Buena Vista (IA)	R	▲ Hood (MD)	S
Butler (IN)	R	Houston, U. of (TX)	L
California State (Fullerton)	L	Idaho, U. of	M
California, U. of (Riverside)	M	Illinois, U. of (Chicago)	L
California, U. of (Santa Barbara)	L	Indiana U. of Pennsylvania	L
Capital U. (OH)	R	Iowa State	XL
Centenary (LA)	S	Iowa, U. of	XL
Christian Brothers (TN)	R	James Madison (VA)	M
Clark (MA)	R	John Carroll (OH)	M
Clemson (SC)	L	Juniata (PA)	R
Coe (IA)	R	Kansas Newman	S
Colorado, U. of (Col. Springs)	M	Kansas State	L
Columbia College (SC)	R	Kentucky, U. of	L
Concordia (MN)	R	LaSalle (PA)	M
Dayton, U. of (OH)	M	Lebanon Valley (PA)	R
Delaware, U. of	L	LeMoyne (NY)	R
Denver, U. of (CO)	M	LeTourneau (TX)	R
DePaul (IL)	M	Lewis & Clark (OR)	R
Dominican (IL)	S	Longwood (VA)	R
Drake (IA)	M	Loras (IA)	R
Eastern Michigan	L	Lowell, U. of (MA)	L
Eckerd (FL)	R	Loyola (MD)	R
Elizabethtown (PA)	R	Loyola (LA)	R
Elon (NC)	R	Loyola Marymount (CA)	M
Erskine (SC)	S	Luther (IA)	R
Flagler (FL)	R	Manhattan (NY)	M
Florida Atlantic	L	Manhattanville (NY)	R
Florida Gulf Coast U.	R	Marietta (OH)	R
Florida Inst. of Tech.	R	Marist (NY)	M
Florida International	M	Marquette (WI)	M
Fredonia (SUNY) (NY)	M	Maryland, U. of	XL
George Mason (VA)	L	Massachusetts, U. of	L
Georgetown College (KY)	R	Master's (CA)	R
Gonzaga (WA)	R	Michigan, U. of (Dearborn)	M
Goucher (MD)	S	Michigan State	XL
Grove City (PA)	R	Michigan Tech	M
Guilford (NC)	R	Millersville (PA)	M
Hampton (VA)	M	Millsaps (MS)	S
Hanover (IN)	R	Minnesota, U. of	XL
Hendrix (AR)	R	Mississippi College	R
Hillsdale (MI)	R	Mississippi, U. of	M
Hofstra (NY)	M		

GROUP II continues next page

Enrollment Code

■ Men Only   S = Small (less than 1000 students)   R = Moderate (1000-3000 students)   M = Medium (3000-8000 students)
▲ Women Only   L = Large (8000-20,000 students)   XL = Extra Large (over 20,000 students)

BUSINESS ADMINISTRATION, *continued*

GROUP II, *Continued*

Mississippi U. for Women .... R	Shaw (NC) .... R
Monmouth (IL) .... S	Shepherd (WV) .... M
Moravian (PA) .... R	Siena (NY) .... R
Nazareth (NY) .... R	▲ Simmons (MA) .... R
New Hampshire, U. of L	Skidmore (NY) .... R
New Paltz (SUNY) (NY) .... M	Southern California, U. of L
North Carolina, U. of (Greensboro) .... M	Southern Methodist (TX) .... M
North Dakota, U. of .... M	Spring Hill (AL) .... R
Northeastern (MA) L	St. Bonaventure (NY) .... R
North Florida .... M	▲ St. Catherine (MN) .... R
Oglethorpe (GA) .... R	St. John's (MN) .... R
Ohio U. L	St. Joseph's U. (PA) .... R
Oklahoma City U. (OK) .... R	St. Mary's Col. of CA .... R
Oklahoma State L	▲ St. Mary's Col. (IN) .... R
Oklahoma, U. of L	St. Mary's Col. (MN) .... R
Old Dominion (VA) L	St. Michael's Col. (VT) .... R
Oregon, U. of L	St. Norbert (WI) .... R
Oswego (SUNY) (NY) .... M	Southern Oregon State U. .... M
Pacific Lutheran (WA) .... R	Stetson (FL) .... R
Pacific University (OR) .... S	Stockton State (NJ) .... M
Pennsylvania State XL	Stonehill (MA) .... R
Pepperdine (CA) .... R	Susquehanna U. (PA) .... R
Pittsburgh, U. of (PA) L	Texas A&M XL
Plattsburgh (SUNY) (NY) .... M	Texas A&M at Galveston .... S
Portland, U. of (OR) .... R	Texas, U. of (Austin) XL
Presbyterian (SC) .... S	Texas Christian .... M
Principia (IL) .... S	Transylvania (KY) .... S
Providence (RI) .... M	▲ Trinity (DC) .... S
Puerto Rico, U. of L	Truman State (MO) .... M
Puget Sound (WA) .... R	Ursinus (PA) .... R
Purdue (IN) XL	Valparaiso (IN) .... M
Queens (NC) .... S	Virginia Military Inst. .... R
Randolph-Macon (VA) .... R	Washington College (MD) .... S
Redlands, U. of (CA) .... R	Washington State L
Ripon (WI) .... R	Washington, U. of XL
Roanoke (VA) .... R	▲ Wells (NY) .... S
Rockhurst (MO) .... R	▲ Wesleyan College (GA) .... S
Rowan (NJ) .... M	Western Maryland .... R
Salem College (NC) .... S	Western Michigan L
Samford (AL) .... R	West Virginia U. L
San Diego State U. (CA) XL	Wilberforce (OH) .... S
San Diego, U. of (CA) .... M	William Jewell Col. (MO) .... R
San Francisco, U. of (CA) .... M	Wisconsin, U. of (Stevens Point) .... M
Santa Clara, U. of (CA) .... M	Wittenberg (OH) .... R
Scranton, U. of (PA) .... M	Wyoming, U. of L
Seton Hall (NJ) .... M	Xavier (OH) .... R

BUSINESS ADMINISTRATION, *continued*

GROUP III
Selective

Abilene Christian (TX)	M	Colorado State	L
Alaska, U. of (Anchorage)	M	Concordia (NE)	R
Alaska, U. of (Fairbanks)	M	Delaware Valley (PA)	R
Alderson-Broaddus (WV)	S	Dillard (LA)	R
American International (MA)	R	Doane (NE)	S
Appalachian State (NC)	L	Eastern (PA)	R
Arkansas, U. of	L	Eastern Connecticut	M
Averett (VA)	S	Eastern Nazarene (MA)	R
Azusa Pacific (CA)	R	Eastern Oregon	R
Baker (KS)	S	Elmhurst (IL)	R
Baldwin-Wallace (OH)	R	Elmira (NY)	R
Barry (FL)	R	Emory & Henry (VA)	S
Baruch (CUNY) (NY)	L	Eureka (IL)	S
Belmont Abbey (NC)	S	Fairleigh Dickinson (NJ)	M
Benedictine (KS)	S	Ferris State (MI)	L
Benedictine (IL)	R	Fisk (TN)	S
▲ Bennett (NC)	S	Florida A&M	M
Bethel (MN)	R	Framingham (MA)	M
Bluffton (OH)	S	Freed-Hardeman (TN)	R
Brescia (KY)	S	Gannon (PA)	M
Brockport (SUNY) (NY)	M	Graceland (IA)	R
Caldwell (NJ)	S	Grambling (LA)	M
California Lutheran	R	Green Mountain (VT)	S
Cal. Poly. State U. (Pomona)	L	Hartford, U. of (CT)	M
California State U. (Bakersfield)	M	Hartwick (NY)	R
California State U. (Domiguez Hills)	M	Hastings (NE)	S
California State U. (Fresno)	L	Hawaii Pacific	M
California State U. (Fullerton)	L	Heidelberg (OH)	S
California State U. (Hayward)	M	Henderson State (AR)	M
California State U. (Los Angeles)	L	Hillsdale (MI)	R
California State U. (Sacramento)	M	Howard (DC)	M
California State U. (San Bernardino)	M	Husson (ME)	S
California State U. (San Marcos)	M	▲ Immaculata (PA)	S
California State U. (Stanislaus)	M	Indiana State U.	L
Canisius (NY)	M	Iona (NY)	M
Carthage (WI)	R	Jacksonville (FL)	R
Castleton (VT)	R	Kennesaw State (GA)	R
Catawba (NC)	S	Kentucky Wesleyan (KY)	S
Cedarville (OH)	R	King's (PA)	R
Central Arkansas	M	LaSell (MA)	S
Central Connecticut	M	LaVerne, U. of (CA)	R
Champlain (VT)	R	Lenoir-Rhyne (NC)	R
Chapman (CA)	R	▲ Lesley (MA)	S
▲ Chatham (PA)	S	Linfield (OR)	R
Chowan (NC)	S	Long Island U. (Southampton)	R

GROUP III continues next page

Enrollment Code

■ Men Only | S = Small (less than 1000 students) | R = Moderate (1000-3000 students) | M = Medium (3000-8000 students)
▲ Women Only | L = Large (8000-20,000 students) | XL = Extra Large (over 20,000 students)

BUSINESS ADMINISTRATION, *continued*

GROUP III, *Continued*

Maine (Farmington)	R
Maine, U. of	M
Malone (OH)	R
Manchester (IN)	R
Marshall (WV)	M
▲ Mary Baldwin (VA)	S
Marygrove (MI)	R
Massachusetts Col. of Lib. Arts (N. Adams)	R
Massachusettes, U. of (Boston)	M
Mercer (GA)	R
Mercyhurst (PA)	R
▲ Meredith (NC)	R
Merrimack (MA)	R
Milligan (TN)	S
Montreat (NC)	S
■ Morehouse (GA)	R
Mount Mercy (IA)	S
Mount St. Joseph (OH)	R
Mount St. Mary's (CA)	R
Mount St. Mary's (MD)	R
Mount Union (OH)	S
Muskingum (OH)	R
Nebraska, U. of	L
Nevada, U. of (Las Vegas)	M
New Orleans, U. of	L
Niagara (NY)	R
North Carolina, U. of (Charlotte)	L
North Carolina, U. of (Wilmington)	M
North Georgia	R
Northeast Louisiana	L
Northern Arizona	L
Northern Colorado	L
Northern Illinois	L
Northern Iowa, U. of	L
Northwood University (MI)	R
Nova Southeastern (FL)	R
Nyack (NY)	R
Ohio State	XL
Oregon Inst. of Tech.	R
Ozarks, College of the (MO)	R
Pace (NY)	R
Phila. Col. of Textiles & Sci. (PA)	R
▲ Pine Manor (MA)	S
Point Loma (CA)	R
Potsdam (SUNY) (NY)	M
Puerto Rico (CAYEY), U. of	M
Quincy (IL)	R
Quinnipiac (CT)	R
Phillips (OK)	R
Radford (VA)	M
Regis (CO)	R
Reinhardt (GA)	S
Rider (NJ)	M
Robert Morris (PA)	M
Roosevelt (IL)	R
Sacred Heart (CT)	R
Schreiner (TX)	S
Seattle U. (WA)	R
Shippensburg (PA)	M
Simpson (IA)	S
Sonoma State (CA)	M
South Alabama	M
South Carolina, U. of	L
South Dakota, U. of	M
Southern Illinois	L
Southern Maine	M
Southern Mississippi	L
South Florida, U. of	XL
Southwest Texas State	L
St. Andrews Presbyterian (NC)	S
St. Francis (NY)	R
St. John Fisher (NY)	L
St. John's (NY)	L
St. Joseph's (IN)	S
St. Joseph's (NY)	R
St. Mary's (TX)	R
St. Rose (NY)	R
St. Thomas, Col. of (MN)	M
Suffolk (MA)	R
Tampa, U. of (FL)	R
Tennessee, U. of	L
Texas Wesleyan	R
Texas, U. of (San Antonio)	L
Thomas More (KY)	S
Toledo, U. of	L
Towson (MD)	L
Utica College of Syracuse U. (NY)	R
Virginia Wesleyan	R
Wagner (NY)	R
Washington & Jefferson (PA)	R
West Chester (PA)	M
West Florida, U. of	M
Western Connecticut State	M
Western New England (MA)	R
Westminster (UT)	R
Whittier (CA)	R
Wichita State (KS)	M
Widener (PA)	R
Wisconsin, U. of (Green Bay)	M
Wisconsin, U. of (Stout)	M
Woodbury (CA)	S
Worcester State (MA)	M
Xavier U. of Louisiana	R

CHEMISTRY

GROUP I
Most Selective

Amherst (MA)	R	Kenyon (OH)	R
▲ Barnard (NY)	R	Lafayette (PA)	R
Bates (ME)	R	Lawrence (WI)	R
Bowdoin (ME)	R	MIT (MA)	M
Brown (RI)	M	▲ Mount Holyoke (MA)	R
▲ Bryn Mawr (PA)	S	New College (FL)	S
Bucknell (PA)	M	North Carolina, U. of	L
California Inst. of Tech.	S	Northwestern (IL)	M
California, U. of (Berkeley)	XL	Notre Dame (IN)	M
California, U. of (Los Angeles)	XL	Oberlin (OH)	R
California, U. of (San Diego)	L	Occidental (CA)	R
Carleton (MN)	R	Pennsylvania State	XL
Carnegie Mellon (PA)	M	Pomona (CA)	R
Case Western Reserve U. (OH)	R	Princeton (NJ)	M
Centre (KY)	R	Reed (OR)	R
Colgate (NY)	R	Rice (TX)	R
Columbia (NY)	M	Rochester, U. of (NY)	M
Dartmouth (NH)	M	Rutgers (NJ)	L
Davidson (NC)	R	Skidmore (NY)	R
Drew (NJ)	R	Southwestern (TX)	R
Duke (NC)	M	St. Olaf (MN)	R
Emory (GA)	R	Stanford (CA)	M
Franklin & Marshall (PA)	R	Trinity (TX)	R
Furman (SC)	R	Tufts (MA)	M
Grinnell (IA)	R	Union (NY)	R
Hamilton (NY)	R	Virginia, U. of	L
Harvard (MA)	M	▲ Wellesley (MA)	R
Harvey Mudd (CA)	S	Wesleyan (CT)	R
Haverford (PA)	S	Wheaton (IL)	R
Illinois, U. of (Urbana-Champaign)	XL	Whitman (WA)	R
Johns Hopkins (MD)	R	Willamette (OR)	R
Kalamazoo (MI)	R	Williams (MA)	R

CHEMISTRY continues next page

CHEMISTRY, *continued*

GROUP II
Very Selective

Albertson (ID)	S	Marquette (WI)	M
Alma (MI)	R	Massachusetts, U. of	L
Baylor (TX)	M	Michigan State	XL
Birmingham-Southern (AL)	R	Minnesota, U. of (Morris)	R
California, U. of (Davis)	L	Monmouth (IL)	S
California, U. of (Santa Cruz)	M	New Hampshire, U. of	L
Carroll (WI)	R	Ohio Northern	R
Centenary (LA)	S	Ohio University	L
Clarke (IA)	S	Ohio Wesleyan	R
Clemson (SC)	L	Oklahoma, U. of	L
Colorado, U. of	L	Oregon, U. of	L
Delaware, U. of	L	Purdue (IN)	XL
Denver, U. of (CO)	M	Ripon (WI)	S
Duquesne (PA)	M	Rochester, U. of (NY)	M
Earlham (IN)	R	Rockhurst (MO)	R
Florida State	L	Rollins (FL)	R
Georgia, U. of	XL	St. John's (MN)	R
Goucher (MD)	S	St. Louis (MO)	M
Hamline (MN)	R	St. Michael's (VT)	R
Hendrix (AR)	R	Shepherd (WV)	M
Hiram (OH)	R	▲ Spelman (GA)	R
Hobart & William Smith (NY)	R	Spring Hill (AL)	R
Hope (MI)	R	Stetson (FL)	R
Houghton (NY)	S	Stony Brook (SUNY) (NY)	L
Huntingdon (AL)	S	Texas A&M	XL
Indiana U.	XL	Truman State (MO)	M
Ithaca Col.	M	Ursinus (PA)	R
Juniata (PA)	R	Vermont, U. of	L
Kansas, U. of	L	Washington & Jefferson (PA)	R
Knox (IL)	R	Washington, U. of	XL
Lake Forest (IL)	S	Wittenberg (OH)	R
Linfield (OR)	R	Wofford (SC)	R
Louisiana State	XL	Wooster (OH)	R

GROUP III
Selective

California State U. (Chico)	L	Southern Connecticut	M
California State U. (Fresno)	L	▲ Sweet Briar (VA)	S
California State U. (San Jose)	L	Temple (PA)	L
College of Charleston (SC)	L	Texas Lutheran	S
Delaware Valley (PA)	R	Wheeling Jesuit (WV)	R
Houston Baptist (TX)	R	Whittier (CA)	R
Marshall (WV)	M	Worcester State (MA)	M
Northwestern (IA)	S	Wyoming, U. of	L
St. Mary's (MN)	R	Xavier U. of Louisiana	R
Salem State (MA)	M		

CLASSICS

GROUP I
Most Selective

▲ Barnard (NY) .... R
Brown (RI) .... M
▲ Bryn Mawr (PA) .... S
Chicago, U. of (IL) .... M
Columbia (NY) .... M
Dallas, U. of (TX) .... R
Drew (NJ) .... R
Duke (NC) .... M
Georgetown (DC) .... M
Harvard (MA) .... M
Holy Cross (MA) .... R
Johns Hopkins (MD) .... R
Kalamazoo (MI) .... R
Macalester (MN) .... R

Michigan, U. of XL
Middlebury (VT) .... R
New York U. .... M
North Carolina, U. of L
Northwestern (IL) .... M
Pennsylvania, U. of L
Princeton (NJ) .... M
Skidmore (NY) .... R
Stanford (CA) .... M
Swarthmore (PA) .... R
Trinity (TX) .... R
Tufts (MA) .... M
Williams (MA) .... R
Yale (CT) .... M

GROUP II
Very Selective

Beloit (WI) .... R
California, U. of (Santa Barbara) L
Catholic U. (DC) .... M
Cincinnati, U. of L
Coe (IA) .... R
Florida, U. of XL
Fordham (NY) L
■ Hampden-Sydney (VA) .... S

Illinois, U. of (Chicago) L
Misericordia, College (PA) .... S
Montana, U. of L
Oklahoma, U. of L
▲ Randolph-Macon Woman's Col. (VA) .. S
Rollins (FL) .... R
St. Amselm (NH) .... R

COMPUTER SCIENCE

GROUP I
Most Selective

Brandeis (MA) .... R	Maryland, U. of (Baltimore County) .... M
Brown (RI) .... M	Michigan, U. of XL
California, U. of (Berkeley) XL	MIT (MA) .... M
California, U. of (Los Angeles) XL	Missouri, U. of (Rolla) .... M
Carnegie Mellon (PA) .... M	Pennsylvania State XL
Case Western Reserve U. (OH) .... M	Rensselaer (NY) .... M
Cornell (NY) L	Rice (TX) .... R
Dallas, U. of (TX) .... R	Rose-Hulman (IN).............................. R
Dartmouth (NH) .... M	Stanford (CA) .... M
Dickinson (PA) .... R	Stevens Inst. of Tech (NJ) .... R
Furman (SC) .... R	Washington, U. of XL
George Washington (DC) .... M	Washington U. (MO) .... M
Georgia Institute of Tech. .... M	William & Mary (VA) .... M
Grinnell (IA)....................................... R	Williams (MA) .... R
Harvard (MA) .... M	Wisconsin, U. of XL
Harvey Mudd (CA) ....S	Worcester Poly. Tech. (MA) .... R
Illinois, U. of XL	Yeshiva (NY) .... R
Iowa State XL	

GROUP II
Very Selective

Allegheny (PA) .... R	Hiram (OH) .... R
Alma (MI) .... R	Hunter (CUNY) (NY) L
Bradley (IL) .... M	Illinois College .... S
Bryant (RI) .... R	LaSalle (PA) .... M
Butler (IN) .... R	Maine, U. of....................................... M
Cal. Poly. State U. (San Luis Obispo) .. L	Marist (NY) .... M
California, U. of (Irvine) L	Marquette (WI) .... M
California, U. of (San Diego) L	Massachusetts, U. of L
California, U. of (Santa Barbara) L	McKendree (IL) .... R
California, U. of (Santa Cruz) .... M	Michigan, U. of (Dearborn) .... M
Central (IA).. R	Millsaps (MS)......................................S
Central Florida, U. of.......................... L	Minnesota, U. of (Morris) .... R
Clarke (IA) ....S	Missouri, U. of (Kansas City) .... M
Clemson (SC) L	Montana College of Min. Sci. & Tech.... R
Cogswell (CA) ....S	Montana, U. of .... M
DePaul (IL) .... M	Moravian (PA) .... R
Drexel (PA) .... M	North Central (IL) .... R
George Mason (VA) L	Northeastern (MA) L
Goucher (MD) .... R	Oklahoma City U. .... R
Hendrix (AR) .... R	

GROUP II continues next page

Enrollment Code		
■ Men Only	S = Small (less than 1000 students)	R = Moderate (1000-3000 students)	M = Medium (3000-8000 students)
▲ Women Only	L = Large (8000-20,000 students)	XL = Extra Large (over 20,000 students)	

COMPUTER SCIENCE, *continued*

GROUP II, *Continued*

Oregon, U. of	L	St. Ambrose (IA)	R
Pace (NY)	M	St. John's (MN)	R
Pacific Lutheran (WA)	R	South Carolina, U. of	L
Pepperdine (CA)	R	Stetson (FL)	R
Pittsburgh, U. of (Johnstown)	R	Stony Brook (SUNY) (NY)	L
Potsdam (SUNY) (NY)	M	Syracuse (NY)	L
Regis (CO)	R	Texas, U. of	XL
Rhode Island, U. of	L	Transylvania (KY)	S
Rochester, U. of (NY)	M	Utah, U. of	L
Rochester Inst. of Tech. (NY)	L	Westminster (PA)	R
Rutgers (Camden) (NJ)	M	Wofford (SC)	R
Santa Clara U. (CA)	M		

GROUP III
Selective

Arizona State	XL	Marygrove (MI)	R
Brockport (SUNY) (NY)	M	Monmouth (NJ)	M
Cal. Poly. State U. (Pomona)	L	■ Morehouse (GA)	R
California State U. (Chico)	L	Mount Union (OH)	S
California State U. (Hayward)	M	Muskingum (OH)	R
California State U. (Monterey Bay)	R	North Florida	M
California State U. (San Jose)	L	Oakland U. (MI)	M
California State U. (San Marcos)	M	Pittsburgh, U. of (Bradford)	S
California State U. (Stanislaus)	M	Quinnipiac (CT)	R
Catawba (NC)	S	Rider (NJ)	M
Chowan (NC)	S	Robert Morris (PA)	R
Colorado, U. of (Col. Springs)	M	St. Joseph's (NY)	R
Colorado, U. of (Denver)	M	St. Mary's (MN)	R
East Stroudsburg (PA)	M	San Jose State U. (CA)	L
Eastern Connecticut	M	Southern Maine	M
Eureka (IL)	S	▲ Spelman (GA)	R
Evansville (IN)	R	Temple (PA)	L
Ferris State (MI)	L	West Florida, U. of	M
Florida Gulf Coast U.	R	West Virginia Wesleyan	R
Hawaii Pacific	M	Western New England (MA)	R
High Point (NC)	R	Wilkes (PA)	R
Husson (ME)	S	William Paterson (NJ)	M
Loyola U. (LA)	M	Wisconsin (LaCrosse)	L

Enrollment Code
■ Men Only   ▲ Women Only   S = Small (less than 1000 students)   R = Moderate (1000-3000 students)   M = Medium (3000-8000 students)   L = Large (8000-20,000 students)   XL = Extra Large (over 20,000 students)

DANCE/DRAMA/THEATER

GROUP I
Most Selective

Allegheny (PA)	R	Macalester (MN)	R
American Acad. of Dramatic Arts (NY)	S	Maryland, U. of (Baltimore County)	M
Amherst (MA)	R	Miami, U. of (FL)	L
▲ Barnard (NY)	R	▲ Mount Holyoke (MA)	R
Boston U. (MA)	L	New York U.	L
Brandeis (MA)	R	North Carolina, U. of	L
California, U. of (Los Angeles)	XL	Northwestern (IL)	M
California, U. of (San Diego)	L	Princeton (NJ)	M
Carleton (MN)	R	Rutgers (NJ)	L
Carnegie Mellon (PA)	M	Sarah Lawrence (NY)	S
Columbia (NY)	M	Skidmore (NY)	R
Connecticut College	R	Southwestern (TX)	R
Cornell (NY)	L	Tufts (MA)	M
Dartmouth (NH)	M	Tulane (LA)	M
Drew (NJ)	R	Vassar (NY)	R
Illinois Wesleyan	R	Wesleyan (CT)	R
Juilliard (NY)	S	Whitman (WA)	R
Kenyon (OH)	R	William & Mary (VA)	R
Lawrence (WI)	R	Yale (CT)	M

GROUP II
Very Selective

Arizona, U. of	XL	Maine, U. of	M
Arizona State	XL	Minnesota, U. of	XL
Bard (NY)	R	Muhlenberg (PA)	R
Baylor (TX)	M	Nevada, U. of (Las Vegas)	M
Beloit (WI)	R	No. Carolina School of the Arts	S
Bennington (VT)	S	Ohio U.	L
Butler (IN)	R	Oklahoma City U.	R
California, U. of (Irvine)	L	Oklahoma State	L
Catholic U. (DC)	M	Purchase (SUNY) (NY)	R
Columbia College (SC)	R	Rollins (FL)	R
Cornish (WA)	S	▲ Scripps (CA)	S
DePaul (IL)	M	Southern California	L
Florida State	L	Southern Methodist (TX)	M
Fordham (NY)	L	Susquehanna (PA)	R
George Mason (VA)	L	Syracuse (NY)	L
Goucher (MD)	S	Texas Christian	M
Hanover (IN)	R	Texas, U. of	XL
Hofstra (NY)	M	Utah, U. of	L
Indiana U.	XL	Virginia Commonwealth U.	L
Kansas, U. of	L	Washington, U. of	XL
LeMoyne (NY)	R	West Virginia U.	L
Linfield (OR)	R	Wheaton (MA)	R
Long Island U. (Southampton Col.) (NY)	R	Wooster (OH)	R
Loyola (IL)	M		
Lyon (AR)	S		

DANCE/DRAMA/THEATER continues next page

DANCE/DRAMA/THEATER, *continued*

GROUP III
Selective

Alaska, U. of (Fairbanks) .... M
Allentown College (PA) .... S
Arts, U. of the (PA) .... R
Barry (FL) .... R
Bethany (WV) .... S
Brenau (GA) .... R
Brockport (SUNY)(NY) .... M
Catawba (NC) .... S
Converse College (SC) .... S
Dana (NB) .... S
Emerson (MA) .... R
Evansville (IN) .... R
Fontbonne (MO) .... R
Franklin (IN) .... S
Humboldt State (CA) .... M
Illinois State L
Jacksonville (FL) .... R
Johnson State (VT) .... R
Keene State (NH) .... R
Longwood (VA) .... R
Niagara (NY) .... R

Northwestern College (IA) .... S
Ohio State XL
Otterbein (OH) .... R
Point Park (PA) .... R
Rockford (IL) .... S
Salem State (MA) .... M
San Francisco State (CA) L
Santa Fe, College of (NM) .... S
Seattle U. (WA) .... R
▲ Seton Hill (PA) .... S
Southern Maine .... M
Southern Utah .... M
South Florida, U. of L
St. Mary's (MN) .... R
Stephens (MO) .... S
Temple (PA) L
Wagner (NY) .... R
Webster (MO) .... R
Western Michigan L
* Western St. Coll. of Colorado .... R

❋ Communication and Theatre - One Major

ECONOMICS

GROUP I
Most Selective

American U. (DC)	M	Michigan, U. of	XL
Amherst (MA)	R	MIT (MA)	M
Babson (MA)	R	Middlebury (VT)	R
▲ Barnard (NY)	R	▲ Mount Holyoke (MA)	R
Bates (ME)	R	Northwestern (IL)	M
Boston University (MA)	L	Occidental (CA)	R
Bowdoin (ME)	R	Pennsylvania, U. of	L
Brandeis (MA)	R	Pomona (CA)	R
▲ Bryn Mawr (PA)	S	Princeton (NJ)	M
Bucknell (PA)	M	Rhodes (TN)	R
California, U. of (Los Angeles)	XL	Rochester, U. of (NY)	M
California, U. of (San Diego)	L	Rose-Hulman (IN)	R
Chicago, U. of (IL)	M	▲ Smith (MA)	R
Claremont McKenna (CA)	R	St. Mary's Col. of Maryland	R
Colby (ME)	R	St. Olaf (MN)	R
Columbia (NY)	M	South, U. of the (TN)	R
Connecticut College	R	Southwestern (TX)	R
Cornell (NY)	L	Stanford (CA)	M
Dallas, U. of (TX)	R	Swarthmore (PA)	R
Dartmouth (NH)	M	Trinity (CT)	R
DePauw (IN)	R	Trinity (TX)	R
Duke (NC)	M	Vanderbilt (TN)	M
Georgetown (DC)	M	Villanova (PA)	M
Georgia Inst. of Tech.	M	Virginia, U. of	L
Grinnell (IA)	R	■ Wabash (IN)	S
Hamilton (NY)	R	Wake Forest (NC)	M
Harvard (MA)	M	Washington & Lee (VA)	R
Haverford (PA)	S	▲ Wellesley (MA)	R
Holy Cross (MA)	R	Wesleyan (CT)	R
Kalamazoo (MI)	R	Whitman (WA)	R
Kenyon (OH)	R	Willamette (OR)	R
Lafayette (PA)	R	Williams (MA)	R
Macalester (MN)	R	Yale (CT)	M

ECONOMICS continues next page

Enrollment Code	
■ Men Only	**S = Small** (less than 1000 students) **R = Moderate** (1000-3000 students) **M = Medium** (3000-8000 students)
▲ Women Only	**L = Large** (8000-20,000 students) **XL = Extra Large** (over 20,000 students)

ECONOMICS, *continued*

GROUP II
Very Selective

▲ Agnes Scott (GA) .... S
  Albion (MI) .... R
  Allegheny (PA) .... R
  Beloit (WI) .... R
  Centre (KY) .... R
  Denison (OH) .... R
  George Mason (VA) L
  Hendrix (AR) .... R
  Hobart & William Smith (NY) .... R
  Illinois Col. .... S
  Illinois, U. of (Chicago) L
  Lake Forest (IL) .... S
  Manhattanville (NY) .... R
  Maryland, U. of XL
  Michigan State..................................XL
  Nebraska, U. of L
  North Carolina State L
  Ohio Wesleyan (OH) .... R

  Oneonta (SUNY) (NY) .... M
  Randolph-Macon (VA) .... R
  Ripon (WI) .... S
▲ Salem Col. (NC) .... S
  San Francisco, U. of .... M
  St. John's (MN) .... R
  St. Lawrence (NY) .... R
  Texas A&M XL
  Ursinus (PA) .... R
  Vermont, U. of L
  Virginia Military Inst. .... R
  Washington & Jefferson (PA) .... R
  Washington, U. of XL
  Westminster Col. (MO) .... S
  Westmont Col. (CA) .... R
  Wheaton (MA) .... R
  Wofford (SC) .... R
  Wooster (OH) .... R

GROUP III
Selective

California State U. (Long Beach) L
California State U. (Northridge) L
Framingham (MA) .... M
Heidelberg (OH) .... S
Monmouth (IL) .... S
St. Anselm (NH) .... R

Toledo, U. of (OH) L
Washington State L
Whittier (CA) .... R
Wilson (PA) .... S
Wyoming, U. of L

EDUCATION

GROUP I
Most Selective

Boston U. (MA) L
Bucknell (PA) .... R
Buffalo (SUNY) (NY) L
Connecticut Col. .... R
Dallas, U. of (TX) .... R
Earlham (IN) .... R
Geneseo (SUNY) (NY) .... M
Illinois, U. of XL
Iowa, U. of..XL
Miami, U. of (FL) .... M
Miami U. (OH) L
Michigan, U. of XL

New Jersey, College of .... M
North Carolina, U. of L
Occidental (CA) .... R
Rutgers (NJ) L
Skidmore (NY) .... R
Swarthmore (PA) .... S
Trinity (TX) .... R
➤ Tufts (MA) .... M
Vanderbilt (TN) .... M
▲ Wellesley (MA) .... R
Wheaton (IL) .... R
William & Mary (VA) .... M

➤ *Child Study*

GROUP II
Very Selective

Adelphi (NY) .... M
Adrian (MI) ....S
Albertson (ID) ....S
Alfred (NY) .... R
Alma (MI) .... R
Arizona, U. of XL
Auburn (AL) L
Augustana (IL) .... R
Augustana (SD) .... R
Austin (TX) .... R
Baylor (TX) L
Berry (GA) .... R
Biola (CA) .... R
Birmingham Southern (AL) .... R
Bridgewater (MA) .... M
Buena Vista (IA) .... R
Butler (IN) .... R
California, U. of (Santa Barbara) L
Calvin (MI) .... M
Capital U. (OH) .... R
Carroll (WI) .... R
Centenary (LA) ....S
Central (IA) .... R
Centre (KY) .... R
Clarke (IA) ....S
Clemson (SC) L
Coe (IA) .... R
Columbia College (SC) .... R

Concordia (MN) .... R
Connecticut, U. of............................... L
Cornell College (IA) .... R
Dayton, U. of (OH) .... M
Delaware, U. of L
Drake (IA) .... M
Eastern Michigan L
Elon (NC) .... R
Erskine (SC) ....S
π Flagler (FL) .... R
Florida International L
Florida State....................................... L
Fredonia (SUNY) (NY) .... M
Georgia, U. of....................................XL
Gonzaga (WA) .... R
Goucher (MD)...................................... R
Grove City (PA) .... R
Guilford (NC) .... R
Gustavus Adolphus (MN) .... R
Hanover (IN) .... R
Harding (AR) .... M
Hillsdale (MI) .... R
Hiram (OH) .... R
▲ Hood (MD) ....S
Houghton (NY) ....S
Hunter (CUNY) (NY) L

π *Especially Deaf Education*
GROUP II continues next page

EDUCATION, *continued*

GROUP II, *Continued*

Illinois College	S
Indiana, U.	XL
Indiana, U. of (PA)	L
Iowa State	XL
James Madison (VA)	M
Juniata (PA)	R
Kansas State	L
Kentucky, U. of	L
Loras (IA)	R
Luther (IA)	R
Lyon (AR)	S
Manhattan (NY)	M
Manhattanville (NY)	R
Maryland, U. of	XL
Mercer (GA)	R
Messiah (PA)	R
Michigan State	XL
Millersville (PA)	M
▲ Mills (CA)	S
Minnesota, U. of	XL
Moravian (PA)	R
Nazareth (NY)	R
New Hampshire, U. of	L
New Paltz (SUNY) (NY)	M
North Carolina, U. of (Asheville)	R
North Dakota, U. of	M
North Florida	M
Ohio U.	L
Oklahoma State	L
Oregon, U. of	L
Pennsylvania State	XL
Potsdam (SUNY) (NY)	R
Principia (IL)	S
Puerto Rico, U. of	L
Queens (CUNY) (NY)	L
Redlands, U. of (CA)	R

Regis (CO)	R
Rowan (NJ)	M
St. Louis (MO)	M
St. Mary's Col. (CA)	R
▲ St. Mary's Col. (IN)	R
St. Mary's Col. (MN)	R
St. Michael's (VT)	R
Salisbury State (MD)	M
San Diego State U. (CA)	XL
Shepherd (WV)	M
Shippensburg (PA)	M
South Carolina, U. of	L
South Florida, U. of	L
Southwest Missouri	L
Stetson (FL)	R
Tennessee, U. of	XL
Texas A&M	XL
Texas, U. of (Austin)	XL
Truman State (MO)	M
Ursinus (PA)	R
Valparaiso (IN)	R
Washington & Jefferson (PA)	R
Washington State	L
Washington, U. of	XL
▲ Wells (NY)	S
Western Maryland College	R
Western Michigan	L
Western Washington U.	L
Whitworth (WA)	R
William Jewell Col. (MO)	R
Wisconsin, U. of	XL
Wisconsin, U. of (Milwaukee)	L
Wisconsin, U. of (Stevens Point)	M
Wittenberg (OH)	R
Wofford (SC)	R
York (PA)	M

GROUP III
Selective

Alaska, U. of (Anchorage)	M
Alderson-Broaddus (WV)	S
Appalachian State (NC)	L
Arkansas, U. of	L
Arizona State	XL
Augsburg (MN)	R
Averett (VA)	S

Avila (MO)	S
Baldwin-Wallace (OH)	R
Ball State (IN)	L
Beaver (PA)	R
▲ Bennett (NC)	S
Berea (KY)	R

GROUP III continues next page

EDUCATION, *continued*

GROUP III, *Continued*

Bethany (WV)	S
Bethel (MN)	R
Blackburn (IL)	S
Bluffton (OH)	S
Bowling Green (OH)	L
Bloomsburg (PA)	M
Brescia (KY)	S
Brockport (SUNY) (NY)	M
Caldwell (NJ)	S
California Lutheran	R
California State U. (Bakersfield)	M
California State U. (Fresno)	L
California State U. (Monterey Bay)	R
California State U. (Los Angeles)	L
California State U. (Sacramento)	M
California State U. (San Marcos)	M
California State U. (Stanislaus)	M
California (PA)	M
Canisius (NY)	M
Catawba (NC)	S
Cedarville (OH)	R
Central Connecticut	M
Central Michigan U.	L
City Col. (CUNY) (NY)	L
College of Charleston (SC)	M
Concordia (NE)	R
▲ Converse (SC)	S
Dana (NB)	S
Dominican (CA)	S
Dordt (IA)	S
Dubuque, U. of (IA)	S
East Carolina (NC)	L
Eastern Connecticut	M
Eastern Illinois	L
Eastern Kentucky	L
Eastern Oregon	R
Edgewood (WI)	S
Edinboro (PA)	M
Elmira (NY)	R
Florida A&M	M
Florida Atlantic	L
Florida Gulf Coast U.	R
Fontbonne (MO)	R
Franklin (IN)	S
Freed-Hardeman (TN)	R
Frostburg (MD)	M
Geneva (PA)	R
George Fox (OR)	S
Georgia Southern	L
Gordon (MA)	R
Graceland (IA)	R
Hardin-Simmons (TX)	R
Hastings (NE)	S
Heidelberg (OH)	S
Henderson State (AR)	M
Herbert Lehman (CUNY) (NY)	L
Huntingdon (AL)	S
Huntington (IN)	S
Husson (ME)	S
Illinois State	L
Indiana State U.	L
Jacksonville State (AL)	M
Johnson State (VT)	R
Kean (NJ)	M
Keene State (NH)	R
Kent State (OH)	L
Kentucky Wesleyan	S
Kutztown (PA)	M
Lamar (TX)	M
LaSell (MA)	S
Laverne, U. of (CA)	R
▲ Lesley (MA)	S
Lewis-Clark State (ID)	R
Linfield (OR)	R
Lock Haven (PA)	M
Longwood (VA)	R
Maine (Farmington)	R
Mansfield (PA)	R
Marshall (WV)	M
Maryville (St. Louis) (MO)	R
Mass. St. Col. System	M
Middle Tennessee	L
Millikin (IL)	R
Misericordia, College (PA)	S
Mississippi State	L

GROUP III continues next page

Enrollment Code
■ Men Only ▲ Women Only S = Small (less than 1000 students) R = Moderate (1000-3000 students) M = Medium (3000-8000 students) L = Large (8000-20,000 students) XL = Extra Large (over 20,000 students)

EDUCATION, *continued*

GROUP III, *Continued*

Monmouth (IL)	S	St. Thomas Aquinas (NY)	R
Montana, U. of	M	Seton Hall (NJ)	M
Montana State (Billings)	R	Simpson (IA)	S
Montclair State (NJ)	M	Southern Connecticut	M
Montevallo (AL)	R	Southern Oregon State U.	M
Mount St. Joseph (OH)	R	Southern Utah	M
Muskingum (OH)	R	Southwest Baptist (MO)	R
Nevada, U. of (Las Vegas)	M	Southwest Texas State	L
Nevada, U. of (Reno)	M	Southwestern Oklahoma	M
New Mexico, U. of	M	Texas Tech. U.	L
Northern Arizona	L	Texas Wesleyan	R
Northern Illinois U.	L	Tougaloo (MS)	S
Northern Iowa	L	Utah State	L
Northwestern (IA)	R	Wagner (NY)	R
Northwestern (MN)	R	Wartburg (IA)	R
Nyack (NY)	R	Western Kentucky	L
Ohio State	L	Western New England (MA)	R
Oklahoma Baptist	R	Westfield State (MA)	M
Ozarks, College of the (MO)	R	West Florida, U. of	M
Peru State (NE)	R	West Virginia Wesleyan	R
Point Loma (CA)	R	▲ Wheelock (MA)	S
Puerto Rico (Cayey), U. of	L	Whittier (CA)	R
Radford (VA)	M	Widener (PA)	R
Roger Williams (RI)	R	Wilmington (OH)	S
Saint Rose (NY)	R	Wisconsin, U. of (Platteville)	M
St. Joseph's (IN)	S	Worcester State (MA)	M
St. Joseph's (ME)	S	Wyoming, U. of	L
St. Joseph's (NY)	R	Xavier U. of Louisiana	R
▲ St. Joseph's Col. (CT)	S		

ENGINEERING

GROUP I
Most Selective

Boston U. (MA)	L	New Jersey, College of	M
Brown (RI)	M	Northwestern (IL)	M
Bucknell (PA)	M	Notre Dame (IN)	M
Buffalo (SUNY) (NY)	L	Olin (MA)	S
California Inst. of Tech.	S	Pennsylvania State	XL
California, U. of (Berkeley)	XL	Pennsylvania, U. of	L
California, U. of (Davis)	L	Princeton (NJ)	M
California, U. of (Los Angeles)	XL	Rensselaer (NY)	M
California, U. of (San Diego)	L	Rice (TX)	R
California, U. of (Santa Barbara)	L	Rochester, U. of	M
Carnegie Mellon (PA)	M	Rose-Hulman (IN)	R
Case Western Reserve U. (OH)	R	Rutgers (NJ)	L
Clarkson (NY)	M	▲ Smith (MA)	R
Colorado School of Mines	R	Southern California, U. of	L
Columbia (NY)	M	Stanford (CA)	M
Cooper Union (NY)	S	Stevens Inst. of Tech. (NJ)	R
Cornell (NY)	L	Swarthmore (PA)	R
Dartmouth (NH)	M	Texas, U. of (Austin)	XL
Duke (NC)	M	Trinity (CT)	R
Georgia Inst. of Tech.	M	Tufts (MA)	M
Harvey Mudd (CA)	S	Tulane (LA)	M
Illinois Inst. of Tech.	R	Union (NY)	R
Illinois, U. of (Urbana-Champaign)	XL	U.S. Air Force Academy (CO)	M
Iowa State	XL	U.S. Coast Guard Academy (CT)	S
Iowa, U. of	XL	U.S. Military Academy (NY)	M
Johns Hopkins (MD)	R	U.S. Naval Academy (MD)	M
Kettering (MI)	R	Vanderbilt (TN)	M
Lafayette (PA)	R	Villanova (PA)	M
Lehigh (PA)	M	Virginia, U. of	L
MIT (MA)	M	Washington U. (MO)	M
Michigan, U. of	XL	Washington, U. of	L
Missouri, U. of (Rolla)	M	Worcester Poly. Tech. (MA)	R
New Mexico Inst. of Mining & Tech.	S		

GROUP II
Very Selective

Alabama, U. of	L	Cal. Poly State U. (Pomona)	L
Alabama, U. of (Huntsville)	M	Cal. Poly. State U. (San Luis Obispo)	L
Alfred (NY)	R	Calvin (MI)	M
Arizona, U. of	XL	Catholic U. (DC)	M
Arizona State	XL	Central Connecticut	M
Arkansas, U. of	L	Central Florida, U. of	L
Auburn (AL)	L	Christian Brothers (TN)	R
Bradley (IL)	M	Cincinnati, U. of (OH)	L
Butler (IN)	R	City College (CUNY)(NY)	L
California, U. of (Irvine)	L	Clemson (SC)	L
California, U. of (Riverside)	M	Cogswell (CA)	S
California Maritime Academy	S		

GROUP II continues next page

ENGINEERING, *continued*

GROUP II, *Continued*

Colorado, U. of	L	North Dakota State	L
Colorado, U. of (Col. Springs)	R	Northeastern (MA)	L
Dayton, U. of (OH)	M	Northern Illinois U.	L
Delaware, U. of	L	Oakland U. (MI)	M
Detroit Mercy (MI)	M	Ohio Northern	R
Drexel (PA)	M	Ohio State	XL
East Carolina (NC)	L	Ohio U.	L
Florida Atlantic	L	Oklahoma, U. of	L
Florida Inst. of Tech.	R	Oklahoma State	L
Florida International	L	Oregon Inst. of Tech.	R
Gannon (PA)	R	Pacific, U. of the (CA)	R
Geneva (PA)	R	Pittsburgh, U. of	L
Gonzaga (WA)	R	Pittsburgh, U. of (Johnstown)	R
Grove City (PA)	R	Polytechnic Univ. of NY	R
Hartford, U. of (CT)	M	Portland, U. of (OR)	R
Houston, U. of (TX)	L	Puerto Rico, U. of (Mayaguez)	L
Idaho, U. of	M	Purdue (IN)	XL
Illinois, U. of (Chicago)	L	+ Rhode Island, U. of	L
Kansas, U. of	L	Rochester Inst. of Tech. (NY)	L
Kansas State	L	Roger Williams (RI)	R
Kentucky, U. of	L	Rowan (NJ)	M
Lamar (TX)	M	San Diego State (CA)	XL
Letourneau College (TX)	S	Santa Clara, U. of (CA)	M
Louisville (KY)	L	Seattle Pacific (WA)	R
Lowell, U. of (MA)	L	Seattle U. (WA)	R
Loyola (MD)	R	South Carolina, U. of	L
Loyola Marymount (CA)	M	So. Dakota School of Mines	R
Maine, U. of	M	South Dakota State U.	M
Manhattan (NY)	M	Southern Maine, U. of	M
Marquette (WI)	M	Stony Brook (SUNY) (NY)	L
Massachusetts, U. of	L	Tennessee, U. of	XL
Massachusetts, U. of (Boston)	M	Texas A&M	XL
Massachusetts, U. of (Lowell)	M	Texas, U. of (Arlington)	L
Mass. Maritime Academy	S	Tri-State (IN)	R
Mercer (GA)	R	Tulsa, U. of (OK)	R
Michigan State	XL	Tuskegee University (AL)	M
Michigan Tech.	M	Utah, U. of	L
Michigan, U. of	XL	Valparaiso (IN)	M
Michigan, U. of (Dearborn)	M	Virginia Military Inst.	R
Milwaukee Sch. of Eng, (WI)	R	Virginia Poly. Inst.	L
Minnesota, U. of	XL	Walla Walla (WA)	R
Mississippi State	L	Washington State	L
Montana College of Min. Sci. & Tech.	R	Wayne State (MI)	L
Montana State	L	West Virginia U.	L
Nevada, U. of (Las Vegas)	M	Western Michigan	L
Nevada, U. of (Reno)	M	Western New England (MA)	R
New Jersey Inst. of Tech.	M	Widener (PA)	R
New Mexico State U.	L	Wisconsin, U. of	XL
New Orleans, U. of	L	Wisconsin, U. of (Platteville)	M
New Paltz (SUNY)(NY)	M	Wyoming, U. of	L
North Carolina State	L		

+ *And International Engineering*

ENGLISH

GROUP I
Most Selective

Allegheny (PA) .... R	Lawrence (WI) .... R
Amherst (MA) .... R	Macalester (MN) .... R
Bard (NY) .... R	Middlebury (VT) .... R
▲ Barnard (NY) .... R	▲ Mount Holyoke (MA) .... R
Boston Col. (MA) L	New (FL) ....S
Bowdoin (ME) .... R	North Carolina, U. of L
Brandeis (MA) .... R	New Jersey, College of .... M
▲ Bryn Mawr (PA) ....S	Northwestern (IL) .... M
Buffalo (SUNY) (NY) L	Oberlin (OH) .... R
California, U. of (Berkeley) XL	Pennsylvania, U. of L
California, U. of (Los Angeles) XL	Pomona (CA) .... R
Carleton (MN) .... R	Princeton (NJ) .... M
Centre (KY) .... R	Reed (OR) .... R
Chicago, U. of (IL) .... M	Rhodes (TN) .... R
Claremont McKenna (CA) .... R	Richmond, U. of (VA) .... R
Colby (ME) .... R	Rochester, U. of (NY) .... M
Colgate (NY) .... R	Rutgers (NJ) L
Colorado College .... R	Sarah Lawrence (NY) ....S
Columbia (NY) .... M	Skidmore (NY) .... R
Connecticut Col. .... R	▲ Smith (MA) .... R
Cornell (NY) L	South, U. of the (TN) .... R
Dallas, U. of (TX) .... R	Southwestern (TX) .... R
Dartmouth (NH) .... M	Stanford (CA) .... M
Davidson (NC) .... R	St. Olaf (MN) .... R
Dickinson (PA) .... R	Swarthmore (PA) .... R
Duke (NC) .... M	Trinity (TX) .... R
Emory (GA) .... R	Tufts (MA) .... M
Florida, U. of XL	Vanderbilt (TN) .... M
Franklin & Marshall (PA) .... R	Vassar (NY) .... R
Gettysburg (PA) .... R	Virginia, U. of L
Grinnell (IA) .... R	Wake Forest (NC) .... M
Hamilton (NY) .... R	Washington & Lee (VA) .... R
Harvard (MA) .... M	Washington U. (MO) .... M
Haverford (PA) ....S	▲ Wellesley (MA) .... R
Holy Cross (MA) .... R	Wesleyan (CT) .... R
Illinois Wesleyan .... R	Wheaton (IL) .... R
Iowa, U. of XL	Whitman (WA) .... R
Kalamazoo (MI) .... R	Willamette (OR) .... R
Kenyon (OH) .... R	Williams (MA) .... R
Knox (IL) .... R	Wisconsin, U. of XL
Lafayette (PA) .... R	Yale (CT) .... M

ENGLISH continues next page

Enrollment Code

■ Men Only	S = Small (less than 1000 students)	R = Moderate (1000-3000 students)	M = Medium (3000-8000 students)
▲ Women Only	L = Large (8000-20,000 students)	XL = Extra Large (over 20,000 students)	

ENGLISH, *continued*

GROUP II
Very Selective

▲ Agnes Scott (GA) .... S	Massachusetts, U. of L
Albany (SUNY) (NY) L	Master's (CA) .... R
Albertson (ID) .... S	Millsaps (MS) .... S
Albion (MI) .... R	Mississippi, U. of .... M
Alfred (NY) .... R	Missouri, U. of XL
Arizona, U. of XL	Muhlenberg (PA) .... R
Augustana (IL) .... R	Nazareth (NY) .... R
Baylor (TX) .... M	New Hampshire, U. of L
Beloit (WI) .... R	New Paltz (SUNY)(NY) .... M
Bennington (VT) .... S	Northeastern (MA) L
Birmingham-Southern (AL) .... R	Ohio U. L
California, U. of (Davis) L	Oklahoma City U. .... R
Cal Poly State U. (San Luis Obispo) L	Oklahoma, U. of L
Calvin (MI) .... M	Oneonta (SUNY)(NY) .... M
Canisius (NY) .... M	Pittsburgh, U. of (PA) L
Cornell Col. (IA) .... R	Presbyterian (SC) .... S
Denison (OH) .... R	Principia (IL) .... S
Denver, U. of (CO) .... M	Puget Sound (WA) .... R
Earlham (IN) .... R	Purchase (SUNY) (NY) .... R
Eckerd (FL) .... R	Queens (NC) .... S
Emerson (MA) .... R	Randolph-Macon (VA) .... R
Fredonia (SUNY)(NY) .... M	▲ Randolph-Macon Woman's Col. (VA) .. S
Fordham (NY) L	Redlands, U. of (CA) .... R
George Mason (VA) L	Ripon (WI) .... S
Georgetown College (KY) .... R	Roanoke (VA) .... R
Georgia, U. of XL	Rollins (FL) .... R
Gonzaga (WA) .... R	Rutgers (Camden) NJ .... M
Gordon (MA) .... R	San Diego State (CA) XL
Goucher (MD) .... R	▲ Scripps (CA) .... S
Grand Valley (MI) L	Spring Hill (AL) .... R
Guilford (NC) .... R	St. Anselm (NH) .... R
Hamline (MN) .... R	St. Joseph's U. (PA) .... R
■ Hampton-Sydney (VA) .... S	St. Lawrence (NY) .... R
Hiram (OH) .... R	▲ St. Mary's Col. (IN) .... R
Hobart & Wm. Smith (NY) .... R	Stetson (FL) .... R
▲ Hollins (VA) .... S	Stony Brook (SUNY) (NY) L
▲ Hood (MD) .... S	Warren Wilson (NC) .... S
Hunter (CUNY) (NY) L	Wartburg (IA) .... R
John Carroll (OH) .... M	Washington & Jefferson (PA) .... R
Kentucky Wesleyan .... S	▲ Wells (NY) .... S
Lake Forest (IL) .... S	Western Michigan L
LaSalle (PA) .... M	Western Washington U. L
LeMoyne (NY) .... R	Wheaton (MA) .... R
Lewis & Clark (OR) .... R	Whitworth (WA) .... R
Loras (IA) .... R	Winona State U. (MN) .... M
Lycoming (PA) .... R	Wittenberg (OH) .... R
Marietta (OH) .... R	Wofford (SC) .... S
Marquette (WI) .... M	

ENGLISH continues next page

ENGLISH, *continued*

GROUP III
Selective

Adrian (MI)	S	Montclair State (NJ)	M
Arkansas, U. of	L	Montevallo (AL)	R
Baldwin-Wallace (OH)	R	Niagara (NY)	R
Brescia (KY)	S	North Carolina, U. of (Wilmington)	M
California State U. (Bakersfield)	M	▲ Regis (MA)	S
California State U. (Monterey Bay)	R	Rhode Island, U. of	L
California State U. (Northridge)	L	Rockford (IL)	S
California State U. (Sacramento)	M	▲ Rosemont (PA)	S
▲ Chestnut Hill (PA)	S	St. Mary (KS)	S
Chowan (NC)	S	▲ Salem Col. (NC)	S
Dana (NB)	S	San Francisco State (CA)	L
Eastern Nazarene (MA)	R	Seattle U. (WA)	R
Edinboro (PA)	M	▲ Spelman (GA)	R
Fairleigh Dickinson (NJ)	M	Temple (PA)	L
Fort Hays (KS)	M	Tennessee, U. of	XL
Fort Lewis (CO)	M	Utah, U. of	L
Johnson State (VT)	R	Western Connecticut	M
Illinois College	S	Western St. Coll. of Colorado	R
Long Island U. (Southampton Col.) (NY)	R	Wichita State (KS)	M
Longwood (VA)	R	Whittier (CA)	R
Mansfield (PA)	R	Wilkes (PA)	R
Massachusetts Coll. of Lib. Arts (N. Adams)	R	William Paterson (NJ)	M
Misericordia (PA)	S	Wisconsin, U. of (Milwaukee)	R

FOREIGN LANGUAGES

GROUP I
Most Selective

Allegheny (PA) .... R	Lawrence (WI) .... R
Bard (NY) .... R	Michigan, U. of XL
▲ Barnard (NY) .... R	Middlebury (VT) .... R
Boston College (MA) L	▲ Mt. Holyoke (MA) .... R
Bowdoin (ME) .... R	New York U. .... M
Brown (RI) .... M	North Carolina, U. of L
▲ Bryn Mawr (PA) ....S	Pennsylvania, U. of L
California, U. of (Berkeley) XL	Pomona (CA) .... R
California, U. of (Los Angeles) XL	Princeton (NJ) .... M
Carleton (MN) .... R	Rochester, U. of (NY) .... M
Chicago, U. of (IL) .... M	Rutgers (NJ) L
Colby (ME) .... R	▲ Scripps (CA) ....S
Columbia (NY) .... M	Skidmore (NY) .... R
Dallas, U. of .... R	▲ Smith (MA) .... R
Dartmouth (NH) .... M	South, U. of the (TN) .... R
Dickinson (PA) .... R	Southwestern (TX) .... R
Drew (NJ) .... R	Trinity (TX) .... R
Emory (GA) .... R	Tulane (LA) .... M
Georgetown (DC) .... M	Wake Forest (NC) .... M
Grinnell (IA) .... R	Washington & Lee (VA) .... R
Gustavus Adolphus (MN) .... R	Washington U. (MO) .... M
Harvard (MA) .... M	▲ Wellesley (MA) .... R
Illinois, U. of (Urbana-Champaign) XL	Whitman (WA) .... R
Kalamazoo (MI) .... R	Yale (CT) .... M

FOREIGN LANGUAGES continues next page

FOREIGN LANGUAGES, *continued*

GROUP II
Very Selective

▲ Agnes Scott (GA) .... S
   Beloit (WI) .... R
   Brigham Young (UT) XL
   California, U. of (Santa Barbara) L
   Calvin (MI) .... M
   Catholic (DC) .... M
   Central (IA) .... R
   Clark (MA) .... R
   Drake (IA) .... M
   Earlham (IN) .... R
   Eckerd (FL) .... R
   Georgia, U. of XL
   Gustavus Adolphus (MN) .... R
   Hawaii, U. of L
▲ Hollins (VA) .... S
   Illinois College .... S
   Illinois, U. of (Chicago) L
   Indiana U. XL
   Iowa, U. of...XL
   James Madison (VA) L
   Kansas, U. of L

   Lewis & Clark (OR) .... R
   Linfield (OR) .... R
▲ Mills (CA) .... S
   Minnesota, U. of (Morris) .... R
   Moravian (PA) .... R
   Nazareth (NY) .... R
   New Paltz (SUNY)(NY) .... M
   Pacific University (OR) .... S
   Pepperdine (CA) .... R
▲ Rosemont (PA) .... S
   St. Anselm (NH) .... R
▲ Sweet Briar (VA) .... S
   Texas, U. of (Austin) XL
▲ Trinity (DC) .... S
   Truman State (MO)............................. M
   Utah, U. of.. L
   Vermont, U. of L
▲ Wells (NY) .... S
   Wheaton (MA) .... R
   Wisconsin, U. of XL
   Wofford (SC) .... R

GROUP III
Selective

Bethany (WV) .... S
Emory & Henry (VA) .... S
Mansfield (PA) .... R
Montana State L
New Mexico, U. of L

Southern Oregon State U. .... M
South Florida, U. of............................. L
Temple (PA) L
Wayne State (MI) L

FOREIGN LANGUAGES continues next page

Enrollment Code
■ Men Only   S = Small (less than 1000 students)   R = Moderate (1000-3000 students)   M = Medium (3000-8000 students)
▲ Women Only   L = Large (8000-20,000 students)   XL = Extra Large (over 20,000 students)

FOREIGN LANGUAGES, *continued*

Some Recommendations by Specific Departments
Compiled initially with the help of Minnesota's Jeff Sheehan, Secondary School Counselor

FRENCH

Arizona, U. of	XL	▲ Mills (CA)	S
California, U. of (Berkeley)	XL	▲ Mount Holyoke (MA)	R
Columbia (NY)	M	Northwestern (IL)	M
Dartmouth (NH)	M	Princeton (NJ)	M
Emory (GA)	R	▲ Scripps (CA)	S
Georgetown (DC)	M	Tufts (MA)	M
Harvard (MA)	M	Tulane (LA)	M
Holy Cross (MA)	M	Washington U. (MO)	M
Indiana U.	XL	▲ Wellesley (MA)	R

GERMAN

Brown (RI)	M	Pennsylvania, U. of	L
California, U. of (Santa Barbara)	L	Princeton (NJ)	M
Colorado, U. of	L	Stanford (CA)	M
Illinois, U. of (Urbana-Champaign)	XL	Texas, U. of (Austin)	XL
Indiana U.	XL	Williams (MA)	R
Michigan State	XL	Wisconsin, U. of	XL
Penn State	XL	Wofford (SC)	R

JAPANESE

Brigham Young (UT)	XL	Pennsylvania, U. of	L
Harvard (MA)	M	Pittsburgh, U. of (PA)	L
Hawaii, U. of (Manoa)	L	Washington, U. of	XL
Ohio State	L	Wisconsin, U. of	XL
Oregon, U. of	L		

SPANISH

Brigham Young (UT)	XL	Massachusetts, U. of (Dartmouth)	M
Buffalo (SUNY) (NY)	L	Pittsburgh, U. of	L
California, U. of (Irvine)	M	Rutgers (NJ)	L
California, U. of (San Diego)	L	▲ Scripps (CA)	S
California, U. of (Santa Barbara)	L	Utah, U. of	L
Colby (ME)	R	Vanderbilt (TN)	M
Indiana U.	XL	Wisconsin, U. of	XL
Kansas, U. of	L		

Enrollment Code		
■ Men Only	S = Small (less than 1000 students)	R = Moderate (1000-3000 students)	M = Medium (3000-8000 students)
▲ Women Only	L = Large (8000-20,000 students)	XL = Extra Large (over 20,000 students)	

FORESTRY

GROUP I
Most Selective

California, U. of (Berkeley) XL

Florida, U. of XL

Michigan, U. of XL

North Carolina State L

SUNY Coll. of Env. Sci. & Forestry .... R

GROUP II
Very Selective

Arizona, U. of XL

Auburn (AL) L

Berry (GA) ....R

Clemson (SC) L

Colorado State L

Georgia, U. of L

Iowa State XL

Maine, U. of......................................M

Michigan State...................................XL

Michigan Tech ....M

Minnesota, U. of XL

Missouri, U. of XL

Montana State L

Oklahoma State L

Pennsylvania State XL

Purdue (IN).......................................XL

South, U. of the (TN) .... R

Syracuse (NY) L

Tennessee, U. of XL

Texas A&M XL

Virginia Poly. Inst. L

Washington, U. of XL

West Virginia U...................................L

Wisconsin, U. of XL

GROUP III
Selective

Humboldt State (CA) .... M

Idaho, U. of ....M

Montana, U. of ....M

Northern Arizona XL

Oregon State L

Stephen F. Austin (TX)........................L

Utah State L

GEOGRAPHY

GROUP I
Most Selective

Buffalo (SUNY)(NY)	L	Florida, U. of	XL
California, U. of (Berkeley)	XL	George Washington (DC)	M
California, U. of (Los Angeles)	XL	Johns Hopkins (MD)	R
Chicago, U. of (IL)	M	Macalester (MN)	R
Clark (MA)	R	Michigan, U. of	XL
Colgate (NY)	R	Middlebury (VT)	R
Dartmouth (NH)	M	Minnesota, U. of	XL

GROUP II
Very Selective

Arizona State	XL	Oklahoma, U. of	L
Bemidji State (MN)	M	Oklahoma State	L
California, U. of (Santa Barbara)	L	Oregon, U. of	L
Colorado, U. of	L	Pennsylvania State	XL
Colorado, U. of (Colorado Springs)	M	Radford (VA)	M
Indiana U.	XL	Texas, U. of (Austin)	XL
Kansas, U. of	L	Vermont, U. of	L
Louisiana State	XL	Western Washington U.	L
Mary Washington (VA)	R	Wisconsin, U. of (Madison)	XL
Michigan State	XL	Wittenberg (OH)	R
Ohio State	XL		

GROUP III
Selective

California State U. (Chico)	L	Mansfield (PA)	R
California State U. (Northridge)	L	Salem State (MA)	M
Central Connecticut	M	Sonoma State (CA)	M
Keene State (NH)	R	Wyoming, U. of	L
Maine (Farmington)	R		

Enrollment Code			
■ Men Only	S = Small (less than 1000 students)	R = Moderate (1000-3000 students)	M = Medium (3000-8000 students)
▲ Women Only	L = Large (8000-20,000 students)	XL = Extra Large (over 20,000 students)	

GEOLOGY

GROUP I
Most Selective

Amherst (MA)	R
▲ Barnard (NY)	R
Bates (ME)	R
Bowdoin (ME)	R
Brown (RI)	M
▲ Bryn Mawr (PA)	R
California Inst. of Tech.	S
California, U. of (Berkeley)	XL
Carleton (MN)	R
Chicago, U. of (IL)	M
Colgate (NY)	R
Colorado Col.	R
Colorado School of Mines	R
Columbia (NY)	M
Dartmouth (NH)	M
Franklin & Marshall (PA)	R
Furman (SC)	R
Geneseo (SUNY) (NY)	M
Harvard (MA)	M
Lafayette (PA)	R
Lehigh (PA)	M
MIT (MA)	M
Pennsylvania, U. of	L
Pomona (CA)	R
Princeton (NJ)	M
Rochester, U. of (NY)	M
Skidmore (NY)	R
▲ Smith (MA)	R
Vanderbilt (TN)	M
Washington & Lee (VA)	R
Washington U. (MO)	M
Whitman (WA)	R
William & Mary (VA)	M

GROUP II
Very Selective

Albany (SUNY) (NY)	L
Alabama, U. of	L
Allegheny (PA)	R
Arizona, U. of	XL
Beloit (WI)	R
California, U. of (Davis)	L
California, U. of (Santa Barbara)	L
Centenary College (LA)	S
Colorado State	L
Colorado, U. of	L
Cornell Col. (IA)	R
Denison (OH)	R
Earlham (IN)	R
Guilford (NC)	R
Hope (MI)	R
Indiana U.	XL
Michigan Tech	M
Millsaps (MS)	S
Minnesota, U. of	XL
New Mexico Inst. of Mining & Tech.	S
Oklahoma, U. of	L
Oklahoma State	L
Purdue (IN)	XL
St. Lawrence (NY)	R
St. Thomas (MN)	M
South Dakota School of Mines	R
Stony Brook (SUNY) (NY)	L
Texas A&M	XL
Texas Christian	M
Texas, U. of (Austin)	XL
Tulsa, U. of (OK)	M
Vermont, U. of	M
Washington, U. of	XL
Wisconsin, U. of	XL
Wooster, College of (OH)	R

GEOLOGY continues next page

Enrollment Code
■ Men Only ▲ Women Only | S = Small (less than 1000 students) R = Moderate (1000-3000 students) M = Medium (3000-8000 students) L = Large (8000-20,000 students) XL = Extra Large (over 20,000 students)

GEOLOGY, *continued*

GROUP III
Selective

Brooklyn Col. (CUNY) (NY) L
California State U. (Bakersfield) .... M
California State U. (Chico) L
California State U. (Hayward) .... M
California State U. (Sacramento) .... M
Fort Lewis (CO) .... M

Hartwick (NY) .... R
Lamar (TX) .... M
Louisiana State XL
Western State Coll. of Colorado .... R
Wyoming, U. of L

HISTORY

GROUP I
Most Selective

Albion (MI)	R		Kenyon (OH)	R
Amherst (MA)	R		Lafayette (PA)	R
▲ Barnard (NY)	R		Lawrence (WI)	R
Bates (ME)	R		Macalester (MN)	R
Boston Col. (MA)	L		Middlebury (VT)	R
Boston U. (MA)	L		▲ Mount Holyoke (MA)	R
Bowdoin (ME)	R		North Carolina, U. of	L
Brandeis (MA)	R		Northwestern (IL)	M
Brown (RI)	M		Notre Dame (IN)	M
▲ Bryn Mawr (PA)	S		Oberlin (OH)	R
Bucknell (PA)	M		Pennsylvania, U. of	L
California, U. of (Berkeley)	XL		Pomona (CA)	R
California, U. of (Los Angeles)	XL		Princeton (NJ)	M
Carleton (MN)	R		Reed (OR)	R
Centre (KY)	R		Rhodes (TN)	R
Chicago, U. of (IL)	M		Rice (TX)	R
Claremont McKenna (CA)	R		▲ Smith (MA)	R
Colgate (NY)	R		South, U. of the (TN)	R
Colorado Col.	R		Southwestern (TX)	R
Columbia (NY)	M		Swarthmore (PA)	R
Connecticut Col.	R		Texas Christian U. (TX)	M
Cornell (NY)	L		Trinity (TX)	R
Dallas, U. of (TX)	R		Tufts (MA)	M
Davidson (NC)	R		Tulane (LA)	M
Dickinson (PA)	R		Union (NY)	R
Drew (NJ)	R		Vanderbilt (TN)	R
Duke (NC)	M		Vassar (NY)	R
Emory (GA)	R		Virginia, U. of	L
George Washington (DC)	M		■ Wabash (IN)	S
Georgetown (DC)	M		Wake Forest (NC)	M
Gettysburg (PA)	R		Washington & Lee (VA)	R
Grinnell (IA)	R		▲ Wellesley (MA)	R
Hamilton (NY)	R		Wesleyan U. (CT)	R
Harvard (MA)	M		Whitman (WA)	R
Haverford (PA)	S		William & Mary (VA)	M
Holy Cross (MA)	R		Williams (MA)	R
Kalamazoo (MI)	R		Yeshiva (NY)	R

HISTORY continues next page

Enrollment Code

■ Men Only	S = Small (less than 1000 students) R = Moderate (1000-3000 students) M = Medium (3000-8000 students)
▲ Women Only	L = Large (8000-20,000 students) XL = Extra Large (over 20,000 students)

HISTORY, *continued*

GROUP II
Very Selective

▲ Agnes Scott (GA) .... S
  Albion (MI) .... R
  Allegheny (PA) .... R
  Alma (MI) .... R
  Baylor (TX) .... M
  Birmingham-Southern (AL) .... R
  California, U. of (Davis) L
  Calvin (MI) .... M
  Canisius (NY) .... M
  Christiandom (VA) .... S
  Coe (IA) .... R
  Covenant (GA) .... S
  Denison (OH) .... R
  Erskine (SC) .... S
  Gonzaga (WA) .... R
  Goucher (MD) .... S
■ Hampden-Sydney (VA) .... S
  Hanover (IN) .... R
  Hillsdale (MI) .... R
  Hiram (OH) .... R
  Hobart & William Smith (NY) .... R
  Illinois College .... S
  Juniata (PA) .... R
  Kansas, U. of L
  Kentucky, U. of L
  Kentucky Wesleyan .... S
  Knox (IL) .... R
  Lake Forest (IL) .... S
  Marquette (WI) .... M
  Maryland, U. of XL
+ Mary Washington (VA) .... R

  Massachusetts, U. of L
  Miami, U. of (FL) .... M
  Millersville (PA) .... M
  Missouri, U. of XL
  Muhlenberg (PA) .... R
  North Carolina (Asheville) .... R
  Northeastern (MA) L
  Ohio U. L
  Oklahoma, U. of L
  Queens (NC) .... S
  Ripon (WI) .... S
▲ Rosemont (PA) .... S
  Rutgers (Camden) (NJ) .... M
  San Diego State U. (CA) XL
  Shepherd (WV) .... M
  Spring Hill (AL) .... R
  Stetson (FL) .... R
  Tennessee, U. of XL
  Texas, U. of (Austin) XL
  Vermont, U. of L
  Warren Wilson (NC) .... S
  Wartburg (IA) .... R
  Washington College (MD) .... S
▲ Wells (NY) .... S
  Western Michigan L
  Wheaton (MA) .... R
  Willamette (OR) .... R
  Wisconsin, U. of XL
  Wittenberg (OH) .... R
  Wofford (SC) .... R
  Wooster (OH) .... R

+ And Historic Preservation Major

GROUP III
Selective

  Alabama, U. of L
  Bridgewater (MA) .... M
  Brockport (SUNY)(NY) .... M
  California State U. (Fullerton)............. L
  Capital U. (OH) .... R
  Carson-Newman (TN) .... R
  Central Connecticut .... M
  Charleston, U. of (WV)........................ S
  Misericordia (PA) .... S
  Muskingum (OH) .... R

  New Mexico, U. of L
  Northwestern (IA) .... S
  St. Joseph's (NY) .... R
  St. Mary's (MN) .... R
  Toledo, U. of L
  Western St. Col. of Colorado .... R
  Wheeling Jesuit (WV) .... R
  Wilkes (PA) .... R
  Wisconsin, U. of (Green Bay) .... M

HOME ECONOMICS/FAMILY STUDIES/FOODS

GROUP I
Most Selective

Florida State L

Wisconsin, U. of XL

GROUP II
Very Selective

Georgia, U. of XL

➤ Kansas State L

Michigan State XL

Northern Illinois U. L

Oneonta (SUNY) (NY) .... M

Utah State L

Wisconsin, U. of (Stout) .... M

➤ *Nutritional & Exercise Sciences*

GROUP III
Selective

California State (Fresno) L

Central Michigan L

Montclair State (NJ) .... M

Montevallo (AL) .... R

Oregon State L

Point Loma (CA) .... R

Texas Tech. U. L

Washington State L

JOURNALISM/COMMUNICATIONS

GROUP I
Most Selective

American U. (DC)	M	North Carolina, U. of	L
Boston U. (MA)	L	Northwestern (IL)	M
California, U. of (Los Angeles)	XL	Ohio U.	L
Creighton (NE)	R	Southern California	L
DePauw (IN)	R	Southwestern (TX)	R
Florida, U. of	XL	Stanford (CA)	M
Gettysburg (PA)	R	Syracuse (NY)	L
Illinois, U. of (Urbana-Champaign)	XL	Trinity (TX)	R
Macalester (MN)	R	Villanova (PA)	M
Miami, U. of (FL)	L	Wheaton (IL)	R
Michigan, U. of	XL	Wisconsin, U. of	XL

GROUP II
Very Selective

Alabama, U. of (Huntsville)	M	John Carroll (OH)	M
Arizona State	XL	Juniata (PA)	R
Arizona, U. of	XL	Kansas, U. of	L
California Poly (SLO)	L	Kansas State	L
Canisius (NY)	M	Kentucky, U. of	L
Central Florida, U. of	L	LeMoyne (NY)	R
Chapman (CA)	R	Linfield (OR)	R
Clark (MA)	R	Loras (IA)	R
Colorado, U. of	L	Louisiana State	XL
Delaware, U. of	L	Loyola (MD)	R
Denver, U. of (CO)	M	Loyola Marymount (CA)	M
DePaul (IL)	M	Marist (NY)	M
Drake (IA)	M	π Marquette (WI)	M
Duquesne (PA)	M	Mary Baldwin (VA)	S
Fairfield (CT)	M	Maryland, U. of	XL
Flagler (FL)	R	Massachusetts, U. of	L
Fordham (NY)	M	Master's (CA)	R
Fredonia (SUNY) (NY)	M	Michigan State	L
Georgetown College (KY)	R	▲ Mills College (CA)	S
Georgia, U. of	XL	Minnesota, U. of	XL
Gonzaga (WA)	R	Mississippi, U. of	M
Hanover (IN)	R	Missouri, U. of	XL
Illinois College	S	Moravian (PA)	R
Indiana U.	XL	Muhlenberg (PA)	R
Iowa, U. of	XL		
James Madison (VA)	M		

π *Especially Broadcasting*
GROUP II continues next page

JOURNALISM/COMMUNICATIONS, *continued*

GROUP II, *continued*

Nevada, U. of (Reno) .... M	South Carolina, U. of L
New Hampshire, U. of L	Southern Methodist (TX) .... M
North Central (IL) .... R	Spring Hill (AL) .... R
Ohio Wesleyan .... R	Susquehanna U. (PA) .... R
Oklahoma, U. of L	Temple (PA) L
Oregon, U. of L	Texas A&M (Galveston) .... S
Pepperdine (CA) .... R	Texas Christian U. .... M
▲ Randolph-Macon Woman's Col. (VA) .. S	Texas, U. of (Austin) XL
Rowan (NJ) .... M	Tulsa, U. of (OK) .... R
St. Ambrose (IA) .... R	Wartburg (IA) .... R
St. Bonaventure (NY) .... R	West Virginia U. L
St. Louis (MO) .... M	Western Michigan L
St. Mary's (IN) .... R	Western Washington U. L
St. Michael's (VT) .... R	Whitworth (WA) .... R
San Diego State U. (CA) XL	Winona State U. (MN) L
Santa Clara U. (CA) .... M	Wisconsin, U. of (Stevens Point) .... M
Scranton, U. of (PA) .... M	Xavier (OH) .... R
▲ Simmons (MA) .... R	

JOURNALISM/COMMUNICATIONS continues next page

Enrollment Code		
■ **Men Only** ▲ **Women Only**	**S = Small** (less than 1000 students) **R = Moderate** (1000-3000 students) **M = Medium** (3000-8000 students) **L = Large** (8000-20,000 students) **XL = Extra Large** (over 20,000 students)	

JOURNALISM/COMMUNICATIONS, *continued*

GROUP III
Selective

Appalachian State (NC)	L	Loyola (IL)	M
Arkansas, U. of	L	Loyola U. (LA)	M
Augsburg (MN)	R	Lynchburg (VA)	R
Bemidji State (MN)	M	Lyndon State (VT)	R
Bethany (WV)	S	Massachusetts Col. of Lib. Arts (N. Adams)	R
Brockport (SUNY) (NY)	M	Minnesota, U. of (Duluth)	M
Buena Vista (IA)	R	Misericordia, College (PA)	S
Butler (IN)	R	Montana, U. of	M
California State U. (Fullerton)	L	Morningside (IA)	S
California State U. (Long Beach)	L	Montevallo (AL)	R
California State U. (Northridge)	L	Nebraska, U. of	L
California State U. (Sacramento)	M	North Carolina, U. of (Greensboro)	M
California State U. (San Bernardino)	M	Oakland U. (MI)	M
▲ Chatham (PA)	S	Oklahoma City U.	R
Elon (NC)	R	▲ Pine Manor (MA)	S
Fitchburg (MA)	R	Regis (CO)	R
Florida Southern	R	▲ Regis (MA)	S
Fontbonne (MO)	R	Reinhardt (GA)	S
Franklin (IN)	S	Robert Morris (PA)	R
Hardin-Simmons (TX)	R	St. John Fisher (NY)	R
Hawaii Pacific	M	St. Mary's College (MN)	R
Hofstra (NY)	M	Salem State (MA)	M
Howard (DC)	M	Samford (AL)	R
Hunter (CUNY) (NY)	L	Santa Fe, College of (NM)	S
Idaho, U. of	M	Seton Hall (NJ)	M
Jacksonville (FL)	R	Southern Connecticut	M
Johnson C. Smith (NC)	R	Southern Maine	M
Keene State (NH)	R	Tampa, U. of (FL)	R
Kent State (OH)	L	Texas Wesleyan	R
Kentucky Wesleyan	S	Wichita State (KS)	M
Lewis-Clark State (ID)	R	Worcester State (MA)	M

MATHEMATICS

GROUP I
Most Selective

American U. (DC)	M	▲ Mount Holyoke (MA)	R
▲ Barnard (NY)	R	New College (FL)	S
Bates (ME)	R	New Jersey, College of	M
Binghamton (SUNY) (NY)	L	New York U.	L
Bowdoin (ME)	R	Northwestern (IL)	M
Bucknell (PA)	M	Occidental (CA)	R
California Inst. of Tech.	S	Pomona (CA)	R
California, U. of (Berkeley)	XL	Princeton (NJ)	M
California, U. of (Los Angeles)	XL	Rensselaer (NY)	M
California, U. of (San Diego)	L	Rice (TX)	R
Carleton (MN)	R	Stanford (CA)	M
Case Western Reserve U. (OH)	R	St. Mary's Col. of Maryland	R
Chicago, U. of (IL)	M	St. Olaf (MN)	R
Colgate (NY)	R	Trinity (CT)	R
Columbia (NY)	M	Tulane (LA)	M
Dartmouth (NH)	M	Union (NY)	R
Davidson (NC)	R	Villanova (PA)	M
Dickinson (PA)	R	■ Wabash (IN)	S
Duke (NC)	M	Washington U. (MO)	M
Florida, U. of	XL	▲ Wellesley (MA)	R
Harvard (MA)	M	Wesleyan (CT)	R
Harvey Mudd (CA)	S	Wheaton (IL)	R
Holy Cross (MA)	R	Whitman (WA)	R
Illinois Inst. of Tech.	R	Willamette (OR)	R
Illinois, U. of (Urbana-Champaign)	XL	Wisconsin, U. of	XL
Kenyon (OH)	R	Yale (CT)	M
MIT (MA)	M		

MATHEMATICS continues next page

Enrollment Code

■ Men Only
▲ Women Only

S = Small (less than 1000 students) **R = Moderate** (1000-3000 students) **M = Medium** (3000-8000 students)
L = Large (8000-20,000 students) **XL = Extra Large** (over 20,000 students)

MATHEMATICS, *continued*

GROUP II
Very Selective

Alabama, U. of (Huntsville)	M	Millsaps (MS)	S
Albion (MI)	R	Muhlenberg (PA)	R
Arizona State	XL	North Carolina State	L
Birmingham-Southern (AL)	R	Ohio U.	L
Bryant (RI)	R	Oregon, U. of	L
California, U. of (Irvine)	L	Potsdam (SUNY) (NY)	R
California, U. of (Riverside)	M	Rochester Inst. of Tech.	L
California, U. of (Santa Cruz)	M	▲ Simmons (MA)	R
Cincinnati, U. of (OH)	L	Southern California, U. of	L
Colorado, U. of	L	Southwest Missouri	L
Concordia (MN)	R	Stetson (FL)	R
Earlham (IN)	R	▲ Sweet Briar (VA)	S
Fairfield (CT)	M	Texas, U. of (Austin)	XL
Florida Atlantic	L	▲ Trinity (DC)	S
Hiram (OH)	R	Valparaiso (IN)	M
Illinois College	S	Washington, U. of	XL
Kansas State	L	Wheaton (MA)	R
Knox (IL)	R	Wofford (SC)	R
Lebanon Valley (PA)	R	Wooster (OH)	R
Michigan State	XL		

GROUP III
Selective

Bluffton (OH)	S	Malone (OH)	R
California State U. (Monterey Bay)	R	St. Joseph's (NY)	R
California State U. (San Jose)	L	Simpson (IA)	S
Eastern Connecticut	M	Southwest Texas State	L
Fisk (TN)	S	Texas Tech. U.	L
Fontbonne (MO)	R	Wisconsin, U. of (Eau Claire)	L
Louisiana State	XL	Worcester State (MA)	M
Lynchburg (VA)	R		

Enrollment Code

■ **Men Only**   **S = Small** (less than 1000 students)   **R = Moderate** (1000-3000 students)   **M = Medium** (3000-8000 students)
▲ **Women Only**   **L = Large** (8000-20,000 students)   **XL = Extra Large** (over 20,000 students)

MUSIC

GROUP I
Most Selective

▲ Barnard (NY) .... R
Beloit (WI) .... R
Boston U. (MA) L
Bowdoin (ME) .... R
Brandeis (MA) .... R
Bucknell (PA) .... R
California, U. of (Berkeley) XL
California, U. of (Los Angeles) XL
California, U. of (San Diego) L
Carnegie-Mellon (PA).......................... M
Case Western Reserve U. (OH) .... R
Cleveland Inst. of Music (OH) ....S
Columbia (NY) .... M
Connecticut College............................ R
π DePauw (IN) .... R
Furman (SC) .... R
Geneseo (SUNY) (NY) .... M
Gustavus Adolphus (MN) .... R
Harvard (MA) .... M
Hofstra (NY) .... M
Illinois, U. of (Urbana-Champaign) XL
Illinois Wesleyan .... R
Iowa, U. of...XL
Johns Hopkins (MD) .... M

Juilliard (NY) ....S
Lawrence (WI) .... R
Miami, U. of (FL) L
Michigan, U. of XL
New York U. L
Northwestern (IL) .... M
Oberlin (OH) .... R
Princeton (NJ) .... M
Rhodes (TN) .... R
Rice (TX) .... R
Rochester, U. of (NY) .... M
Skidmore (NY) .... R
▲ Smith (MA) .... R
Southwestern (TX) .... R
Stanford (CA) .... M
St. Mary's College of Maryland .... R
St. Olaf (MN) .... R
Vanderbilt (TN) .... M
Vassar (NY) .... R
Wheaton (IL) .... R
Whitman (WA) .... R
Willamette (OR) .... R
Yale (CT) .... M

π *Music and Music Business*

MUSIC continues next page

Enrollment Code			
■ Men Only	S = Small (less than 1000 students)	R = Moderate (1000-3000 students)	M = Medium (3000-8000 students)
▲ Women Only	L = Large (8000-20,000 students)	XL = Extra Large (over 20,000 students)	

MUSIC, *continued*

GROUP II
Very Selective

Augustana (IL) .... R	Manhattan School of Music (NY) .... S
Bard (NY) .... R	Mercer (GA) .... R
Berklee College of Music (MA) .... R	Milliken (IL) .... R
Birmingham-Southern (AL) .... R	▲ Mills (CA) .... S
Boston Conservatory .... S	Millsaps (MS) .... S
Butler (IN) .... R	Missouri, U. of (Kansas City) .... M
Cal. Inst. of the Arts .... S	Moravian (PA) .... R
California, U. of (Riverside) .... M	Nebraska, U. of L
California, U. of (Santa Barbara) L	New England Conservatory (MA) .... S
California, U. of (Santa Cruz) .... M	New Hampshire, U. of L
Capital (OH) .... R	North Florida .... M
Catholic U. (DC) .... M	North Texas L
Chapman (CA) .... R	Ohio U. L
Clark (MA) .... R	π Oklahoma City U. .... R
Coe (IA) .... R	π Oneonta (SUNY)(NY) .... M
Colorado, U. of L	Oregon, U. of L
Concordia (CA) .... R	Pacific, U. of the (CA) .... R
Concordia (MN) .... R	Potsdam (SUNY) (NY) .... M
▲ Converse (SC) .... S	Purchase (SUNY) (NY) .... R
Cornish (WA) .... S	Queens (NC) .... R
Curtis Institute of Music (PA) .... S	Redlands, U. of (CA) .... R
Denver, U. of .... R	Rowan (NJ) .... M
Drake (IA) .... M	San Francisco Conservatory (CA) .... S
Drury (MO) .... S	Santa Clara, U. of (CA) .... M
Florida State L	Shepherd (WV) .... R
Fredonia (SUNY) (NY) .... M	Southern California, U. of L
Gordon (MA) .... R	▲ St. Catherine (MN) .... R
Hope (MI) .... R	Stetson (FL) .... R
Houghton (NY) .... S	Syracuse (NY) L
Houston, U. of (TX) L	Temple (PA) .... M
Indiana U. XL	Valparaiso (IN) .... R
Ithaca (NY) .... M	Wartburg (IA) .... R
James Madison (VA) L	West Chester (PA) .... M
▲ Judson (AL) .... S	West Virginia, U. of L
Lake Forest (IL) .... S	Western Michigan L
Lebanon Valley (PA) .... R	Whitworth (WA) .... R
Louisiana State XL	William Jewell Col. (MO) .... R
Loyola (IL) .... M	Wittenberg (OH) .... R
Luther (IA) .... R	Wooster, College of (OH) .... R
Maine, U. of .... M	
Manhattanville (NY) .... R	*π Music and Music Business*

MUSIC continues next page

MUSIC, *continued*

GROUP III
Selective

Anna Maria (MA) .... S	Longwood (VA).................................. R
Arkansas, U. of L	Loyola (LA).. M
Arts, U. of the (PA) .... R	Massachusetts, U. of (Boston) .... M
π Baldwin-Wallace (OH) .... R	Massachusetts, U. of (Lowell) .... M
Belhaven (MS) .... S	Memphis, U. of (TN) L
➤ Belmont (TN)..................................... R	▲ Meredith (NC)................................... R
Bethany (WV) .... R	π Monmouth (NJ) .... R
Bowling Green (OH) L	Moorhead (MN) .... M
Brenau (GA) .... R	Mount St. Mary's (CA) .... R
California State U. (Fresno) L	Nevada, U. of (Reno) .... M
California State U. (Fullerton).............. L	Northern Colorado L
California State U. (Hayward) .... M	Northwestern College (IA).................... S
California State U. (Northridge)........... L	Nyack (NY).. R
California State U. (Sacramento) .... M	Oklahoma Baptist .... R
California State U. (San Jose) L	Rider (NJ).. M
Carson-Newman (TN) .... R	Roosevelt (IL).................................... R
Central Connecticut .... M	▲ Seton Hill (PA).................................. S
Central Washington L	Shenandoah (VA) .... R
Duquesne (PA) .... M	Simpson (IA) .... S
East Carolina L	Southern Maine .... M
➤ Five Towns College (NY) .... S	Southwest Baptist (MO) .... R
Fort Hays (KS) .... M	Tampa, U. of (FL) .... R
Hardin-Simmons (TX) .... R	Western Connecticut .... M
Hartford, U. of (CT) .... M	Western St. Coll. of Colorado .... R
Hartwick (NY) .... R	Westfield (MA) .... M
Heidelberg (OH) .... S	William Paterson (NJ) .... M
Humboldt State (CA) .... M	Xavier U. of Louisiana .... R
Jacksonville (FL) .... R	
Keene State (NH) .... R	➤ *Music Business*
Kent State (OH).................................. L	π *Music and Music Business*

NURSING

GROUP I
Most Selective

▲ Barnard (NY) .... R
Binghamton (SUNY) (NY) L
Boston Col. (MA) L
Case Western Reserve U. (OH) .... R
Colorado, U. of L
Columbia (NY) .... M
DePauw (IN) .... R
Duke (NC) .... M
Emory (GA) .... R
Florida, U. of XL
Gustavus Adolphus (MN) .... R
Illinois, U. of XL

Illinois Wesleyan .... R
Missouri, U. of (Rolla) .... M
New York U. L
Pennsylvania, U. of L
Rochester, U. of (NY) .... M
St. Olaf (MN) .... R
Vanderbilt (TN) .... M
Villanova (PA) .... M
Virginia, U. of L
Washington, U. of XL
Wisconsin, U. of L

NURSING continues next page

NURSING, *continued*

GROUP II
Very Selective

Adelphi (NY)	M		Minnesota, U. of	XL
Alabama, U. of (Huntsville)	M		Mississippi U. for Women	R
Arizona, U. of	XL		Moravian (PA)	R
Augustana (SD)	R		Morningside (IA)	S
Barry (FL)	R		Mount Mercy (IA)	S
Baylor (TX)	M		New Jersey, College of	M
Bethel (MN)	R		North Dakota, U. of	M
Capital (OH)	R		Ohio State	XL
Carroll (WI)	R		Pace (NY)	M
Catholic U. (DC)	M		Pacific Lutheran (WA)	R
Clarke (IA)	S		Pennsylvania State	XL
Creighton (NE)	R		Pittsburgh, U. of (PA)	L
Daemen (NY)	R		Portland, U. of (OR)	R
Delaware, U. of	L		Samford (AL)	R
Detroit Mercy (MI)	M		San Diego, U. of (CA)	M
Duquesne (PA)	M		San Francisco, U. of (CA)	M
Evansville (IN)	R		Seattle Pacific (WA)	R
Fairfield (CT)	M		Seton Hall (NJ)	M
Florida Gulf Coast U.	R		▲ Simmons (MA)	R
Franciscan U. of Steubenville (OH)	R		South Dakota School of Mines	R
George Mason (VA)	M		▲ St. Catherine (MN)	R
Georgetown (DC)	M		St. Louis (MO)	M
Gwynedd Mercy (PA)	S		▲ St. Mary's College (IN)	R
Hunter (CUNY) (NY)	L		Texas Christian U.	M
Illinois, U. of (Chicago)	L		Truman State (MO)	M
Iowa, U. of	XL		Union University (TN)	R
Lebanon Valley (PA)	R		Valparaiso U. (IN)	M
Loyola (IL)	M		Viterbo (WI)	R
Luther (IA)	R		Webster (MD)	R
Marquette (WI)	M		Western Michigan	L
➤ Maryland, U. of (Baltimore County)	M		Westminster (UT)	R
Massachusetts, U. of	L		William Jewell (MO)	R
McKendree (IL)	R		Wisconsin, U. of (Milwaukee)	XL
Michigan, U. of	XL		York (PA)	M

➤ *Health Policy, also*

NURSING continues next page

NURSING, *continued*

GROUP III
Selective

Alaska, U. of (Fairbanks)	M	Marshall (WV)	M
Alderson-Broaddus (WV)	S	Marymount (VA)	R
Alverno (WI)	R	Maryville (St. Louis) (MO)	R
Arizona State	XL	Massachusetts, U. of (Boston)	M
Avila (MO)	S	Massachusetts, U. of (Dartmouth)	M
Azusa Pacific (CA)	R	Mercy (NY)	M
Ball State (IN)	L	Midwestern State U. (TX)	M
Bellarmine (KY)	R	Milligan (TN)	R
Berea (KY)	R	Misericordia, College (PA)	S
California State U. (Bakersfield)	M	Mississippi College	R
California State U. (Chico)	L	Mount St. Joseph (OH)	R
California State U. (Dominguez Hills)	M	Mount St. Mary's (CA)	R
California State U. (Fresno)	L	Mount St. Mary's (NY)	S
California State U. (Fullerton)	L	North Carolina, U. of (Charlotte)	L
California State U. (Los Angeles)	L	North Carolina, U. of (Greensboro)	M
California State U. (San Jose)	L	Northeast Louisiana	L
Carroll (MT)	R	Northern Illinois U.	L
Carson-Newman (TN)	R	Oakland (MI)	M
▲ Cedar Crest (PA)	S	Oklahoma Baptist	R
Cedarville (OH)	R	Plattsburgh (SUNY) (NY)	M
Central Arkansas	M	Point Loma (CA)	R
Dominican (CA)	S	Rhode Island, U. of	L
D'Youville (NY)	R	Russell Sage (The Sage Colleges)(NY)	R
East Carolina (NC)	L	St. Scholastica (MN)	R
Eastern (PA)	R	St. Joseph's (ME)	S
Eastern Kentucky	L	San Diego State (CA)	L
Edgewood (WI)	S	Seattle U. (WA)	R
Elms (MA)	S	Shenandoah (VA)	R
Ferris State (MI)	L	Sonoma State (CA)	M
Fitchburg (MA)	R	South Alabama	M
Gannon (PA)	M	South Dakota, U. of	M
Goshen (IN)	R	South Florida, U. of	L
Graceland (IA)	R	Southern Maine, U. of	M
Grambling (LA)	M	St. Anselm (NH)	R
Hartwick (NY)	R	Tuskegee University (AL)	M
Hawaii Pacific	M	Walla Walla (WA)	R
Henderson State (AR)	M	Wayne State (MI)	L
Howard (DC)	M	Western Connecticut State	M
Husson (ME)	S	Western Kentucky	L
▲ Immaculata (PA)	S	Wheeling Jesuit (WV)	R
Ind.U.-Purdue U.-Indianapolis (IN)	L	Widener (PA)	R
Jacksonville (FL)	R	Wilkes (PA)	R
Lewis-Clark State (ID)	R	Wisconsin, U. of (Eau Claire)	L
MacMurray (IL)	S	Worcester State (MA)	M

Enrollment Code	
■ Men Only	S = Small (less than 1000 students) R = Moderate (1000-3000 students) M = Medium (3000-8000 students)
▲ Women Only	L = Large (8000-20,000 students) XL = Extra Large (over 20,000 students)

PHARMACY

GROUP I
Most Selective

Buffalo (SUNY) (NY)	L	Michigan, U. of	XL
Butler (IN)	R	North Carolina, U. of	L
Creighton (NE)	R	Purdue (IN)	XL
Florida, U. of	XL	Rutgers (NJ)	L
Illinois, U. of	XL	Wisconsin, U. of	L

GROUP II
Very Selective

Albany Col. of Pharmacy (NY)	S	Ohio Northern U.	R
Cincinnati, U. of (OH)	L	Ohio State	XL
Connecticut, U. of	L	Pacific, U. of the (CA)	R
Drake (IA)	M	Pittsburgh, U. of	L
Duquesne (PA)	M	Rhode Island, U. of	L
Ferris State (MI)	L	Samford (AL)	R
Florida A&M	L	Sciences in Philadelphia, U. of (PA)	R
Georgia, U. of	L	South Carolina, U. of	L
Illinois, U. of (Chicago)	L	Southern California, U. of	L
Kansas, U. of	L	Southwestern Oklahoma	M
Kentucky, U. of	L	St. John's (NY)	L
Maryland, U. of	XL	St. Louis Col. of Pharmacy (MO)	S
Mass. College of Pharmacy	R	Temple (PA)	L
Mercer (GA)	R	Texas, U. of (Austin)	XL
Minnesota, U. of	XL	Toledo, U. of	L
Mississippi, U. of	M	Utah, U. of	L
Montana, U. of	M	Virginia Commonwealth U.	L
New Mexico, U. of	M	Washington State	L
Northeastern (MA)	L	Wayne State (MI)	L
Northeast Louisiana	L	Wyoming, U. of	L
North Dakota State	L	Xavier (LA)	R

	Enrollment Code		
■ Men Only	S = Small (less than 1000 students)	R = Moderate (1000-3000 students)	M = Medium (3000-8000 students)
▲ Women Only	L = Large (8000-20,000 students)	XL = Extra Large (over 20,000 students)	

PHILOSOPHY

GROUP I
Most Selective

▲ Barnard (NY) .... R	Johns Hopkins (MD) .... R
Bates (ME) .... R	Kenyon (OH) .... R
Binghamton (SUNY) (NY) L	Macalester (MN) .... R
Boston Col. (MA) L	Michigan, U. of XL
Boston U. (MA) L	New College (FL) .... S
Bowdoin (ME) .... R	New York U. L
Bucknell (PA) .... M	Oberlin (OH) .... R
California, U. of (Berkeley) XL	Pennsylvania, U. of L
California, U. of (Los Angeles) XL	Pittsburgh, U. of (PA) L
Chicago, U. of (IL) .... M	Pomona (CA) .... R
Claremont McKenna (CA) .... R	Princeton (NJ) .... M
Colgate (NY) .... R	Reed (OR) .... R
Colorado Col. .... R	Rochester, U. of (NY) .... M
Columbia (NY) .... M	▲ Smith (MA) .... R
Connecticut Col. .... R	Southwestern (TX) .... R
Cornell (NY) L	St. Olaf (MN) .... R
Davidson (NC) .... R	Swarthmore (PA) .... R
Duke (NC) .... M	Trinity (CT) .... R
Florida State L	Trinity (TX) .... R
Florida, U. of XL	Tulane (LA) .... M
George Washington (DC) .... M	Vanderbilt (TN) .... M
Georgetown (DC) .... M	Washington U. (MO) .... M
Hamilton (NY) .... R	Wheaton (IL) .... R
Harvard (MA) .... M	Whitman (WA) .... R
Haverford (PA) .... S	Yale (CT) .... M
Holy Cross (MA) .... R	

GROUP II
Very Selective

Allegheny (PA) .... R	Lycoming (PA) .... R
Asbury (KY) .... R	Mansfield (PA) .... R
Biola (CA) .... R	Marquette (WI) .... M
California, U. of (Santa Barbara) L	Milligan (TN) .... S
California State U. (Dominguez Hills) . M	Muhlenberg (PA) .... R
California State U. (Fresno) L	Northeastern (MA) L
California State U. (Northridge) L	Oneonta (SUNY)(NY) .... M
Christiandom (VA) .... S	Regis (CO) .... R
Clarke (IA) .... S	St. Andrews Presbyterian (NC) .... S
Cornell Col. (IA) .... R	St. Bonaventure (NY) .... R
Denison (OH) .... R	St. Louis (MO) .... M
Fordham (NY) L	St. Thomas (MN) .... M
Franciscan U. of Steubenville (OH) ..... R	Salisbury State (MD) .... M
▲ Hood (MD) .... S	Skidmore (NY) .... R
Indiana U. XL	Stony Brook (SUNY) (NY) L
Kansas Newman .... S	Wheeling Jesuit (WV) .... R
Loyola (LA) .... M	Wofford (SC) .... R

PHYSICS

GROUP I
Most Selective

Amherst (MA) .... R
▲ Barnard (NY) .... R
Bates (ME) .... R
Binghamton (SUNY) (NY) L
Boston U. (MA) L
▲ Bryn Mawr (PA) .... S
California Inst. of Tech. .... S
California, U. of (Berkeley) XL
California, U. of (San Diego) L
Carleton (MN) .... R
Case Western Reserve U. (OH) .... R
Centre (KY) .... R
Chicago, U. of (IL) .... M
Colorado School of Mines .... R
Columbia (NY) .... M
Cornell (NY) L
Dartmouth (NH) .... M
Dickinson (PA) .... R
Florida, U. of XL
Franklin & Marshall (PA) .... R
Geneseo (SUNY) (NY) .... M
Georgetown (DC) .... M
Georgia Inst. of Tech. .... M
Grinnell (IA) .... R
Gustavus Adolphus (MN) .... R
Harvard (MA) .... M
Harvey Mudd (CA) .... S

Haverford (PA) .... S
Illinois, U. of (Urbana-Champaign) XL
Kalamazoo (MI) .... R
Lawrence (WI) .... R
Macalester (MN) .... R
MIT (MA) .... M
New College (FL) .... S
New Mexico Inst. of Mining & Tech. .... S
Occidental (CA) .... R
Princeton (NJ) .... M
Reed (OR) .... R
Rensselaer (NY) .... M
Rhodes (TN) .... R
Rice (TX) .... R
St. Olaf (MN) .... R
▲ Smith (MA) .... R
Stanford (CA) .... M
Swarthmore (PA) .... R
Wake Forest (NC) .... M
Washington U. (MO) .... M
▲ Wellesley (MA) .... R
Wheaton (IL) .... R
Whitman (WA) .... R
William & Mary (VA) .... M
Worcester Poly. Inst. (MA) .... R
Yeshiva (NY) .... R

PHYSICS continues next page

PHYSICS, *continued*

GROUP II
Very Selective

Adelphi (NY) .... M	Ohio State XL
Beloit (WI) .... R	Ohio U. L
California, U. of (Irvine) L	Oklahoma State L
California, U. of (Santa Barbara) L	Oregon State L
California, U. of (Santa Cruz) .... M	Rollins (FL) .... R
Colorado, U. of L	St. John's (MN) .... R
Colorado, U. of (Colorado Springs) .... M	Shippensburg (PA) .... M
Denver, U. of (CO) .... M	Stockton State (NJ) .... M
Evansville, U. of (IN) .... R	Stony Brook (SUNY) (NY) L
Fairfield (CT) .... M	Texas, U. of (Austin) XL
Guilford (NC) .... R	Ursinus (PA) .... R
Lewis & Clark (OR) .... R	Vermont, U. of .... M
Loyola (IL) .... M	Whitworth (WA) .... R
Mississippi, U. of .... M	Wisconsin, U. of XL

GROUP III
Selective

Brooklyn Col. (CUNY) (NY) L	Jacksonville (FL) .... R
California State U. (Northridge) L	Louisiana State XL
California State U. (San Jose) L	Northwestern (IA) .... S
City Col. (CUNY) (NY) L	Southern Connecticut .... M
Goshen (IN) .... R	

Enrollment Code

■ Men Only   **S = Small** (less than 1000 students)   **R = Moderate** (1000-3000 students)   **M = Medium** (3000-8000 students)

▲ Women Only   **L = Large** (8000-20,000 students)   **XL = Extra Large** (over 20,000 students)

POLITICAL SCIENCE

GROUP I
Most Selective

American U. (DC)	M	▲ Mount Holyoke (MA)	R
Amherst (MA)	R	Northwestern (IL)	M
Boston U. (MA)	L	Notre Dame (IN)	M
Brandeis (MA)	R	Occidental (CA)	R
Brown (RI)	M	Pennsylvania, U. of	L
California, U. of (Los Angeles)	XL	Pomona (CA)	R
California, U. of (San Diego)	L	Princeton (NJ)	M
Centre (KY)	R	Rhodes (TN)	R
Chicago, U. of (IL)	M	Richmond, U. of (VA)	M
Claremont McKenna (CA)	R	Rochester, U. of (NY)	M
Colby (ME)	R	▲ Smith (MA)	R
Colgate (NY)	R	South, U. of the (TN)	R
Colorado Col.	R	Southwestern (TX)	R
Columbia (NY)	M	Stanford (CA)	M
Connecticut Col.	R	Swarthmore (PA)	R
Dartmouth (NH)	M	Trinity (TX)	R
Dickinson (PA)	R	Tufts (MA)	M
Drew (NJ)	R	Union (NY)	R
Duke (NC)	M	U.S. Naval Academy (MD)	M
Emory (GA)	R	Ursinus (PA)	R
Franklin & Marshall (PA)	R	Vanderbilt (TN)	M
Furman (SC)	R	Villanova (PA)	M
Georgetown (DC)	M	■ Wabash (IN)	S
George Washington (DC)	M	Wake Forest (NC)	M
Grinnell (IA)	R	Washington & Lee (VA)	R
Hamilton (NY)	R	▲ Wellesley (MA)	R
Harvard (MA)	M	Wesleyan (CT)	R
Johns Hopkins (MD)	R	Whitman (WA)	R
Kenyon (OH)	R	Willamette (OR)	R
Macalester (MN)	R	Williams (MA)	R
MIT (MA)	M	Yale (CT)	M
Middlebury (VT)	R	Yeshiva (NY)	R

POLITICAL SCIENCE continues next page

Enrollment Code

■ Men Only   **S = Small** (less than 1000 students)   **R = Moderate** (1000-3000 students)   **M = Medium** (3000-8000 students)

▲ Women Only   **L = Large** (8000-20,000 students)   **XL = Extra Large** (over 20,000 students)

POLITICAL SCIENCE, *continued*

GROUP II
Very Selective

Austin (TX)	R	Ohio Wesleyan	R
California, U. of (Davis)	L	Oklahoma City U.	R
California, U. of (Riverside)	M	Oklahoma, U. of	L
California, U. of (Santa Barbara)	L	Oklahoma State	L
Catholic U. (DC)	M	Presbyterian (SC)	S
Creighton (NE)	R	Providence (RI)	M
Dayton, U. of	M	Randolph Macon (VA)	R
Denison (OH)	R	Redlands, U. of (CA)	R
DePaul (IL)	M	Ripon (WI)	S
Drake (IA)	M	Siena (NY)	R
Gonzaga (WA)	R	Skidmore (NY)	R
Hawaii, U. of	L	Spring Hill (AL)	R
Hobart & William Smith (NY)	R	St. Bonaventure (NY)	R
Hofstra (NY)	M	St. John's (MN)	R
Hope (MI)	R	St. Lawrence (NY)	R
Howard (DC)	M	Stonehill (MA)	R
Knox (IL)	R	Syracuse (NY)	L
Manhattan (NY)	M	▲ Trinity (DC)	S
Marquette (WI)	M	Vermont, U. of	L
Maryland, U. of (Baltimore County)	M	Washington & Jefferson (PA)	R
Millersville (PA)	M	Wheaton (MA)	R
Minnesota, U. of	XL	Wilberforce (OH)	S
North Central (IL)	R	Wittenberg (OH)	R
Oglethorpe (GA)	S		

GROUP III
Selective

Adrian (MI)	S	Michigan State	XL
Albright (PA)	R	Mt. St. Mary's (MD)	R
Arizona State	XL	▲ Pine Manor (MA)	S
Belmont Abbey (NC)	S	Radford (VA)	M
Brockport (SUNY)(NY)	M	Rhode Island, U. of	L
California State U. (Long Beach)	L	St. Mary's (TX)	R
California State U. (Northridge)	L	▲ Spelman (GA)	R
California State U. (Sacramento)	M	Texas, U. of (Arlington)	L
▲ Chatham (PA)	S	Virginia Wesleyan	R
Eastern Connecticut	M	Westfield (MA)	M
Hartwick (NY)	R	Whittier (CA)	R

Enrollment Code

■ Men Only   **S = Small** (less than 1000 students)   **R = Moderate** (1000-3000 students)   **M = Medium** (3000-8000 students)

▲ Women Only   **L = Large** (8000-20,000 students)   **XL = Extra Large** (over 20,000 students)

PRE-LAW

Author's Note: *Law School Associations usually recommend that a student choose a major dependent upon one's own individual intellectual interests and upon "the quality of undergraduate education" provided by various departments and colleges. The following recommended colleges have been taken primarily from our recommended departments in English, Economics, and Political Science.*

GROUP I
Most Selective

Albany (SUNY) (NY)	L	Florida, U. of	XL
Allegheny (PA)	R	Franklin & Marshall (PA)	R
American U. (DC)	M	Furman (SC)	R
Amherst (MA)	R	Georgetown (DC)	M
Bard (NY)	R	George Washington (DC)	M
▲ Barnard (NY)	R	Gettysburg (PA)	R
Bates (ME)	R	Grinnell (IA)	R
Binghamton (SUNY) (NY)	L	Hamilton (NY)	R
Boston Col. (MA)	L	Harvard (MA)	M
Boston U. (MA)	L	Haverford (PA)	S
Bowdoin (ME)	R	Holy Cross (MA)	R
Brandeis (MA)	R	Illinois Wesleyan	R
Brown (RI)	M	Iowa, U. of	XL
▲ Bryn Mawr (PA)	S	Johns Hopkins (MD)	R
Bucknell (PA)	M	Kalamazoo (MI)	R
Buffalo (SUNY) (NY)	L	Kenyon (OH)	R
California, U. of (Berkeley)	XL	Lafayette (PA)	R
California, U. of (Los Angeles)	XL	Macalester (MN)	R
California, U. of (San Diego)	L	Maryland, U. of (Baltimore County)	M
Carleton (MN)	R	MIT (MA)	M
Centre (KY)	R	Michigan, U. of	XL
Chicago, U. of (IL)	M	Middlebury (VT)	R
Claremont McKenna (CA)	R	▲ Mount Holyoke (MA)	R
Clark (MA)	R	Muhlenberg (PA)	R
Colby (ME)	R	New Jersey, College of	M
Colgate (NY)	R	North Carolina, U. of	L
Colorado Col.	R	Northwestern (IL)	M
Columbia (NY)	M	Notre Dame (IN)	M
Connecticut Col.	R	Oberlin (OH)	R
Dallas, U. of (TX)	R	Occidental (CA)	R
Dartmouth (NH)	M	Pennsylvania, U. of	L
Davidson (NC)	R	Pomona (CA)	R
DePauw (IN)	R	Princeton (NJ)	M
Dickinson (PA)	R	Providence (RI)	M
Drew (NJ)	R	Reed (OR)	R
Duke (NC)	M	Rhodes (TN)	R
Emory (GA)	R		

GROUP I continues next page

Enrollment Code

■ Men Only
▲ Women Only

S = **Small** (less than 1000 students) **R** = **Moderate** (1000-3000 students) **M** = **Medium** (3000-8000 students)
L = **Large** (8000-20,000 students) **XL** = **Extra Large** (over 20,000 students)

PRE-LAW, *continued*

GROUP I, *continued*

Rice (TX) .... R	Vanderbilt (TN) .... M
Richmond, U. of (VA) .... M	Vassar (NY) .... R
Rochester, U. of (NY) .... M	Villanova (PA) .... M
Rutgers (NJ) L	Virginia, U. of L
Sarah Lawrence (NY) .... S	■ Wabash (IN) .... S
Skidmore (NY) .... R	Wake Forest (NC) .... M
▲ Smith (MA) .... R	Washington & Lee (VA) .... R
South, U. of the (TN) .... R	Washington U. (MO) .... M
Southwestern (TX) .... R	▲ Wellesley (MA) .... R
Stanford (CA) .... M	Wesleyan U. (CT) .... R
St. Olaf (MN) .... R	Wheaton (IL) .... R
Swarthmore (PA) .... R	Whitman (WA) .... R
Trinity (CT) .... R	Williams (MA) .... R
Trinity (TX) .... R	Wisconsin, U. of XL
Tufts (MA) .... M	Worcester Poly. Inst. (MA) .... R
Union (NY) .... R	Yale (CT) .... M

GROUP II
Very Selective

▲ Agnes Scott (GA) .... S	Denver, U. of (CO) .... M
Albertson (ID) .... S	DePaul (IL) .... M
Albion (MI) .... R	Drake (IA) .... M
Alfred (NY) .... R	Evansville (IN) .... R
Alma (MI) .... R	Flagler (FL) .... R
Arizona, U. of XL	Fordham (NY) L
Augustana (IL) .... R	George Mason (VA) L
Baylor (TX) .... R	Georgetown College (KY) .... R
Bennington (VT) .... S	Georgia, U. of XL
Birmingham-Southern (AL) .... R	Gonzaga (WA) .... R
Butler (IN) .... R	Goucher (MD) .... R
California, U. of (Davis) L	Grand Valley (MI) L
California, U. of (Irvine) L	Guilford (NC) .... R
California, U. of (Riverside) .... M	Hamline (MN) .... R
California, U. of (Santa Barbara) L	■ Hampden-Sydney (VA) .... S
Calvin (MI) .... M	Hartwick (NY) .... R
Catholic (DC) .... R	Hendrix (AR) .... R
Chapman (CA) .... R	Hiram (OH) .... R
Clark (MA) .... R	Hobart & Wm. Smith (NY) .... R
Columbia Col. (SC) .... R	Hofstra (NY) .... M
Cornell Col. (IA) .... R	Hope (MI) .... R
Creighton (NE) .... R	Howard (DC) .... M
Denison (OH) .... R	*GROUP II continues next page*

GROUP II continues next page

Enrollment Code

■ Men Only	S = Small (less than 1000 students)	R = Moderate (1000-3000 students)	M = Medium (3000-8000 students)
▲ Women Only	L = Large (8000-20,000 students)	XL = Extra Large (over 20,000 students)	

PRE-LAW, *continued*

GROUP II, *continued*

Hunter (CUNY) (NY) L	▲ Randolph-Macon Woman's Col. (VA) .. S
Illinois College .... S	Redlands, U. of (CA) .... R
Kansas State L	Ripon (WI) .... S
Knox (IL) .... R	Rutgers (Camden) (NJ) .... M
Lake Forest (IL) .... R	▲ Salem College (NC) .... S
LaSalle (PA) .... M	Salisbury State (MD) .... M
Lawrence (WI) .... R	San Diego, U. of .... M
Loras (IA) .... R	San Francisco, U. of (CA) .... M
Loyola (LA) .... R	Santa Clara (CA) .... R
Loyola (MD) .... M	▲ Scripps (CA) .... S
Manhattan (NY) .... M	Siena (NY) .... R
Marietta (OH) .... R	Spring Hill (AL) .... R
Marquette (WI) .... M	St. Bonaventure (NY) .... R
Maryland, U. of XL	St. John's (MN) .... R
Massachusetts, U. of L	St. Lawrence (NY) .... R
Michigan State XL	▲ St. Mary's Col. (IN) .... R
Millersville (PA) .... M	Stetson (FL) .... R
Millsaps (MS) .... S	Stonehill (MA) .... R
Minnesota, U. of XL	Stony Brook (SUNY) (NY) L
Minnesota, U. of (Morris) .... R	Syracuse (NY) L
Mississippi, U. of .... M	▲ Trinity (DC) .... S
Nebraska, U. of L	Ursinus (PA) .... R
New Hampshire, U. of L	Vermont, U. of L
North Carolina State L	Virginia Commonwealth U. L
North Central (IL) .... R	Virginia Military Inst. .... R
Oglethorpe (GA) .... S	Warren Wilson (NC) .... S
Ohio U. L	Washington & Jefferson (PA) .... R
Ohio Wesleyan .... R	Washington, U. of XL
Oklahoma City U. .... R	▲ Wells (NY) .... S
Oklahoma, U. of L	Western Washington U. L
Oneonta (SUNY) (NY) .... M	Westminster Col. (MO) .... S
Pittsburgh, U. of (PA) L	Westmont (CA) .... R
Presbyterian (SC) .... S	Wheaton (MA) .... R
Principia (IL) .... S	Wilberforce (OH) .... S
Puget Sound (WA) .... R	Wittenberg (OH) .... R
Purchase (SUNY) (NY) .... R	Wofford (SC) .... R
Queens (NC) .... S	Wooster (OH) .... R
Randolph-Macon (VA) .... R	

PRE-LAW continues next page

PRE-LAW, *continued*

GROUP III
Selective

Adrian (MI)	S	Mount St. Mary's (MD) .... R
Albright (PA)	R	Niagara (NY) .... R
Arkansas, U. of	L	North Carolina, U. of (Wilmington) ..... M
Baldwin-Wallace (OH)	R	Radford (VA) .... M
Belmont Abbey (NC)	S	Rhode Island, U. of L
▲ Bennett (NC)	S	Roanoke (VA) .... R
California State U. (Long Beach)	L	Rockford (IL) .... S
California State U. (Monterey Bay)	R	▲ Rosemont (PA) .... S
California State U. (Northridge)	L	San Francisco State (CA) L
▲ Chatham (PA)	S	Seattle U. (WA) .... R
▲ Chestnut Hill (PA)	S	▲ Spelman (GA) .... R
Emerson (MA)	R	St. Anselm (NH) .... R
Fairleigh Dickinson (NJ)	M	St. Mary's (TX) .... R
Fisk (TN)	S	Temple (PA) L
Florida A&M	M	Tennessee, U. of XL
Fort Lewis (CO)	M	Utah, U. of L
Hawaii, U. of	L	Virginia Wesleyan .... R
Heidelberg (OH)	S	Whittier (CA) .... R
▲ Hollins (VA)	S	Wilson (PA) .... S
Longwood (VA)	R	Wisconsin, U. of (Milwaukee) L
Lynchburg (VA)	R	Wyoming, U. of L
Mount St. Joseph (OH)	R	

Enrollment Code		
■ Men Only	S = Small (less than 1000 students)	R = Moderate (1000-3000 students)	M = Medium (3000-8000 students)
▲ Women Only	L = Large (8000-20,000 students)	XL = Extra Large (over 20,000 students)	

PRE-MED/PRE-DENTAL

Author's Note: *In addition to general college requirements and requirements of their major department, premedical and predental students must usually pass with a good grade the following: general chemistry, zoology, organic chemistry, general biology, English composition or literature, and general physics.*

Other required or highly recommended courses are: advanced biology, psychology or sociology, physical chemistry, calculus, and quantitative chemistry. Of course, the wise path to follow is to consult the exact course requirements of the school you expect to apply to. The recommended colleges below are taken primarily from our recommended departments in biology and chemistry.

GROUP I
Most Selective

Albany (SUNY) (NY)	L	Furman (SC)	R
Allegheny (PA)	R	Geneseo (SUNY) (NY)	M
Amherst (MA)	R	Georgetown (DC)	M
Bates (ME)	R	Gettysburg (PA)	R
Binghamton (SUNY) (NY)	L	Grinnell (IA)	R
Boston Col. (MA)	L	Hamilton (NY)	R
Bowdoin (ME)	R	Harvard (MA)	M
Brandeis (MA)	R	Harvey Mudd (CA)	S
Brown (RI)	M	Haverford (PA)	S
▲ Bryn Mawr (PA)	S	Holy Cross (MA)	R
Bucknell (PA)	M	Illinois, U. of (Urbana-Champaign)	XL
Buffalo (SUNY) (NY)	L	Illinois Wesleyan	R
California Inst. of Tech.	S	Iowa State	XL
California, U. of (Berkeley)	XL	Iowa, U. of	XL
California, U. of (Los Angeles)	XL	Johns Hopkins (MD)	R
California, U. of (San Diego)	L	Kalamazoo (MI)	R
Carleton (MN)	R	Kenyon (OH)	R
Carnegie-Mellon (PA)	M	Knox (IL)	R
Case Western Reserve U. (OH)	R	Lafayette (PA)	R
Centre (KY)	R	Lawrence (WI)	R
Chicago, U. of (IL)	M	Macalester (MN)	R
Claremont McKenna (CA)	R	Miami, U. of (FL)	L
Clark (MA)	R	MIT (MA)	M
Colby (ME)	R	Michigan, U. of	XL
Colgate (NY)	R	Middlebury (VT)	R
Colorado Col.	R	▲ Mount Holyoke (MA)	R
Colorado School of Mines	R	New College (FL)	S
Cornell (NY)	L	New Jersey, College of	M
Dallas, U. of (TX)	R	North Carolina, U. of	L
Dartmouth (NH)	M	Northwestern (IL)	M
Davidson (NC)	R	Notre Dame (IN)	M
Dickinson (PA)	M	Oberlin (OH)	R
Duke (NC)	R	Occidental (CA)	R
Emory (GA)	R	Pitzer (CA)	S
Fairfield (CT)	M	Pomona (CA)	R
Franklin & Marshall (PA)	R		

GROUP I continues next page

Enrollment Code

■ **Men Only**   **S = Small** (less than 1000 students)   **R = Moderate** (1000-3000 students)   **M = Medium** (3000-8000 students)
▲ **Women Only**   **L = Large** (8000-20,000 students)   **XL = Extra Large** (over 20,000 students)

PRE-MED/PRE-DENTAL, *continued*

GROUP I, *continued*

Princeton (NJ)	M	Tulane (LA)	M
Reed (OR)	R	Union (NY)	R
Rhodes (TN)	R	Ursinus (PA)	R
Rice (TX)	R	Vanderbilt (TN)	M
Rochester, U. of (NY)	M	Villanova (PA)	M
Rutgers (NJ)	L	■ Wabash (IN)	S
Skidmore (NY)	R	Wake Forest (NC)	M
▲ Smith (MA)	R	Wartburg (IA)	R
South, U. of the (TN)	R	Washington U. (MO)	M
Southwestern (TX)	R	▲ Wellesley (MA)	R
Stanford (CA)	M	Wesleyan (CT)	R
Stetson (FL)	R	Wheaton (IL)	R
St. Mary's College of Maryland	R	Whitman (WA)	R
St. Olaf (MN)	R	Willamette (OR)	R
Swarthmore (PA)	S	William & Mary (VA)	M
Texas, U. of (Austin)	XL	Williams (MA)	R
Trinity (CT)	R	Yale (CT)	M
Trinity (TX)	R	Yeshiva (NY)	R
Tufts (MA)	M		

GROUP II
Very Selective

▲ Agnes Scott (GA)	S	College of Charleston (SC)	L
Albertson (ID)	S	Columbia Col. (SC)	R
Albright (PA)	R	Colorado, U. of	L
Alma (MI)	R	Concordia (MN)	R
Arizona State	XL	Connecticut, U. of	L
Augustana (SD)	M	Cornell (IA)	R
Austin (TX)	R	Creighton (NE)	R
Baylor (TX)	M	Delaware, U. of	L
Berry (GA)	R	Denison (OH)	R
Bethany (WV)	S	Denver, U. of (CO)	M
Birmingham-Southern (AL)	R	Duquesne (PA)	M
Butler (IN)	R	Earlham (IN)	R
California, U. of (Davis)	L	Eckerd (FL)	R
California, U. of (Irvine)	L	Erskine (SC)	S
California, U. of (Riverside)	M	Evansville (IN)	R
California, U. of (Santa Cruz)	M	Florida State	L
Canisius (NY)	M	Fordham (NY)	M
Carroll (WI)	R	Georgia, U. of	XL
Chapman (CA)	R	Guilford (NC)	R

GROUP II continues next page

Enrollment Code	
■ **Men Only**	**S = Small** (less than 1000 students) **R = Moderate** (1000-3000 students) **M = Medium** (3000-8000 students)
▲ **Women Only**	**L = Large** (8000-20,000 students) **XL = Extra Large** (over 20,000 students)

PRE-MED/PRE-DENTAL, *continued*

GROUP II, *continued*

Hamline (MN) .... R	Pittsburgh, U. of (PA) L
■ Hampden-Sydney (VA) .... S	Presbyterian (SC) .... S
Hendrix (AR) .... R	Puget Sound (WA) .... R
Hiram (OH) .... R	Randolph-Macon (VA) .... R
Hobart & Wm. Smith (NY) .... R	▲ Randolph-Macon Woman's Col. (VA) .. S
Hofstra (NY) .... M	Redlands, U. of (CA) .... R
▲ Hood (MD) .... S	Regis (CO) .... R
Hope (MI) .... R	Ripon (WI) .... S
Houghton (NY) .... S	San Diego, U. of (CA) .... M
Houston Baptist (TX) .... R	San Francisco, U. of (CA) .... M
Howard (DC) .... M	Scranton, U. of (PA) .... M
Huntingdon (AL) .... S	▲ Scripps (CA) .... S
Illinois, U. of (Chicago) L	Siena (NY) .... R
Indiana U. XL	Spring Hill (AL) .... R
Ithaca Col. (NY) .... M	St. John's (MN) .... R
Juniata (PA) .... R	St. Joseph's U. (PA) .... R
Kansas, U. of L	St. Louis (MO) .... M
Kansas State L	St. Louis Col. of Pharmacy (MO) .... S
Kentucky, U. of L	St. Thomas, U. of (MN) .... S
Knox (IL) .... R	St. Thomas, U. of (TX) .... R
Lake Forest (IL) .... S	Stetson (FL) .... R
Lewis & Clark (OR) .... R	Stony Brook (SUNY) (NY) L
Loyola (IL) .... M	Tennessee, U. of XL
Loyola (LA) .... R	Texas A&M XL
Loyola (MD) .... M	Transylvania (KY) .... S
Marquette (WI) .... M	Truman State (MO) .... M
Mary Washington (VA) .... R	Utah, U. of....................................... L
Massachusetts, U. of L	Vermont, U. of L
Michigan State XL	Washington College (MD) .... S
Millsaps (MS) .... R	Washington & Jefferson (PA) .... R
Minnesota, U. of (Morris) .... R	Washington, U. of XL
Monmouth (IL) .... S	▲ Wells (NY) .... S
Morningside (IA) .... S	Western Maryland .... R
Muhlenberg (PA) .... R	Westminster (PA) .... R
Nebraska Wesleyan .... R	Westmont (CA) .... R
Nevada, U. of (Reno) L	Wheaton (MA) .... R
New Hampshire, U. of L	Winona State U. (MN) .... M
New York U. L	Wisconsin, U. of XL
North Central (IL) .... R	Wittenberg (OH) .... R
Ohio State XL	Wofford (SC) .... R
Ohio Wesleyan .... R	Wooster (OH) .... R
Pacific Lutheran (OR) .... R	Wyoming, U. of L
Pennsylvania State XL	

PRE-MED/PRE-DENTAL continues next page

Enrollment Code

■ Men Only ▲ Women Only | **S = Small** (less than 1000 students) **R = Moderate** (1000-3000 students) **M = Medium** (3000-8000 students) **L = Large** (8000-20,000 students) **XL = Extra Large** (over 20,000 students)

PRE-MED/PRE-DENTAL, *continued*

GROUP III
Selective

American International (MA)	R	Kentucky Wesleyan	S
Benedictine (IL)	R	Louisiana State	XL
▲ Bennett (NC)	S	Lynchburg (VA)	R
Blackburn (IL)	S	Mount St. Joseph (OH)	R
Brooklyn Col. (SUNY) (NY)	L	Mount St. Mary's (MD)	R
California State U. (Fullerton)	L	Nova Southeastern (FL)	R
California State U. (Monterey Bay)	R	▲ Spelman (GA)	R
California State U. (San Jose)	L	St. Mary's (TX)	R
Carroll (MT)	R	St. Vincent (PA)	R
Carson-Newman (TN)	R	Temple (PA)	L
Delaware Valley (PA)	R	Texas, U. of (San Antonio)	L
DePaul (IL)	M	Thomas More (KY)	S
East Carolina (NC)	L	Virginia Commonwealth	L
Florida A&M	M	Virginia Wesleyan	R
Florida Southern	R	Walla Walla (WA)	R
Freed-Hardeman (TN)	R	Wayne State (MI)	L
Heidelberg (OH)	S	Wilkes (PA)	R
Ind.U.-Purdue U.-Indianapolis (IN)	L	Xavier U. of Louisiana	R
Jacksonville (FL)	R		

PSYCHOLOGY

GROUP I
Most Selective

Allegheny (PA)	R	
Amherst (MA)	R	
▲ Barnard (NY)	R	
Bates (ME)	R	
Binghamton (SUNY) (NY)	L	
Boston U. (MA)	L	
Brandeis (MA)	R	
▲ Bryn Mawr (PA)	S	
Bucknell (PA)	M	
California, U. of (Berkeley)	XL	
California, U. of (Los Angeles)	XL	
California, U. of (San Diego)	L	
Carnegie-Mellon (PA)	M	
Case Western Reserve U. (OH)	R	
Chicago, U. of (IL)	M	
Claremont McKenna (CA)	R	
Colby (ME)	R	
Columbia (NY)	M	
Connecticut Col.	R	
Drew (NJ)	R	
Duke (NC)	M	
Emory (GA)	R	
Furman (SC)	R	
George Washington (DC)	M	
Gettysburg (PA)	R	
Grinnell (IA)	R	
Gustavus Adolphus (MN)	R	
Harvard (MA)	M	
Haverford (PA)	S	
Illinois, U. of (Urbana-Champaign)	XL	
Kenyon (OH)	R	
Lafayette (PA)	R	
Macalester (MN)	R	
Michigan, U. of	XL	

▲ Mount Holyoke (MA)	R	
New College (FL)	S	
New Jersey, College of	M	
New York U.	L	
North Carolina, U. of	L	
Notre Dame, U of (IN)	M	
Occidental (CA)	R	
Pennsylvania, U. of	L	
Pitzer (CA)	S	
Reed (OR)	R	
Rhodes (TN)	R	
Rochester, U. of (NY)	M	
▲ Simmons (MA)	R	
▲ Smith (MA)	R	
Southwestern (TX)	R	
Stanford (CA)	M	
St. Mary's College of Maryland	R	
St. Olaf (MN)	R	
Swarthmore (PA)	R	
Tufts (MA)	M	
Tulane (LA)	M	
Union (NY)	R	
Vanderbilt (TN)	M	
Vassar (NY)	R	
Virginia, U. of	L	
■ Wabash (IN)	S	
Wake Forest (NC)	M	
Wesleyan (CT)	R	
Whitman (WA)	R	
Willamette (OR)	R	
Williams (MA)	R	
Yale (CT)	M	
Yeshiva (NY)	M	

PSYCHOLOGY continues next page

Enrollment Code

■ Men Only	S = Small (less than 1000 students)	R = Moderate (1000-3000 students)	M = Medium (3000-8000 students)
▲ Women Only	L = Large (8000-20,000 students)	XL = Extra Large (over 20,000 students)	

PSYCHOLOGY, *continued*

GROUP II
Very Selective

▲ Agnes Scott (GA) .... S	Lake Forest (IL) .... S
Albany (SUNY) (NY) L	Lebanon Valley (PA) .... R
Alfred (NY) .... R	LeMoyne (NY) .... R
Arizona, U. of XL	Loras (IA) .... R
Beloit (WI) .... R	Louisiana State U. L
Berry (GA) .... R	Loyola (IL) .... M
California, U. of (Riverside) .... M	Luther (IA) .... R
California, U. of (Santa Cruz) .... M	Lycoming (PA) .... R
Carroll (WI) .... R	Manhattanville (NY) .... R
Central Florida, U. of......................... L	Marist (NY) .... M
Chapman (CA) .... R	Marquette (WI) .... R
Cincinnati, U. of L	Maryville (TN) .... S
Clark (MA) .... R	Mary Washington (VA) .... R
Colorado State L	Michigan State XL
Concordia (MN) .... R	Millersville (PA) .... M
Cornell Col. (IA) .... R	▲ Mills (CA) .... S
Denison (OH) .... R	Minnesota, U. of XL
Denver, U. of (CO) .... M	Missouri, U. of XL
Earlham (IN) .... R	Missouri, U. of (Kansas City) .... M
Eastern Michigan L	Muhlenberg (PA) .... R
Elmira (NY) .... R	Nevada, U. of (Las Vegas) .... M
Fairfield (CT) .... M	New Paltz (SUNY) (NY) .... M
Flagler (FL) .... R	North Carolina (Asheville) .... R
Florida Inst. of Tech. .... R	Ohio U. L
Florida International L	Ohio Wesleyan .... R
Florida State..................................... L	Oklahoma City U. .... R
George Mason (VA) L	Oklahoma, U. of L
Grand Valley (MI) L	Oregon, U. of L
Guilford (NC) .... R	Oswego (SUNY) (NY) .... M
Hamline (MN) .... R	Pace (NY) .... M
Hanover (IN) .... R	Pittsburgh, U. of (PA)......................... L
Herbert Lehman (CUNY) (NY) L	Queens (CUNY) (NY) L
Hobart & Wm. Smith (NY) .... R	Randolph-Macon (VA) .... R
Hood (MD) ....S	▲ Randolph-Macon Woman's Col. (VA) ..S
Hope (MI) .... R	Roanoke (VA) .... R
Houghton (NY) ....S	Rollins (FL)....................................... R
Houston, U. of (TX) L	Salisbury State (MD) .... M
Hunter (CUNY) (NY) L	San Francisco, U. of (CA) .... M
Illinois, U. of (Chicago) L	Santa Clara, U. of (CA)....................... M
Indiana U. XL	Shepherd (WV) .... R
Iowa, U. of.......................................XL	Siena (NY) .... R
Kean (NJ) .... M	Southern California L
Kentucky, U. of.................................. L	*GROUP II continues next page*

GROUP II continues next page

Enrollment Code		
■ Men Only	S = Small (less than 1000 students)	R = Moderate (1000-3000 students)	M = Medium (3000-8000 students)
▲ Women Only	L = Large (8000-20,000 students)	XL = Extra Large (over 20,000 students)	

PSYCHOLOGY, *continued*

GROUP II, *continued*

St. Lawrence (NY) .... R

Stetson (FL) .... R

Stonehill (MA) .... R

Stony Brook (SUNY) (NY) L

Susquehanna (PA) .... R

▲ Sweet Briar (VA) .... S

Syracuse (NY) L

Texas, U. of (Austin) XL

Transylvania (KY) .... R

Tulsa, U. of (OK) .... R

Virginia Poly. Inst. L

Washington College (MD) ....S

Washington & Jefferson (PA) .... R

Washington, U. of XL

Webster (MO) .... R

▲ Wells (NY) .... S

Western Michigan L

Westminster (MO) ....S

Westmont (CA) .... R

Wheaton (MA) .... R

Whitworth (WA) .... R

Wisconsin, U. of XL

Wittenberg (OH) .... R

Wofford (SC) .... R

PSYCHOLOGY continues next page

Enrollment Code

■ Men Only   **S = Small** (less than 1000 students)   **R = Moderate** (1000-3000 students)   **M = Medium** (3000-8000 students)

▲ Women Only   **L = Large** (8000-20,000 students)   **XL = Extra Large** (over 20,000 students)

PSYCHOLOGY, *continued*

GROUP III
Selective

American International (MA) .... R	Manchester (IN) .... R
Aquinas (MI) .... R	▲ Mary Baldwin (VA) .... S
Baker (KS) .... S	Marymount (VA) .... R
Beaver (PA) .... R	Massachusetts, U. of (Dartmouth) .... M
Bethel (MN) .... R	Mercy (NY) .... M
Biola (CA) .... R	Middle Tennessee L
Blackburn (IL) .... S	Montclair State (NJ) .... M
Bridgewater (MA) .... M	New Hampshire, U. of L
Bridgewater (VA) .... R	Northern Arizona L
Brockport (SUNY)(NY) .... M	North Carolina (Wilmington) .... M
Caldwell (NJ) .... S	Northwestern (IA) .... R
California Lutheran .... R	Nyack (NY) .... R
California State U. (Bakersfield) .... M	Oklahoma Baptist .... R
California State U. (Chico) L	Otterbein (OH) .... R
California State U. (Dominguez Hills) . M	Ozarks, College of the (MO) .... R
California State U. (Chico) L	Palm Beach Atlantic (FL) .... R
California State U. (Long Beach) L	▲ Pine Manor (MA) .... S
California State U. (Los Angeles) L	Purchase (SUNY) (NY) .... R
California State U. (Northridge) L	Regis (CO) .... R
California State U. (Sacramento) .... M	Roger WIlliams (RI) .... R
California State U. (San Bernardino) .. M	▲ Rosemont (PA) .... S
California State U. (San Marcos) .... M	Sacred Heart (CT) .... R
California State U. (Stanislaus) .... M	St. Anselm (NH) .... R
Canisius (NY) .... M	St. Francis (NY) .... R
Carson-Newman (TN) .... R	St. Joseph's (IN) .... S
Carthage (WI) .... R	St. Joseph's (NY) .... R
▲ Cedar Crest (PA) .... S	St. Scholastica (MN) .... R
Central Connecticut .... M	St. Thomas Aquinas (NY) .... R
Chapman (CA) .... R	St. Vincent (PA) .... R
Colorado, U. of (Colorado Springs) .... M	Seton Hall (NJ) .... M
Colorado, U. of (Denver) .... M	Siena Heights (MI) .... S
Dominican (CA) .... S	Shippensburg (PA) .... M
Dominican (IL) .... S	Sonoma State (CA) .... M
Eastern Connecticut .... M	Southern Connecticut .... M
Eastern Illinois L	Springfield (MA) .... R
Fitchburg (MA) .... R	Taylor (IN) .... R
Framingham (MA) .... M	Virginia Commonwealth U. L
Franciscan U. of Steubenville (OH) ..... R	Virginia Wesleyan .... R
▲ Hollins (VA) .... S	Western New England (MA) .... R
John Jay College (CUNY)(NY) .... M	Westfield (MA) .... M
▲ Judson (AL) .... S	Wheeling Jesuit (WV) .... R
Keene State (NH) .... R	Wilkes (PA) .... R
Kentucky Wesleyan .... S	William Paterson (NJ) .... M
Lindenwood (MO) .... S	Wisconsin, U. of (Green Bay) .... M
Longwood (VA) .... R	Worcester State (MA) .... M
Lyon (AR) .... S	Wyoming, U. of L
Maine, U. of (Farmington) .... R	Xavier University of Louisiana .... R

RELIGIOUS STUDIES

GROUP I
Most Selective

▲ Barnard (NY) .... R
Bates (ME) .... R
Brown (RI) .... M
California, U. of (Berkeley) XL
Chicago, U. of (IL) .... M
Colgate (NY) .... R
Columbia (NY) .... M
Dartmouth (NH) .... M
Davidson (NC) .... R
Dickinson (PA) .... R
Duke (NC) .... M
Emory (GA) .... R
Furman (SC) .... R
Georgetown (DC) .... M
Hamilton (NY) .... R
Haverford (PA) .... S
Kenyon (OH) .... R
Lawrence (WI) .... R

Northwestern (IL) .... M
Notre Dame (IN) .... M
Oberlin (OH) .... R
Occidental (CA) .... R
Pomona (CA) .... R
Princeton (NJ) .... M
South, U. of the (TN) .... R
Southwestern (TX) .... R
Stanford (CA) .... M
Trinity (CT) .... R
Virginia, U. of L
Wake Forest (NC) .... M
▲ Wellesley (MA) .... R
Wesleyan (CT) .... R
Wheaton (IL) .... R
William & Mary (VA) .... M
Yale (CT) .... M

GROUP II
Very Selective

Arizona State XL
Baylor (TX) .... M
Birmingham-Southern (AL) .... R
Brigham Young (UT) XL
California, U. of (Santa Barbara) L
Catholic U. (DC) .... M
Christiandom (VA) .... S
Concordia (CA) .... R
Eckerd (FL) .... R
Florida State L
Fordham (NY) .... M
Gordon (MA) .... R
Guilford (NC) .... R
Harding (AR) .... M
Hendrix (AR) .... R
Hiram (OH) .... R
Houghton (NY) .... S

Iowa, U. of XL
Loyola (LA) .... R
Lycoming (PA) .... R
Marquette)WI) .... M
Master's (CA) .... R
Roanoke (VA) .... R
Rollins (FL) .... R
San Diego, U. of (CA) .... M
Southern Methodist (TX) L
St. Bonaventure (NY) .... R
Stetson (FL) .... R
Stony Brook (SUNY) (NY) L
Texas Christian U. .... M
Wartburg (IA) .... R
Westmont (CA) .... R
Whitworth (WA) .... R
Wooster (OH) .... R

RELIGIOUS STUDIES continues next page

Enrollment Code
■ Men Only   S = Small (less than 1000 students)   R = Moderate (1000-3000 students)   M = Medium (3000-8000 students)
▲ Women Only   L = Large (8000-20,000 students)   XL = Extra Large (over 20,000 students)

RELIGIOUS STUDIES, *continued*

GROUP III
Selective

California State U. (Chico)	L		Oklahoma Baptist	R
Franciscan U. of Steubenville (OH)	R		Regis (CO)	R
King (TN)	S	▲	St. Catherine (MN)	R
Milligan (TN)	S		Southwest Baptist (MO)	R
Mississippi College	R		Taylor (IN)	R
Northwestern (IA)	S		Union University (TN)	R
Northwestern (MN)	R		Virginia Commonwealth U.	L
Nyack (NY)	R		Wheeling Jesuit (WV)	R

SOCIOLOGY

GROUP I
Most Selective

Amherst (MA) .... R	Illinois, U. of (Urbana-Champaign) XL
▲ Barnard (NY) .... R	Kalamazoo (MI) .... R
▲ Bryn Mawr (PA) ....S	Michigan, U. of XL
Bucknell (PA) .... M	North Carolina, U. of L
California, U. of (Berkeley) XL	Northwestern (IL) .... M
California, U. of (Los Angeles) XL	Oberlin (OH) .... R
Chicago, U. of (IL) .... M	Pennsylvania, U. of L
Clarkson (NY) .... M	Pitzer (CA) ....S
Colby (ME) .... R	Southwestern (TX) .... R
Columbia (NY) .... M	Stanford (CA) .... M
Dartmouth (NH) .... M	Virginia, U. of L
Florida, U. of XL	Wheaton (IL) .... R
Franklin & Marshall (PA) .... R	Willamette (OR) .... R
Gettysburg (PA) ....S	Yale (CT) .... M
Grinnell (IA).. R	

GROUP II
Very Selective

Albany (SUNY) (NY) L	Pace (NY) .... M
Asbury (KY) .... R	Principia (IL).......................................S
Beloit (WI) .... R	Puget Sound (WA) .... R
California, U. of (Santa Barbara) L	Queens (CUNY)(NY) L
Clemson(SC) L	Regis (CO) .... R
Concordia (MN) .... R	Roanoke (VA) .... R
Cornell Col. (IA) .... R	Rutgers (Camden) (NJ) .... M
Covenant (GA) ....S	▲ Salem Col. (NC) ....S
Denison (OH) .... R	San Diego State U. (CA) XL
Earlham (IN) .... R	▲ Simmons (MA) .... R
Hamline (MN) .... R	St. Lawrence (NY) .... R
Hanover (IN) .... R	St. Mary's Col. (CA) .... R
Hendrix (AR) .... R	South Dakota School of Mines .... R
Hofstra (NY) .... M	Syracuse (NY) L
Howard (DC) .... M	▲ Trinity (DC) ....S
Illinois College ....S	▲ Wells (NY) ....S
Iowa State XL	Westminster (PA) .... R
Knox (IL) .... R	Western Maryland College .... R
Lake Forest (IL) ....S	Western Washington U. L
Lewis & Clark (OR) .... R	Wheaton (MA) .... R
Manhattanville (NY) .... R	Winona State U. (MN) .... M
Minnesota, U. of XL	Wisconsin, U. of XL
Moravian (PA) .... R	Wisconsin, U. of (Stevens Point) .... M
North Carolina (Asheville) .... R	Wofford (SC) .... R
Oklahoma State L	Wooster (OH) .... R

SOCIOLOGY continues next page

SOCIOLOGY, *continued*

GROUP III
Selective

Adrian (MI) .... S
Belmont Abbey (NC) .... S
Benedictine (KS) .... S
Biola (CA) .... R
Bridgewater State (MA) .... M
California State U. (Fresno) L
California State U. (Fullerton) L
California State U. (Northridge) L
California State U. (Sacramento) .... M
California State U. (San Bernardino) .. M
Central Connecticut .... M
Doane (NE) .... S
D'Youville (NY) .... R
Eastern (PA) .... R
Eastern Connecticut .... M
Fisk (TN) .... S
George Fox (OR) .... S
Grambling (LA) .... M
Hartwick (NY) .... R
Johnson C. Smith (NC) .... R
Kean (NJ) .... M
Lamar (TX) .... M
Lenoir-Rhyne (NC) .... R
Lynchburg (VA) .... R
▲ Mary Baldwin (VA) .... S
Massachusetts Col. of Lib. Arts. (N. Adams) R

Massachusetts, U. of (Boston) .... M
Massachusetts, U. of (Dartmouth) .... M
Michigan State XL
North Carolina, U. of (Wilmington) ..... M
Northern Colorado L
Quincy (IL) .... R
St. Anselm (NH) .... R
▲ St. Catherine (MN) .... R
St. Mary's U. of San Antonio (TX) ...... R
St. Rose (NY) .... R
San Francisco State (CA) L
Shaw (NC) .... R
Shippensburg (PA) .... M
Southern Connecticut .... M
Southern Oregon State U. .... M
▲ Spelman (GA) .... R
Suffolk (MA) .... R
Temple (PA) L
Virginia Wesleyan .... R
Wagner (NY) .... R
Western Connecticut State .... M
Western Kentucky L
Whitman (WA) .... R
William Paterson (NJ) .... M
Wilson (PA) .... S

ZOOLOGY

GROUP I
Most Selective

California, U. of (Berkeley) XL
Cornell (NY) L
Florida, U. of XL
Miami, U. of (OH) L

Michigan, U. of XL
North Carolina, U. of L
Pennsylvania State XL
Wisconsin, U. of XL

GROUP II
Very Selective

Albertson (ID) ....S
California, U. of (Davis) L
California, U. of (Santa Barbara) L
Connecticut, U. of...............................L
Georgia, U. of L
Indiana U. XL
Iowa State XL
Kansas, U. of L
Kentucky, U. of..................................XL
Maryland, U. of XL

Massachusetts, U. of L
North Carolina State L
Ohio U. L
Oklahoma, U. of L
Texas A&M XL
Texas, U. of (Austin) XL
Vermont, U. of L
Washington State L
Washington, U. of XL

GROUP III
Selective

Cal. Poly. State U. (Pomona) L
California State U. (San Jose) L
Colorado State L
Eastern Illinois L
Howard (DC) .... M
Louisiana State...................................XL

Montana, U. of .... M
Oregon State L
San Jose State (CA)............................L
Southern Illinois U. (Carbondale) L
Tennessee, U. of XL
Wyoming, U. of L

SECTION TWO

MISCELLANEOUS MAJORS

AFRO-AMERICAN STUDIES

Bates (ME)
California, U. of (Berkeley)
California, U. of (Santa Barbara)
Chicago, U. of (IL)
Coe (IA)
Columbia (NY)
Denison (OH)
Duke (NC)
Earlham (IN)
Emory (GA)
Harvard (MA)
Howard (DC)
Kalamazoo (MI)
Loyola Marymount (CA)
Luther (IA)
Macalester (MN)
Mercer (GA)
New York U.
North Carolina (Chapel Hill)

Oberlin (OH)
Ohio State U.
Pennsylvania, U. of
Pomona (CA)
Princeton (NJ)
Rutgers (NJ)
San Diego State (CA)
San Francisco State (CA)
▲ Spelman (GA)
Stanford (CA)
Tuskegee University (AL)
Vassar (NY)
Washington U. (MO)
▲ Wellesley (MA)
Wesleyan (CT)
Wooster (OH)
Wisconsin, U. of
Xavier (LA)
Yale (CT)

ALTERNATIVE COLLEGES *(see page ix)*

Antioch (OH)
Atlantic, College of the (ME)
Deep Springs (CA)
Eugene Lang (NY)
Evergreen (WA)
Hampshire (MA)
Marlboro (VT)
New College (FL)

New School for Social Research
  (NY)
Prescott (AZ)
St. John's (MD) (NM)
Shimer (IL)
Simon's Rock (MA)
Sterling (VT)
Thomas Aquinas (CA)

ARCHAEOLOGY

Baylor (TX)
Boston U. (MA)
Brown (RI)
▲ Bryn Mawr (PA)
Cornell (NY)
Dartmouth (NH)
Evansville (IN)
Haverford (PA)
Hunter (CUNY) (NY)
Kansas, U. of
Michigan, U. of

Missouri, U. of
North Carolina, U. of (Greensboro)
New York U.
Oberlin (OH)
Pennsylvania, U. of
Texas, U. of
Washington & Lee (VA)
Washington U. (MO)
Washington, U. of
Wheaton (IL)

ART THERAPY

Alverno (WI)
Anna Maria (MA)
Art Institute of Chicago (IL)
Barat (IL)
Beaver (PA)
Bowling Green (OH)
Brescia (KY)
Capital U. (OH)
Carlow (PA)
▲ Converse (SC)
▲ Edgewood (WI)
Harding (AR)
Indianapolis, U. of

▲ Lesley (MA)
Long Island U. (CW Post)(NY)
Marygrove (MI)
Marian Col. of Fond du Lac (WI)
Millikin (IL)
Pittsburg (KS)
Russell Sage (NY)
Santa Fe, Col. of (NM)
▲ Seton Hill (PA)
Spring Hill (AL)
Springfield (MA)
St. Thomas Aquinas (NY)
Wisconsin (Superior)

■ Men Only
▲ Women Only

ATMOSPHERIC SCIENCES

Albany (SUNY) (NY)
Arizona, U. of
California, U. of (Davis)
Colorado State
Cornell (NY)
Florida Inst. of Tech.
Florida State
Hawaii
Iowa State
Kansas
Lyndon State (VT)
Metropolitan State (CO)
Nebraska
North Carolina State
North Dakota, U. of

Northern Illinois
Northland (WI)
Oklahoma, U. of
Oneonta (SUNY) (NY)
Pennsylvania State
Purdue (IN)
San Francisco State (CA)
San Jose State (CA)
St. Louis University (MO)
Stony Brook (SUNY)(NY)
Texas A&M
Utah, U. of
Washington, U. of
Western Connecticut
Wisconsin, U. of

AUDIOLOGY/SPEECH/LANGUAGE THERAPY

Arizona
Arizona State
Ball State (IN)
Boston U.
Buffalo (SUNY) (NY)
California, U. of (Santa Barbara)
Florida
Florida State
Geneseo (SUNY) (NY)
George Washington
Hardin-Simmons (TX)
Hawaii
Hofstra (NY)
Iowa, U. of
James Madison (VA)
Kansas
Kean (NJ)
Longwood (VA)
Michigan State
Misericordia, College (PA)
Montana
Montevallo (AL)
Moorhead (MN)
Nazareth (NY)
Nebraska

New Hampshire, U. of
No. Colorado
No. Iowa
No. Michigan
Oklahoma
Oregon State
Pace (NY)
Purdue (IN)
Richard Stockton (NJ)
Rhode Island
St. John's (NY)
S. Dakota, U. of
Syracuse (NY)
Tennessee
Texas
Tulsa (OK)
Utah State
Vanderbilt (TN)
Washington, U. of
Wayne State (MI)
Western Michigan
Western Washington
Worcester State (MA)
Wisconsin
Wyoming

CERAMICS

Alfred (NY)
Arts, U. of the (PA)
California State U. (Long Beach)
Clemson (SC)
Cleveland Institute of Art (OH)
East Carolina (NC)
Florida, U. of
Hartford, U. of (CT)
Illinois, U. of
Iowa State

Kansas City Art Institute (MO)
Maryland Inst. College of Art
Massachusetts College of Art
North Texas
Otis College of Art & Design (CA)
Parsons School of Design (NY)
Rhode Island School of Design
Ringling School of Art & Design (FL)
Temple (PA)
Washington, U. of

■ Men Only
▲ Women Only

CINEMATOGRAPHY/FILM STUDIES

Arizona State
Bard (NY)
Beloit (WI)
Bowling Green (OH)
Boston U. (MA)
Brooks Institute of Photography (CA)
California State U. (Northridge)
California, U. of (Berkeley)
California, U. of (Irvine)
California, U. of (Los Angeles)
California, U. of (Santa Barbara)
California, U. of (Santa Cruz)
California Institute of the Arts
Carleton (MN)
Chapman (CA)
Cincinnati, U. of (OH)
Cogswell (CA)
Colorado, U. of
Columbia (IL)
Columbia (NY)
Delaware, U. of
Denison (OH)
Duke (NC)
Emerson (MA)
Florida
Florida State
Hampshire (MA)
Hofstra (NY)
Howard (DC)
Ithaca (NY)

Kansas
Massachusetts College of Art
Memphis State (TN)
Montana State
New York U.
Northwestern (IL)
Oklahoma
Pennsylvania State
Pittsburgh, U. of (PA)
Pitzer (CA)
Point Park (PA)
Purchase (SUNY) (NY)
Purdue (IN)
Rhode Island College
Rochester Inst. of Tech. (NY)
Rutgers (NJ)
St. Lawrence (NY)
St. Olaf (MN)
San Diego State
Santa Fe (NM)
Sarah Lawrence (NY)
Southern California
Syracuse (NY)
Temple (PA)
Texas, U. of
Toledo (OH)
Wayne State (MI)
Webster (MO)
Wesleyan (CT)

CREATIVE WRITING

▲ Agnes Scott (GA)
Alabama, U. of
Albertson (ID)
Bard (NY)
▲ Barnard (NY)
Beloit (WI)
Bennington (VT)
Brown (RI)
Carlow (PA)
Carnegie Mellon (PA)
Columbia (NY)
Creighton (NE)
Dana (NB)
Denison (OH)
Dominican (CA)
Eckerd (FL)
Emerson (MA)
Florida State
Grinnell (IA)
Hamilton (NY)
Hobart & Wm. Smith (NY)
Iowa
Johns Hopkins (MD)
Lewis-Clark State (ID)
Linfield (OR)

Long Island U. (Southampton) (NY)
Lycoming (PA)
Maine (Farmington)
Michigan, U. of
New Paltz (SUNY)(NY)
North Carolina State
Northwestern (IL)
Oberlin (OH)
Oregon, U. of
Pittsburgh, U. of (PA)
Redlands (CA)
St. Andrews (NC)
San Francisco State (CA)
Santa Fe, College of (NM)
Sarah Lawrence (NY)
▲ Stephens (MO)
Susquehanna (PA)
▲ Sweet Briar (VA)
Temple (PA)
Virginia
Washington College (MD)
Webster (MO)
Wheaton (MA)
Wichita State (KS)
Wittenberg (OH)

■ Men Only
▲ Women Only

CRIMINAL JUSTICE

Albany (SUNY) (NY)
Anna Maria (MA)
Bowling Green (OH)
California State U. (Fresno)
California State U. (Fullerton)
California State U. (Long Beach)
California State U. (Los Angeles)
California State U. (Sacramento)
California State U. (San
    Bernardino)
California, U. of (Irvine)
Castleton (VT)
Dayton, U. of (OH)
Delaware, U. of
Eastern Kentucky
Edinboro (PA)
Elmira (NY)
Florida Southern
Florida State
Gannon (PA)
George Washington (DC)
Grambling (LA)
Guilford (NC)
Hamline (MN)
Indiana
Iona (NY)
Juniata (PA)
Kentucky Wesleyan
Lindenwood (MO)
Loras (IA)
Loyola (LA)
Lycoming (PA)
Madonna (MI)
Mansfield (PA)
Marist (NY)
Marshall (WV)
Maryland
Massachusetts State College
  (Westfield)

Mercy (NY)
Mercyhurst (PA)
Michigan State
New Haven (CT)
North Carolina (Chapel Hill)
North CarolinaWesleyan
Northeastern (MA)
No. Florida
Ohio Northern
Portland, U. of (OR)
Potsdam (SUNY) (NY)
Radford (VA)
Regis (CO)
Richmond (VA)
Ripon (WI)
Roanoke (VA)
Rowan (NJ)
St. Anselm (NH)
St. Edward's (TX)
Salem State (MA)
Salve Regina- The Newport
  College (RI)
St. Francis (NY)
St. John's (NY)
St. Leo (FL)
Sam Houston State (TX)
San Diego State (CA)
Seton Hall (NJ)
Simpson (IA)
South Dakota, U. of
Southern Oregon
Southwest Texas
Tampa, U. of
Toledo (OH)
Wilmington (OH)
Wisconsin (Platteville)
Youngstown State (OH)

DESIGN/COMMERCIAL ART

Alfred (NY)
Art Center College of Design (CA)
Auburn (AL)
Bradford (MA)
Brenau (GA)
Brigham Young (UT)
Brooks Institute of
    Photography (CA)
Calif. Inst. of the Arts
California Poly (SLO)
California State U. (Chico)
California State U. (Long Beach)
California, U. of (Davis)
California, U. of (Los Angeles)
Champlain (VT)

Chowan (NC)
Columbia (IL)
Cincinnati, U. of (OH)
Cornish (WA)
Creighton (NB)
Drake (IA)
Edgewood (WI)
Fashion Inst. of Tech. (NY)
Flagler (FL)
Fort Hays (KS)
Frostburg (MD)
Illinois Institute of Technology
Illinois, U. of
Kansas City Art Institute (MO)

■ Men Only
▲ Women Only

DESIGN /COMMERCIAL ART continues next page

DESIGN/COMMERCIAL ART *CONTINUED*

Kean (NJ)
Kendall Coll. of Art & Design (MI)
Kent State (OH)
Maryland, U. of
Massachusetts College of Art
Massachusetts, U. of (Dartmouth)
Memphis College of Art
Moore (PA)
Moravian (PA)
Morningside (IA)
North Carolina State
North Florida, U. of
Ohio State

Otis College of Art and Design (CA)
Parsons School of Design (NY)
▲ Pine Manor (MA)
Pratt Institute (NY)
Rhode Island School of Design
Ringling (FL)
Rochester Inst. of Tech. (NY)
St. Mary's (MN)
San Jose State (CA)
Shepherd (WV)
Southern Illinois U.
Texas Christian
West Virginia Wesleyan

EAST ASIAN STUDIES

▲ Bryn Mawr (PA)
Bucknell (PA)
Buffalo (SUNY) (NY)
California, U. of (Davis)
California, U. of (Los Angeles)
California, U. of (San Diego)
Chicago, U. of (IL)
Coe (IA)
Columbia (NY)
Cornell (NY)
Denison (OH)
DePauw (IN)
East Michigan
Furman (SC)
Hamline (MN)
Harvard (MA)
Indiana
Lawrence (WI)

Lewis & Clark (OR)
Macalester (MN)
Manhattanville (NY)
Middlebury (VT)
Oberlin (OH)
Pennsylvania, U. of
Redlands (CA)
Stanford (CA)
Trinity (TX)
Ursinus (PA)
Vassar (NY)
Washington & Lee (VA)
Washington, U. of
▲ Wellesley (MA)
Wesleyan (CT)
Western Washington
Westmont (CA)
Wittenberg (OH)

ENTREPRENEUR STUDIES

American International (MA)
Arizona, U. of
Babson (MA)
Ball State U. (IN)
Baylor (TX)
Black Hills State U. (SD)
Boise State U. (ID)
Buena Vista (IA)
California State U. (San
  Bernardino)
Canisius (NY)
Chowan (NC)
Colorado State
Colorado, U. of
Columbia College (SC)
Eastern Michigan
Fairleigh Dickinson (NJ)
Ferris State U. (MI)
Georgia, U. of
Gonzaga (WA)
Hartford, U. of (CT)
Hawaii Pacific

Houston, U. of (TX)
Illinois
Indiana
Kennesaw (GA)
Louisiana State U.
Lyndon State (VT)
Lynn (FL)
Maryland, U. of
Miami (FL)
Michigan, U. of
Mississippi U. for Women
Muhlenberg (PA)
New Mexico
New York U.
Northeastern (MA)
North Carolina (Greensboro)
Ohio University
Pennsylvania, U. of
Reinhardt (GA)
Rensselaer (NY)
St. Mary's (TX)

■ Men Only
▲ Women Only

ENTREPRENEUR STUDIES continues next page

ENTREPRENEUR STUDIES *CONTINUED*

▲ Seton Hill (PA)
Southern California, U. of
Syracuse (NY)
Texas, U. of
Virginia Commonwealth

Washington & Jefferson (PA)
Wheeling Jesuit (WV)
Wichita State (KS)
Wyoming
Xavier (OH)

ENVIRONMENTAL STUDIES

Adelphi (NY)
Alaska Pacific
Allegheny (PA)
Bates (ME)
Berry (GA)
Bethany (WV)
Bowdoin (ME)
Brenau (GA)
Brown (RI)
▲ Bryn Mawr (PA)
California, U. of (Davis)
California, U. of (Irvine)
California, U. of (Riverside)
California, U. of (Santa Barbara)
California, U. of (Santa Cruz)
California State U. (Humboldt)
Case Western Reserve
Catholic (DC)
Centenary (LA)
Chicago, U. of (IL)
Clark (MA)
Clemson (SC)
Colby (ME)
Colorado, U. of
Connecticut College
Cornell (NY)
Davis & Elkins (WV)
Delaware Valley (PA)
Denison (OH)
Dickinson (PA)
Doane (NB)
Drake (IA)
Dubuque (IA)
Earlham (IN)
Eastern Connecticut
Eastern Kentucky
Eckerd (FL)
Findlay (OH)
Florida Gulf Coast
Florida, U. of
Florida Institute of Technology
Fredonia (SUNY) (NY)
Green Mountain (VT)
Harvard (MA)
Hawaii Pacific
Idaho
Johnson State (VT)
Juniata (PA)
Kalamazoo (MI)

Kentucky Wesleyan
Lake Forest (IL)
Long Island U. (Southampton)(NY)
Lynchburg (VA)
Macalester (MN)
Michigan, U. of
Michigan State
Middlebury (VT)
Millsaps (MS)
Minnesota, U. of
Monmouth (IL)
Montreat (NC)
New Hampshire, U. of
New Mexico Inst. of Min. & Tech.
π New Mexico State
North Carolina (Asheville)
Northland (WI)
Oberlin (OH)
Ohio Wesleyan
Oregon State
Pennsylvania State
Pennsylvania, U. of
Pittsburgh (Bradford)
Pittsburgh, U. of (PA)
Pitzer (CA)
Plattsburgh (SUNY)(NY)
Ramapo (NJ)
Randolph-Macon (VA)
Ripon (WI)
Rutgers (NJ)
Sacred Heart (CT)
St. Anselm (NH)
St. John's (MN)
St. Lawrence (NY)
St. Michael's (VT)
Salisbury State (MD)
San Francisco State (CA)
Santa Fe, College of (NM)
Sarah Lawrence (NY)
Shepherd (WV)
South Florida
Southwestern (TX)
Stanford (CA)
Stockton State (NJ)
SUNY Coll. of Env. Sci. & Forestry
Susquehanna (PA)

π *Environmental & Occupational Health*

■ Men Only
▲ Women Only

ENVIRONMENTAL STUDIES continues next page

ENVIRONMENTAL STUDIES CONTINUED

Tufts U. (MA)
Valparaiso (IN)
Vermont, U. of
Warren Wilson (NC)
Washington State
Washington, U. of
Webster (MO)
Wesleyan (CT)
Western Washington

West Virginia Wesleyan
Westfield State (MA)
Whitman (WA)
Wisconsin, U. of (Stevens Point)
Wittenberg (OH)
Worcester Poly (MA)
Wyoming, U. of
Yale (CT)

EQUESTRIAN STUDIES

Averett (VA)
Bluefield College (VA)
Centenary (NJ)
Colorado State
Delaware Valley (PA)
Findlay (OH)
Lake Erie (OH)
Otterbein (OH)

St. Andrews (NC)
Salem-Teikyo (WV)
▲ Stephens (MO)
Truman State (MO)
Virginia Intermont
William Woods (MO)
Wilson (PA)

EXERCISE SCIENCE / WELLNESS / MOVEMENT

Abilene Christian (TX)
Adrian (MI)
Alma (MI)
Ball State (IN)
Baptist U.
Bluffton (OH)
Bridgewater (VA)
California State U. (Fresno)
California State U. (Long Beach)
Castleton (VT)
Chapman (CA)
Colby-Sawyer (NH)
Concordia (NE)
Drury (MO)
Eastern Nazarene (MA)
Evansville (IN)
Fitchburg (MA)
Florida Atlantic
Fort Lewis (CO)
Greensboro (NC)
Gordon (MA)
Houston (TX)
Humboldt State (CA)
High Point (NC)
Idaho, U. of
Illinois, U. of (Chicago)
▲ Immaculata (PA)
James Madison (VA)

Kennesaw State (GA)
Linfield (OR)
Lourdes (OH)
Lynchburg (VA)
▲ Meredith (NC)
Mississippi U. for Women
North Texas
Nebraska
New Hampshire, U. of
Oklahoma
Ohio Northern
Otterbein (OH)
▲ St. Catherine (MN)
Southwestern (TX)
Slippery Rock (PA)
San Francisco State (CA)
Shaw (NC)
Stetson (FL)
Tennessee, U. of
Transylvania(KY)
Texas Lutheran
Texas Women's
Westfield (MA)
Willamette (OR)
Western State College of
    Colorado
Western Maryland

■ Men Only
▲ Women Only

FASHION DESIGN / MERCHANDISING

Arkansas, U. of
Auburn (AL)
Baylor (TX)
Bradley (IL)
Brenau (GA)
Cincinnati (OH)
Davis & Elkins (WV)
Delaware, U. of
Florida State
High Point (NC)
Indiana (PA)
Iowa State
Kent State (OH)
LaSell (MA)
Lynn (FL)
Madonna (MI)

▲ Meredith (NC)
New Hampshire College
Ohio U.
Oregon State
Philadelphia Col. Tex. & Sci. (PA)
Pratt (NY)
Purdue (IN)
Rhode Island School of Design
Rhode Island, U. of
Sanford (AL)
▲ Stephens (MO)
Texas Christian
Vermont, U. of
Virginia Commonwealth
Western Washington
Wisconsin, U. of

FORENSIC SCIENCES / TECHNOLOGY

Central Florida
Defiance (OH)
Eastern Kentucky
Edinboro (PA)
Hamline (MN)
John Jay (CUNY)(NY)

Kansas State
Miami, U. of (FL)
Mississippi, U. of
New Haven, U. of (Connecticut)
West Virginia

GENETICS

Ball State (IN)
California, U. of (Berkeley)
California, U. of (Davis)
California, U. of (Irvine)
California, U. of (Los Angeles)
Carnegie Mellon (PA)
▲ Cedar Crest (PA)
Chicago, U. of (IL)
Connecticut, U. of
Cornell (NY)
Florida State
Fredonia (SUNY)(NY)
Georgia, U. of
Harvard (MA)
Illinois, U. of
Illinois, U. of (Chicago)

Iowa State
Kansas
Minnesota
Ohio State
Ohio Wesleyan
Otterbein (OH)
Purdue (IN)
Rochester, U. of (NY)
Rutgers (NJ)
Sarah Lawrence (NY)
Texas A & M
Vermont, U. of
Washington State
Western Kentucky
Wisconsin, U. of

GERONTOLOGY / GERIATRIC SERVICES

Arkansas, U. of (River Bluff)
Bowling Green (OH)
Cal State (Sacramento)
California (PA)
Central Washington
Gwynedd-Mercy (PA)
Kent State (OH)
Lindenwood (VA)
Lourdes (OH)
Lynchburg (VA)
Madonna (MI)
Massachusetts (Boston)
Mount St. Mary's (CA)

Mount St. Joseph (OH)
North Texas
Oregon, U. of
Quinnipiac (CT)
St. Edward's (TX)
St. Mary's (CA)
San Diego State (CA)
Shaw (NC)
South Florida
Southern California
Springfield (MA)
Stephen F. Austin (TX)
Weber State (UT)

■ Men Only
▲ Women Only

HEALTH SERVICES ADMINISTRATION

Alfred (NY)
Appalachian State (NC)
Arizona
Detroit Mercy (MI)
Eastern Michigan
Herbert Lehman (CUNY) (NY)
Kentucky
Missouri, U. of
North Carolina (Chapel Hill)
Northeastern (MA)
Northern Michigan

Oregon State
Pennsylvania State
Providence College (RI)
Quinnipiac (CT)
Saint Scholastica (MN)
Scranton (PA)
Spring Arbor (MI)
Stonehill (MA)
Washington, U. of
Winona State (MN)

HISPANIC STUDIES / LATIN AMERICAN STUDIES

American (DC)
Arizona, U. of
California, U. of (Berkeley)
California, U. of (Santa Barbara)
California, U. of (Santa Cruz)
California State (Long Beach)
Flagler (FL)
Hunter (CUNY)(NY)
Loyola Marymount (CA)
▲ Mount Holyoke (MA)
North Carolina
Northern Colorado
Northridge State (CA)
Northwestern (IL)
Rice (TX)

Rollins (FL)
Rutgers (NJ)
San Diego State (CA)
San Francisco State (CA)
▲ Scripps (CA)
▲ Smith (MA)
Sonoma State (CA)
Stetson (FL)
Texas, U. of
Tulane (LA)
Wheaton (MA)
Whittier (CA)
Willamette (OR)
Wisconsin, U. of

HOTEL AND RESTAURANT MANAGEMENT

Ashland (OH)
Auburn (AL)
Cal Poly (Pomona)
Cornell (NY)
Delaware
Denver, U. of (CO)
Fairleigh Dickinson (NJ)
Florida International U.
Florida State
Georgia State
Hawaii, U. of
Houston, U. of (TX)
Illinois, U. of
Iowa State
James Madison (VA)
Johnson State (VT)
Kansas State
Massachusetts, U. of
Michigan State
Missouri, U. of
Nevada (Las Vegas)
New Hampshire College
New Hampshire, U. of

New Haven (CT)
New York University
Niagara (NY)
North Dakota State
Northern Arizona
North Texas
Ohio U.
Oklahoma State
Ozarks (MO)
Penn State
Plattsburgh (SUNY)(NY)
Purdue (IN)
Rochester Inst. of Tech. (NY)
St. Leo (FL)
San Jose State (CA)
South Carolina, U. of
Texas Tech
Transylvania (KY)
Virginia Poly. Inst.
Washington State
Widener (PA)
Wisconsin (Stout)

■ Men Only
▲ Women Only

HUMAN RESOURCES MANAGEMENT

American (DC)
Birmingham-Southern (AL)
Boston College (MA)
Bowling Green (OH)
Cabrini (PA)
Cal. Poly. State U. (Pomona)
Duquesne (PA)
Florida State
Hastings (NB)
Houston (TX)
Indiana (PA)
Loras (IA)
LeMoyne (NY)
Lindenwood (MO)
Marietta (OH)
Michigan State

Muhlenberg (PA)
Nevada, U. of (Las Vegas)
New Mexico, U. of
Northeastern (MA)
Oakland (MI)
Ohio State
Ohio University
Point Park (PA)
Puerto Rico, U. of (Rio Piedras)
Rockhurst (MO)
St. Leo (FL)
St. Mary's (TX)
Utah State
Washington U. (MO)
Widener (PA)
Wisconsin (Oshkosh)

INDUSTRIAL ARTS

Berea (KY)
California (PA)
California State U. (Fresno)
Cheyney (PA)
Cincinnati, U. of (OH)
Clemson (SC)
Colorado State
Ferris State (MI)
Fitchburg (MA)
Idaho
Louisiana State U.
Millersville (PA)
Montclair (NJ)

Nebraska, U. of
New Mexico, U. of
Northern Colorado
Northern Illinois
Oklahoma State
Oswego (SUNY) (NY)
Pittsburgh, U. of (PA)
Purdue (IN)
Southern Illinois
Texas A&M
Western Michigan
Wisconsin, U. of (Stout)
Wyoming

INTERNATIONAL RELATIONS/STUDIES

▲ Agnes Scott (GA)
Alma (MI)
American U. (DC)
Arizona State
Beaver (PA)
Beloit (WI)
● Bentley (MA)
Bethany (WV)
☎ Bethune-Cookman (FL)
Boston U. (MA)
Brown (RI)
▲ Bryn Mawr (PA)
Bucknell (PA)
☎ Butler (IN)
☎ Caldwell (NJ)
California State U. (Los Angeles)
California State U. (Sacramento)
California, U. of (Davis)
▲ Chatham (PA)
☎ College of Charleston (SC)
Claremont McKenna (CA)
Colby (ME)

Colgate (NY)
Colorado
Connecticut College
☎ Cornell (IA)
Dartmouth (NH)
Davidson (NC)
Dayton (OH)
Denison (OH)
Denver, U. of (CO)
DePaul (IL)
☎ Dickinson (PA)
Dominican (CA)
☎ Drake (IA)
Eckerd (FL)
☎ Elizabethtown (PA)
☎ Elmira (NY)
Emory (GA)
Evansville (IN)
☎ Florida International
George Washington (DC)
+ Georgetown (DC)

■ **Men Only**
▲ **Women Only**

INTERNATIONAL RELATIONS continues next page

INTERNATIONAL RELATIONS/STUDIES, *continued*

π Georgia Tech.
Goucher (MD)
Hamline (MN)
☎ Hawaii
Hawaii Pacific
☎ Hiram (OH)
☎ Husson (ME)
Johns Hopkins (MD)
Juniata (PA)
☎ Illinois
Indiana
Kalamazoo (MI)
★ Kansas State
Kenyon (OH)
Knox (IL)
☎ Lenoir-Rhyne (NC)
Lewis & Clark (OR)
Linfield (OR)
Macalester (MN)
Maine (Farmington)
Manhattanville (NY)
☎ Marygrove (MI)
Miami, U. of (FL)
☎ Michigan, U. of
Middlebury (VT)
Mississippi, U. of
☎ Moravian (PA)
Mt. Holyoke (MA)
Mt. St. Mary's (MD)
Nebraska
North Carolina (Chapel Hill)
π Northeastern (MA)
Oglethorpe (GA)
Ohio Wesleyan
π Oklahoma City U.
Pacific, U. of the (CA)
Pennsylvania, U. of
Pepperdine (CA)
Pittsburgh, U. of
Pitzer (CA)
☎ Plattsburgh (SUNY)(NY)
Pomona (CA)
Princeton (NJ)
▲ Randolph-Macon Woman's
Col. (VA)
Redlands (CA)

☎ Regis (CO)
Richmond (VA)
Rhodes (TN)
☎ Rochester Inst. of Tech. (NY)
San Diego, U. of (CA)
☎ Santa Clara U. (CA)
Scranton, U. of (PA)
▲ Scripps (CA)
☎ South Carolina, U. of
☎ Southern California, U. of
Southwestern (TX)
Spring Hill (AL)
☎ St. Andrews (NC)
▲ St. Catherine (MN)
☎ St. Louis U. (MO)
☎ St. Mary's (MN)
St. Mary's (TX)
St. Michael's (VT)
☎ St. Norbert (WI)
St. Olaf (MN)
☎ St. Peter's (NJ)
☎ Stetson (FL)
▲ Sweet Briar (VA)
▲ Trinity (DC)
Tufts (MA)
Tulane (LA)
U. S. Air Force Academy
(CO)
U. S. Military Academy (NY)
Vassar (NY)
Virginia Wesleyan (GA)
Washington College (MD)
Washington, U. of
☎▲ Wesleyan (GA)
Westminster (MO)
π Westmont (CA)
☎ Westminster (UT)
Wheaton (MA)
Whittier (CA)
William & Mary (VA)
William Jewell (MO)
Wilson (PA)
Wisconsin, U. of
Wisconsin (Oshkosh)
Wittenberg (OH)

☎ *International Business*
★ *International Marketing*
● *International Culture and Economy*
π *International Business and Global Affairs*
+ *International Relations, also International Business*

■ **Men Only**
▲ **Women Only**

JAPANESE STUDIES

Bucknell (PA)
California, U. of (Los Angeles)
California, U. of (Santa Barbara)
Earlham (IN)
Georgetown (DC)
Hawaii, U. of
Macalester (MN)
Michigan, U. of

Minnesota, U. of
North Central (IL)
Oregon, U. of
Pacific, U. of the (CA)
San Francisco State (CA)
Stanford (CA)
Washington, U. of
Washington U. (MO)

JAZZ

Arizona State
Arizona, U. of
Auburn (AL)
Augustana (IL)
Bennington College (VT)
Berklee College of Music (MA)
Bowling Green (OH)
California Institute of the Arts
California State U. (Los Angeles)
California State U. (Northridge)
Cincinnati
Delaware
Denver, U. of
DePaul U. (IL)
Duquesne U. (PA)
Five Towns College (NY)
Florida Atlantic
Georgia State
Hampshire College (MA)
Hartford (CT)
Idaho
Iowa
Indiana U.
Indiana U. (PA)
Loyola U. (New Orleans) (LA)
Manhattan School of Music (NY)
Mannes College of Music (NY)

Marlboro College (VT)
Miami (FL)
Minnesota (Duluth)
Minnesota
New England Conservatory of
  Music (MA)
New York U. (NY)
North Florida
North Texas
Oberlin College (OH)
Ohio State U. (OH)
Rochester (NY)
Rowan (NJ)
Rutgers (NJ)
San Diego State (CA)
Shenandoah U. (VA)
South Florida
Southern California
Temple U. (PA)
Tennessee
Virginia Commonwealth
Washington, U. of
Webster U. (MO)
Western Michigan U.
Western Washington
Westfield State (MA)

MARINE SCIENCE

Barry (FL)
Brown (RI)
California State U. (Long Beach)
California State U. (Sonoma)
California, U. of (Santa Barbara)
California, U. of (Santa Cruz)
College of Charleston (SC)
Eckerd (FL)
Farleigh Dickinson (NJ)
Florida Inst. of Technology
Hawaii Pacific
Idaho, U. of
Jacksonville U. (FL)
Juniata (PA)
Long Island U. (Southampton)
  (NY)
Maine, U. of
Miami, U. of (FL)

New College (FL)
North Carolina, U. of (Wilmington)
Northern Michigan
Occidental (CA)
Rhode Island, U. of
Richard Stockton (NJ)
Roger Williams (RI)
Samford (AL)
San Diego, U. of (CA)
South Carolina, U. of
Spring Hill (AL)
Tampa, U. of (FL)
Texas A&M
Texas A&M (Galveston)
U. S. Coast Guard Academy (CT)
Washington, U. of
West Florida
Wittenberg (OH)

■ Men Only
▲ Women Only

MEDICAL TECHNOLOGY

American International (MA)
Bowling Green (OH)
Bradley (IL)
Buffalo (SUNY) (NY)
California State U. (Bakersfield)
California, U. of (Davis)
Carroll (WI)
Case Western Reserve U. (OH)
Creighton (NE)
Detroit Mercy (MI)
Elon (NC)
Florida State
Florida, U. of
▲ Hood (MD)
Humboldt (CA)
Maine, U. of
Marquette (WI)
▲ Mary Baldwin (VA)
Massachusetts, U. of
   (Dartmouth)
Mercy (NY)

Miami U. (OH)
Miami, U. of (FL)
Michigan State
Minnesota, U. of
Moravian (PA)
New Hampshire, U. of
North Carolina (Chapel Hill)
North Dakota State
North Dakota, U. of
Northeastern (MA)
Quinnipiac (CT)
St. Leo (FL)
▲ St. Mary's (IN)
San Francisco State (CA)
Suffolk (MA)
Texas Tech
Utah, U. of
Virginia Commonwealth
Washington & Jefferson (PA)
Washington, U. of
Wisconsin, U. of

MUSIC THERAPY

Alabama, U. of
Alverno (WI)
Anna Maria (MA)
Arizona State
Augsburg (MN)
Baldwin-Wallace (OH)
Berklee Coll. of Music (MA)
Charleston Southern (SC)
Colorado State
Dayton (OH)
Duquesne (PA)
East Carolina (NC)
Eastern Michigan (MI)
Elizabethtown (PA)
Evansville (IN)
Florida State
Fredonia (SUNY)(NY)
Georgia
Howard (DC)
▲ Immaculata (PA)
Incarnate Word (TX)
Iowa
Kansas
Loyola (LA)

Mansfield (PA)
Maryville, U. of (St. Louis)(MO)
Miami, U. of (FL)
Michigan State
Minnesota
Mississippi U. for Women
Montclair (NJ)
Nazareth (NY)
New Paltz (SUNY)(NY)
Ohio U.
Queens (NC)
Shenandoah (VA)
Slippery Rock (PA)
Southern Methodist (TX)
Southwestern Oklahoma
Temple (PA)
Texas Women's
Utah State
Wartburg (IA)
Western Illinois
Western Michigan
Wisconsin, U. of (Eau Claire)
Wisconsin, U. of (Oshkosh)
Wooster (OH)

NAVAL ARCHITECTURE

California Maritime Academy
Iowa State
Michigan, U. of
SUNY Maritime College (NY)
Texas A&M (Galveston)

U. S. Coast Guard Academy (CT)
U. S. Merchant Marine Academy (NY)
U. S. Naval Academy
Webb Institute (NY)
Wisconsin, U. of

■ Men Only
▲ Women Only

NUTRITIONAL SCIENCE

Alabama, U. of
Arizona, U. of
Ball State (IN)
Bluffton (OH)
Bridgewater (VA)
California, U. of (Berkeley)
California, U. of (Davis)
Colorado State
Connecticut, U. of
Cornell (NY)
Dominican (IL)
Framingham State (MA)
Georgia, U. of
Hawaii, U. of
Kansas State

Long Island U. (C.W. Post)(NY)
Marygrove (MI)
Marymount-Tarrytown (NY)
Missouri, U. of
New Hampshire, U. of
Oklahoma State
Park (MO)
Purdue (IN)
Rutgers (NJ)
▲ Sage Colleges (Russell Sage)(NY)
San Jose State
▲ Simmons (MA)
Viterbo (WI)
Wisconsin (Green Bay)
Wisconsin, U. of

OCCUPATIONAL THERAPY

American International (MA)
Boston U. (MA)
Brenau (GA)
Buffalo (SUNY) (NY)
Cleveland State (OH)
Colorado State
Creighton (NB)
Dominican (CA)
Eastern Kentucky
Elizabethtown (PA)
Florida Gulf Coast
Florida, U. of
Illinois (Chicago)
I.U. - P.U. - Indianapolis (IN)
Kansas, U. of
Maryville (St. Louis)(MO)
Minnesota, U. of
Misericordia, College (PA)
New England, U. of (ME)
New Hampshire, U. of
New Mexico, U. of
New York University
North Carolina, U. of
North Dakota, U. of

Nova Southeastern (FL)
Ohio State
Puget Sound (WA)
Rockhurst (MO)
Sage Colleges (NY)
St. Ambrose (IA)
▲ St. Catherine (MN)
St. Louis U. (MO)
San Jose State (CA)
Sciences, U. of the (PA)
Scranton (PA)
Southern California
Springfield (MA)
▲ Texas Woman's
Tufts (MA)
Utica College (NY)
Washington U. (MO)
Washington, U. of
Wayne State (MI)
Western Michigan
Wisconsin, U. of
Wisconsin, U. of (Green Bay)
Wisconsin, U. of (La Crosse)
Worcester State (MA)

PARKS AND RECREATION SERVICES

Alderson-Broaddus (WV)
Arizona State
Aurora (IL)
Ball State (IN)
Bowling Green (OH)
Cal. Poly. State U. (Pomona)
Cal. Poly. State U. (San Luis Obispo)
California State (Chico)
California State (Dominguez Hills)
California State (Fresno)
California State (Los Angeles)
Catawba (NC)
Clemson (SC)

Colorado State
Delaware, U. of
Florida International
Florida State
Idaho
Illinois State
Illinois, U. of
Indiana U.
Kansas State
Kean (NJ)
Longwood (VA)

■ Men Only
▲ Women Only

PARKS AND RECREATION SERVICES
continues next page

PARKS AND RECREATION SERVICES, *continued*

Maine, U. of
Maryland, U. of
Mesa State (CO)
Michigan State
Minnesota
Missouri
Montana
Nevada (Reno)
North Carolina State
Northern Arizona
Ohio U.
Pennsylvania State
Pepperdine (CA)
Pfeiffer (NC)
Purdue (IN)

San Diego State (CA)
San Jose State (CA)
Shepherd (WV)
Slippery Rock (PA)
Springfield College (MA)
Taylor (IN)
Texas A&M
Virginia Wesleyan
West Virginia U.
Western State College of Colorado
Western Washington
Wingate (NC)
Winona State (MN)
Wisconsin (LaCrosse)
Wisconsin (Stevens Point)

PHYSICAL EDUCATION

Alderson-Broaddus (WV)
Augsburg (MN)
Bemidji State (MN)
Blackburn (IL)
Bridgewater (MA)
California, U. of (Santa Barbara)
Castleton (VT)
Chowan (NC)
Coe (IA)
Colorado, U. of
Colorado State
Cortland State (NY)
Dana (NB)
Davis & Elkins (WV)
Denison (OH)
Doane (NB)
East Stroudsburg (PA)
Elon (NC)
Eureka (IL)
Florida State
Florida, U. of
Franklin (IN)
Georgia, U. of
Goshen (IN)
Grambling (LA)
Hamline (MN)
Hardin-Simmons (TX)
Illinois College
Illinois, U. of (Chicago)
Iowa, U. of
Ithaca (NY)
Jacksonville (FL)
Johnson C. Smith (NC)
Kansas State
Kansas, U. of

Kean (NJ)
Kennesaw State (GA)
LeTourneau (TX)
Longwood (VA)
Linfield (OR)
Luther (IA)
Maine, U. of
Michigan State
Monmouth (IL)
Nebraska, U. of
Nevada (Reno)
North Carolina, U. of
Norwich (VT)
Oberlin (OH)
Occidental (CA)
Oregon State
Pacific U. (OR)
Pennsylvania State
Purdue (IN)
Rockford (IL)
St. Leo (FL)
▲ Simmons (MA)
Skidmore (NY)
Slippery Rock (PA)
South Florida, U. of
Springfield (MA)
Texas, U. of
Ursinus (PA)
Washington State
Wesley (DE)
Westerm Washington
Westmont (CA)
West Virginia U.
William & Mary (VA)
Wisconsin (LaCrosse)

■ Men Only
▲ Women Only

PHYSICAL THERAPY

American International (MA)
Boston U. (MA)
Bowling Green (OH)
Buffalo (SUNY) (NY)
California State U. (Fresno)
California State U. (Long Beach)
California State U. (Northridge)
Central Arkansas
Central Florida
Chapman (CA)
Clarke (IA)
Colorado, U. of
Connecticut, U. of
D'Youville (NY)
Daemen (NY)
Duquesne (PA)
Eastern Washington
Evansville (IN)
Florida Gulf Coast U.
Florida, U. of
Grand Valley (MI)
Hunter (CUNY) (NY)
Husson (ME)
Illinois (Chicago)
I.U. - P.U. - Indianapolis (IN)
Iowa, U. of
Ithaca (NY)
Kentucky, U. of
* LaSell (MA)
Louisville, U. of (KY)
Marquette (WI)
Maryville (St. Louis) (MO)
Miami, U. of (FL)
Minnesota, U. of
Misericordia College (PA)
Montana, U. of
Mount St. Joseph (OH)
Mt. St. Mary's (CA)
Nazareth (NY)
Nebraska, U. of
New England, U. of (ME)

New Mexico, U. of
North Dakota, U. of
Northeastern (MA)
Northern Illinois
Northwestern (IL)
Oakland (MI)
Ohio State U.
Ohio University
Pacific U. (OR)
Pepperdine (CA)
Philadelphia College of
    Pharmacy & Science (PA)
Pittsburgh, U. of (PA)
Puget Sound (WA)
Quinnipiac (CT)
Regis (CO)
Rockhurst (MO)
Sacramento State (CA)
Sage Colleges (NY)
Saint Scholastica (MN)
St. Louis U. (MO)
Scranton, U. of (PA)
Seton Hall (NJ)
Slippery Rock (PA)
South Alabama
Southern California
Southern Oregon
Southwest Texas State
Springfield College (MA)
Stony Brook (SUNY)(NY)
Temple (PA)
Texas Tech
▲ Texas Woman's
Toledo (OH)
Utah
Vermont, U. of
Washington U. (MO)
Wayne State (MI)
Wisconsin (LaCrosse)
Wisconsin, U. of

* *Physical Therapy Assisting*

PHYSICIAN ASSISTANT

Alabama, U. of (Birmingham)
Alderson-Broaddus (WV)
Colorado, U. of (Denver)
Daeman (NY)
Duquesne (PA)
D'Youville (NY)
East Carolina
Florida, U. of
Gannon (PA)
George Washington (DC)
High Point (NC)
Howard (DC)
Kentucky
King's (PA)
LeMoyne (NY)
Massachusetts Coll. of Pharmacy

Miami, U. of (FL)
Nova Southeastern (FL)
Pace (NY)
Quinnipiac (CT)
St. Francis (NY)
St. Francis (PA)
St. Louis (MO)
▲ Seton Hill (PA)
South Dakota
Southern California
Springfield (MA)
Stony Brook (SUNY)(NY)
Western Michigan
Wichita State (KS)
Wisconsin

■ Men Only
▲ Women Only

PRE-VETERINARY

Auburn (AL)
California, U. of (Davis)
Cal. Poly. State U. (San Luis Obispo)
Clemson (SC)
Colorado State
Delaware Valley (PA)
Evansville, U. of (IN)
Fort Lewis (CO)
Georgia, U. of
Humboldt State (CA)
Idaho, U. of
Juniata (PA)
Kansas State
Lawrence (WI)
Loyola (CA)
MacMurray (IL)
Maryland, U. of
Michigan State
Minnesota, U. of
Montana, U. of
Moravian (PA)
Muskingham (OH)

Nevada, U. of (Reno)
New Hampshire, U. of
New Mexico State
Northland (WI)
Oklahoma State
Purdue (IN)
▲ Russell Sage (The Sage Colleges) (NY)
▲ Salem (NC)
South Dakota State U.
Southern Mississippi, U. of
Susquehanna (PA)
Tennessee, U. of
Texas A & M
Utah State
Virginia Wesleyan
Washington & Jefferson (PA)
Washington State
West Virginia Wesleyan
Wilmington (OH)
Wingate (NC)
Winona State (MN)

SOCIAL AND REHABILITATION SERVICES

Arizona, U. of
Assumption (MA)
Auburn (AL)
Boston U. (MA)
California State (Los Angeles)
Florida State
Gustavus Adolphus (MN)
Iowa, U. of
Louisiana State
Maine (Farmington)
Marshall (WV)
Montana, U. of

Northern Colorado
North Texas
Ohio State
Seattle (WA)
South Florida, U. of
Springfield College (MA)
Texas, U. of (Austin)
Virginia Commonwealth
West Virginia Wesleyan
Wisconsin
Wright State (OH)

SOCIAL WORK

Alaska, U. of (Anchorage)
Alaska, U. of (Fairbanks)
Arizona State
Ashland (OH)
Augsburg (MN)
Azusa Pacific (CA)
Baylor (TX)
Bemidji State (MN)
▲ Bennett (NC)
Bethany (WV)
Boise State (ID)
Bowie State (MD)
Brescia (KY)
Brockport (SUNY) (NY)
Buena Vista (IA)
California (Berkeley)
California State U. (Chico)

California State U. (Fresno)
California State U. (Fullerton)
California State U. (Sacramento)
Carroll (WI)
Castleton (VT)
Colorado State
Cornell (NY)
Creighton (NB)
Dana (NB)
David Lipscomb (TN)
Eastern Michigan
Eastern Nazarene (MA)
Elmira (NY)
Elms (MA)
Ferris State (MI)
Florida Atlantic

■ Men Only
▲ Women Only

SOCIAL WORK continues next page

SOCIAL WORK, *continued*

Florida State
Franciscan U. of Steubenville (OH)
Fredonia (SUNY) (NY)
Gordon (MA)
Goucher (MD)
Hawaii Pacific
▲ Hood (MD)
Hope (MI)
Humboldt State (CA)
Illinois College
Illinois, U. of
Illinois, U. of (Chicago)
Indiana
Juniata (PA)
Kansas State
Kansas, U. of
Kean (NJ)
Kentucky
Lindenwood (MO)
Longwood (VA)
Lourdes (OH)
Madonna (MI)
Marquette (WI)
Marygrove (MI)
Maryland (Baltimore County)
▲ Meredith (NC)
Michigan State
Michigan, U. of
Missouri, U. of
Mount St. Joseph (OH)
Nazareth (NY)
New York University
Niagara (NY)
North Carolina (Greensboro)
North Carolina State

Penn State
Pittsburgh, U. of (PA)
Portland, U. of (OR)
Providence (RI)
Radford (VA)
Rhode Island College
Richard Stockton (NJ)
Rochester Inst. of Tech. (NY)
Rockford (IL)
Sacramento State (CA)
Sacred Heart (CT)
St. Leo (FL)
St. Louis (MO)
St. Mary (KS)
St. Olaf (MN)
Salisbury State (MD)
San Francisco State (CA)
Shepherd (WV)
Shippensburg U. of (PA)
South Connecticut
South Florida, U. of
Southern Connecticut
Tennessee, U. of
Texas, U. of (Austin)
Texas Women's
Valparaiso (IN)
Vermont, U. of
Warren Wilson (NC)
Washington U. (MO)
Washington, U. of
Wayne State (MI)
Western Michigan
Western New England (MA)
William Woods (MO)
Wisconsin, U. of
Wyoming, U. of

SPECIAL EDUCATION

Adelphi (NY)
American International (MA)
Arizona State
Arkansas
Augustana (SD)
Boston U. (MA)
Brenau (GA)
California State (Chico)
California State (Fresno)
π California State (Northridge)
California State (Sonoma)
California State (Stanislaus)
Clarke (IA)
Connecticut, U. of
▲ Converse (SC)
Curry (MA)
Dana (NB)
Denver, U. of (CO)

Doane (NB)
Eastern Montana
Edinboro (PA)
π Flagler (FL)
Florida State
Geneseo (SUNY) (NY)
Hofstra (NY)
▲ Hood (MD)
Illinois State
Juniata (PA)
Kansas, U. of
Kean (NJ)
Kutztown (PA)
Landmark College (VT)
Lenoir-Rhyne (NC)
Lesley (MA)
Lindenwood (MO)

■ Men Only
▲ Women Only

SPECIAL EDUCATION continues next page

SPECIAL EDUCATION CONTINUED

Loras (IA)
Loyola (MD)
Maine, U. of (Farmington)
Marygrove (MI)
Maryland, U. of
Muskingum (OH)
Nebraska
Nevada (Reno)
North Texas
Northern Colorado, U. of
Pacific, U. of (CA)
Pennsylvania State
Presbyterian (SC)
Rhode Island College
Rowan (NJ)

St. Elizabeth (NJ)
▲ Simmons (MA)
Southern Illinois U. (Carbondale)
Southern Utah
Texas, U. of
Texas Christian
Toledo (OH)
▲ Trinity (DC)
Virginia, U. of
West Chester (PA)
Wisconsin, U. of (Oshkosh)
Winona (MN)
Wittenberg (OH)
Wyoming, U. of
π *Also Deaf Studies*

SPORTS MEDICINE / ATHLETIC TRAINING

Adelphi (NY)
Alderson-Broaddus (WV)
Baldwin Wallace (OH)
Ball State (IN)
Bethany (WV)
Boise State (ID)
Bridgewater (MA)
California (PA)
California Lutheran
Canisius (NY)
Castleton (VT)
Catawba (NC)
Centre (KY)
Charleston, U. of (WV)
Chowan (NC)
Clarke (IA)
Coe (IA)
Colby-Sawyer (NH)
Colorado State
Denver, U. of (CO)
Eastern Nazarene (MA)
Elon (NC)
Eureka (IL)
Evansville (IN)
Guilford (NC)
Gustavus Adolphus (MN)
Heidelberg (OH)
High Point (NC)
Illinois (Chicago)
Indiana U.
LaSell (MA)
Lees-McCrae (NC)
Lindenwood (MO)

Linfield (OR)
Lynchburg (VA)
Manchester (IN)
Manhattan (NY)
Marietta (OH)
Mercyhurst (PA)
Mount Union (OH)
New Mexico State
North Dakota
Northwestern (IA)
Norwich (VT)
Occidental (CA)
Ohio Northern
Otterbein (OH)
Pacific, U. of the (CA)
Pepperdine (CA)
Quincy (IL)
Radford (VA)
Roanoke (VA)
St. Andrews (NC)
Salisbury State (MD)
Sanford (AL)
Southern Maine
Springfield (MA)
Taylor (IN)
Tusculum (TN)
Tulsa (OK)
Union (TN)
West Virginia Wesleyan
Wilmington (OH)
Wingate (NC)
Winona State (MN)
Xavier (OH)

SPORTS SCIENCES / MANAGEMENT

Alabama, U. of
Alderson-Broaddus (WV)
Arizona State
Averett (VA)
Belmont Abbey (NC)
Bemidji (MN)
Berry (GA)
Bowling Green (OH)
Buena Vista (IA)
Cabrini (PA)
Central Washington
Chowan (NC)
Colby-Sawyer (NH)
Connecticut, U. of
Dallas, U. of (TX)
Denver, U. of (CO)
Eastern Connecticut
Elon (NC)
Flagler (FL)
Florida Southern
Florida, U. of
Guilford (NC)
High Point (NC)
Husson (ME)
Idaho, U. of
Incarnate Word (TX)
Indiana U.
Kansas, U. of
Kentucky Wesleyan
Louisville (KY)
Lynchburg (VA)
Lynn (FL)
MacMurray (IL)
Malone (OH)
Marian (WI)
Massachusetts, U. of

Michigan, U. of
Misericordia (PA)
Mount Union (OH)
North Carolina State
North Michigan
Ohio Northern
Ohio State
Oklahoma
Oregon, U. of
Pfeiffer (NC)
Richmond (VA)
Robert Morris (PA)
Rutgers (NJ)
Seton Hall (NJ)
Shepherd (WV)
Simpson (IA)
South Carolina, U. of
Springfield (MA)
St. Ambrose (IA)
St. John's (NY)
St. Leo (FL)
St. Olaf (MN)
St. Thomas U. (FL)
Stetson (FL)
Southwest Baptist (MO)
Taylor (IN)
Temple (PA)
Tennessee
Texas Christian
Tulsa (OK)
Union (TN)
West Virginia U.
Western New England (MA)
Wingate (NC)
Xavier (OH)

URBAN STUDIES

Arizona State
Augburg (MN)
Boston U. (MA)
Brown (RI)
Buffalo (SUNY) (NY)
Cal. Poly. State U. (Pomona)
California, U. of (Los Angeles)
California, U. of (San Diego)
Canisius (NY)
Case Western Reserve (OH)
Cleveland State (OH)
College of Charleston (SC)
Columbia (NY)
Cornell (NY)
David Lipscomb (TN)
Evansville (IN)
Georgia State
Hamline (MN)

Illinois (Chicago)
Lake Forest (IL)
Loyola Marymount (CA)
Macalester (MN)
Malone (OH)
Maryland, U. of
Michigan State
New York U.
North Carolina (Greensboro)
Pennsylvania, U. of
Pittsburgh, U. of
Rockford (IL)
Rutgers (NJ)
St. Louis (MO)
St. Olaf (MN)
San Francisco State U. (CA)
Seattle Pacific (WA)

■ Men Only
▲ Women Only

URBAN STUDIES continues next page

URBAN STUDIES *CONTINUED*

Shippensburg (PA)
Stanford (CA)
Tampa, U. of (FL)
Tennessee (Knoxville)
Trinity (TX)
Virginia Commonwealth
Virginia Poly
Washington U. (MO)
Wayne State (MI)

Western Washington
π Westfield State (MA)
Wisconsin, U. of (Green Bay)
Wittenberg (OH)
Wooster (OH)
Worcester State (MA)
Wright State (OH)

π Regional Planning

WOMEN'S STUDIES

Alfred (NY)
Arizona, U. of
▲ Barnard (NY)
Bates (ME)
Beloit (WI)
Bowling Green (OH)
Brockport (SUNY) (NY)
Brown (RI)
California, U. of (Berkeley)
California, U. of (Davis)
California, U. of (Santa Barbara)
California, U. of (Santa Cruz)
Carleton (MN)
Chicago, U. of (IL)
Colorado, U. of
DePauw (IN)
Emory (GA)
Florida, U. of
Goucher (MD)
Harvard (MA)
Hobart & William Smith (NY)
▲ Hollins (VA)
Kalamazoo (MI)
Macalester (MN)
Maine, U. of
Massachusetts, U. of
Michigan, U. of
Middlebury (VT)

▲ Mills (CA)
▲ Mt. Holyoke (MA)
Mount St. Joseph (OH)
Northwestern (IL)
Pennsylvania, U. of
Pitzer (CA)
Portland State (OR)
Rochester, U. of (NY)
Rollins (FL)
▲ Rosemont (PA)
San Francisco State (CA)
Sarah Lawrence (NY)
▲ Simmons (MA)
▲ Smith (MA)
Southern California
Southwestern (TX)
▲ Spelman (GA)
Stanford (CA)
Tennessee, U. of
Texas, U. of
Vanderbilt (TN)
Washington U. (MO)
Washington, U. of
▲ Wellesley (MA)
Wheaton (MA)
Wisconsin, U. of
Wooster (OH)

SECTION THREE

AVERAGE SAT-1/ACT TOTALS
RECOMMENDED MAJORS

ABILENE CHRISTIAN UNIVERSITY (TX) 1000/21
Bus Admin

ADELPHI COLLEGE (NY) 1070/23
Ed, Nurs, Physics

ADRIAN COLLEGE (MI) 1035/22
Ed, English, Poli Sci, Pre-Law, Soc

AGNES SCOTT COLLEGE (GA) 1199/26
Art, Bio, Econ, English, For Lang, Hist, Pre-Law, Pre-Med/Pre-Dental, Psych

ALABAMA, UNIVERSITY OF (AL) 1070/23
Art, Bot, Bus Admin, Engine, Geol, Hist

ALABAMA, UNIVERSITY OF (HUNTSVILLE) 1100/24
Communic, Engine, Math, Nurs

ALASKA PACIFIC UNIVERSITY (AK) 1125/25
Bus Admin

ALASKA, UNIVERSITY OF (ANCHORAGE) (AK) 1020/22
Art, Bus Admin, Ed

ALASKA, UNIVERSITY OF (FAIRBANKS) (AK) 1060/23
Bus Admin, Drama, Nurs

ALBANY COLLEGE OF PHARMACY (NY) 1110/24
Pharm

ALBERTSON COLLEGE (ID) 1160/25
Bio, Bus Admin, Chem, Ed, English, Pre-Law, Pre-Med/Pre-Dental, Zoo

ALBION COLLEGE (MI) 1185/26
Econ, English, Hist, Math, Pre-Law

ALBRIGHT COLLEGE (PA) 1060/23
Biochem, Bio, Bus Admin, Poli Sci, Pre-Law, Pre-Med/Pre-Dental

ALDERSON-BROADDUS COLLEGE (WV) 1000/21
Bus Admin, Ed, Nurs

ALFRED UNIVERSITY (NY) 1130/25
Art, Bus Admin, Ed, Engine, English, Pre-Law, Psych

ALLEGHENY COLLEGE (PA) 1199/26
*Bio, Comp Sci, Drama, Econ, English, For Lang, Geol, Hist, Philo, Pre-Law,
Pre-Med/Pre-Dental, Psych*

ALLENTOWN COLLEGE (PA) 1060/23
Drama

ALMA COLLEGE (MI) 1170/26
Art, Bio, Bus Admin, Chem, Comp Sci, Ed, Hist, Pre-Law, Pre-Med/Pre-Dental

ALVERNO COLLEGE (WI) 1000/21
Nurs

AMERICAN ACADEMY OF DRAMATIC ARTS (NY) **1205/27**
Drama

AMERICAN INTERNATIONAL COLLEGE (MA) **1000/21**
Bus Admin, Pre-Med/Pre-Dental, Psych

AMERICAN UNIVERSITY (DC) **1185/26**
Amer St, Bus Admin, Econ, Communic, Math, Poli Sci, Pre-Law

AMHERST COLLEGE (MA) **1400/31**
*Amer St, Bio, Chem, Drama, Econ, English, Geol, Hist, Physics, Poly Sci, Pre-Law,
Pre-Med/Pre-Dental, Psych, Soc*

ANNA MARIA COLLEGE (MA) **1000/21**
Art, Music

APPALACHIAN STATE UNIVERSITY (NC) **1090/24**
Bus Admin, Communic, Ed

AQUINAS COLLEGE (MI) **1033/22**
Psych

ARIZONA, UNIVERSITY OF (AZ) **1100/24**
*Ag, Amer St, Anthro, Arch, Art, Astro, Bus Admin, Communic, Drama, Ed, Engine,
English, Forest, Geol, Nurs, Pre-Law, Psych*

ARIZONA STATE UNIVERSITY (AZ) **1090/24**
*Arch, Art, Bus Admin, Communic, Comp Sci, Drama, Ed, Engine, Geog, Math,
Nurs, Pre-Med, Poli Sci, Reli Sci*

ARKANSAS, UNIVERSITY OF (AR) **1095/24**
Ag, Arch, Bus Admin, Communic, Ed, Engine, English, Music, Pre-Law

ART CENTER COLLEGE OF DESIGN (CA) **1100/24**
Art

ART INSTITUTE OF CHICAGO (IL) **1100/24**
Art

ARTS, UNIVERSITY OF THE (PA) **1000/21**
Art, Drama, Music

ASBURY COLLEGE (KY) **1110/24**
Bus Admin, Philo, Soc

AUBURN UNIVERSITY (AL) **1145/25**
Ag, Arch, Art, Bus Admin, Ed, Engine, Forest

AUGSBURG COLLEGE (MN) **1040/22**
Communic, Ed

AUGUSTANA COLLEGE (IL) **1170/27**
Art, Bus Admin, Ed, English, Music, Pre-Law

AUGUSTANA COLLEGE (SD) **1120/24**
Bio, Ed, Nurs, Pre-Med/Pre-Dental

AUSTIN COLLEGE (TX) 1199/26
Bus Admin, Ed, Poly Sci, Pre-Med/Pre-Dental

AVERETT COLLEGE (VA) 1050/22
Bus Admin, Ed

AVILA COLLEGE (MO) 1050/22
Ed, Nurs

AZUSA PACIFIC (CA) 1040/22
Bus Admin, Nurs

BABSON COLLEGE (MA) 1175/26
Bus Admin, Econ

BAKER UNIVERSITY (KS) 1075/23
Bus Admin, Psych

BALDWIN-WALLACE COLLEGE (OH) 1075/23
Bus Admin, Ed, English, Music, Pre-Law

BALL STATE UNIVERSITY (IN) 1040/22
Art, Ed, Nurs

BARD COLLEGE (NY) 1250/28
Art, Drama, English, For Lang, Music, Pre-Law

BARRY UNIVERSITY (FL) 1100/24
Bus Admin, Drama, Nurs

BATES COLLEGE (ME) 1320/30
Art, Bio, Chem, Econ, Geol, Hist, Math, Philo, Physics, Pre-Law, Pre-Med/Pre-Dental, Psych, Rel Stu

BAYLOR UNIVERSITY (TX) 1145/25
Bus Admin, Chem, Drama, Ed, English, Hist, Nurs, Pre-Law, Pre-Med/Pre-Dental, Reli Stu

BEAVER COLLEGE (PA) 1075/23
Art, Ed, Psych

BELHAVEN COLLEGE (MS) 1099/24
Art, Music

BELLARMINE COLLEGE (KY) 1095/24
Nurs

BELMONT ABBEY COLLEGE (NC) 1040/22
Bus Admin, Poli Sci, Pre-Law, Soc

BELMONT UNIVERSITY (TN) 1090/24
Music

BELOIT COLLEGE (WI) 1240/28
Anthro, Biochem, Classics, Drama, Econ, English, For Lang, Geol, Music, Physics, Psych, Soc

BEMIDJI STATE UNIVERSITY (MN) 1035/22
Communic, Geog

BENEDICTINE COLLEGE (KS) 1050/22
Astro, Bus Admin, Soc

BENEDICTINE UNIVERSITY (IL) 1030/22
Bio, Bus Admin, Pre-Med/Pre-Dental

BENNETT COLLEGE (NC) 1000/21
Bus Admin, Ed, Pre-Law, Pre-Med/Pre-Dental

BENNINGTON COLLEGE (VT) 1175/26
Drama, English, Pre-Law

BENTLEY COLLEGE (MA) 1125/25
Bus Admin

BEREA COLLEGE (KY) 1099/24
Ag, Ed, Nurs

BERKLEE COLLEGE OF MUSIC (MA) 1100/24
Music

BERRY COLLEGE (GA) 1155/25
Bio, Ed, Forest, Pre-Med/Pre-Dental, Psych

BETHANY COLLEGE (WV) 1080/23
Bio, Communic, Drama, Ed, For Lang, Music, Pre-Med/Pre-Dental

BETHEL COLLEGE (MN) 1099/24
Bus Admin, Ed, Nurs, Psych

BIOLA UNIVERSITY (CA) 1090/24
Ed, Philo, Psych, Soc

BIRMINGHAM-SOUTHERN COLLEGE (AL) 1190/26
Art, Bio, Bus Admin, Chem, Ed, English, Hist, Math, Music, Pre-Law, Pre-Med/Pre-Dental, Reli Stu

BLACKBURN COLLEGE (IL) 1000/21
Bio, Ed, Pre-Med/Pre-Dental, Psych

BLOOMSBURG UNIVERSITY (PA) 1050/22
Art, Ed

BLUFFTON COLLEGE (OH) 1060/22
Bus Admin, Ed, Math

BOSTON COLLEGE (MA) 1280/29
Bio, Bus Admin, English, For Lang, Hist, Nurs, Philo, Pre-Law, Pre-Med/Pre-Dental

BOSTON CONSERVATORY OF MUSIC (MA) 1050/22
Music

BOSTON UNIVERSITY (MA) 1280/29
Art, Astro, Bus Admin, Communic, Drama, Econ, Ed, Engine, Hist, Music, Philo, Physics, Poli Sci, Pre-Law, Psych

BOWDOIN COLLEGE (ME) 1340/30
Art Hist, Biochem, Bio, Chem, Econ, English, For Lang, Geol, Hist, Math, Music, Philo, Pre-Law, Pre-Med/Pre-Dental

BOWLING GREEN STATE UNIVERSITY (OH) 1050/22
Art, Bus Admin, Ed, Music

BRADLEY UNIVERSITY (IL) 1160/25
Art, Comp Sci, Engine

BRANDEIS UNIVERSITY (MA) 1320/30
Anthro, Biochem, Bio, Comp Sci, Drama, Econ, English, Hist, Music, Poli Sci, Pre-Law, Pre-Med/Pre-Dental, Psych

BRENAU UNIVERSITY (GA) 1050/22
Drama, Music

BRESCIA UNIVERSITY (KY) 1030/22
Art, Bus Admin, Ed, English

BRIDGEWATER COLLEGE (VA) 1000/21
Psych

BRIDGEWATER STATE COLLEGE (MA) 1000/21
Ed, Hist, Psych, Soc

BRIGHAM YOUNG UNIVERSITY (UT) 1199/26
Art, Astro, For Lang, Reli Stu

BROWN UNIVERSITY (RI) 1390/31
Art, Art Hist, Bio, Biochem, Chem, Classics, Comp Sci, Engine, For Lang, Geol, Hist, Poli Sci, Pre-Law, Pre-Med/Pre-Dental, Reli Stu

BRYANT COLLEGE (RI) 1080/23
Bus Admin, Comp Sci, Math

BRYN MAWR COLLEGE (PA) 1325/30
Art, Art Hist, Astro, Bio, Chem, Classics, Econ, English, For Lang, Geol, Hist, Physics, Pre-Law, Pre-Med/Pre-Dental, Psych, Soc

BUCKNELL UNIVERSITY (PA) 1250/28
Bio, Bus Admin, Chem, Econ, Ed, Engine, Hist, Math, Music, Philo, Pre-Law, Pre-Med/Pre-Dental, Psych, Soc

BUENA VISTA UNIVERSITY (IA) 1120/24
Communic, Ed

BUTLER UNIVERSITY (IN) 1170/26
Bus Admin, Communic, Comp Sci, Drama, Ed, Engine, Music, Pharm, Pre-Law, Pre-Med/ Pre-Dental

CALDWELL COLLEGE (NJ) 1030/22
Bus Admin, Ed, Psych

CALIFORNIA INSTITUTE OF TECHNOLOGY (CA) 1480/33
Astro, Bio, Chem, Engine, Geol, Math, Physics, Pre-Med/Pre-Dental

CALIFORNIA INSTITUTE OF THE ARTS (CA) 1100/24
Art, Music

CALIFORNIA, UNIVERSITY OF, AT
> **BERKELEY** 1340/30
> *Anthro, Arch, Biochem, Bot, Bus Admin, Chem, Comp Sci, Engine, English,*
> *For Lang, Forest, Geog, Geol, Hist, Math, Music, Philo, Physics, Pre-Law,*
> *Pre-Med/Pre-Dental, Psych, Reli Stu, Soc, Zoo*
> **DAVIS** 1165/26
> *Ag, Anthro, Bio, Biochem, Bot, Chem, Engine, English, Geol, Hist, Poli Sci,*
> *Pre-Law, Pre-Med/Pre-Dental, Zoo*
> **IRVINE** 1130/25
> *Art, Bio, Comp Sci, Drama, Engine, Math, Physics, Pre-Law, Pre-Med/Pre-Dental*
> **LOS ANGELES** 1280/29
> *Anthro, Art Hist, Bio, Biochem, Chem, Communic, Comp Sci, Drama, Econ,*
> *Engine, English, For Lang, Geog, Hist, Math, Music, Philo, Poli Sci,*
> *Pre-Law, Pre-Med/Pre-Dental, Psych, Soc*
> **RIVERSIDE** 1100/24
> *Ag, Art Hist, Biochem, Bio, Bot, Bus Admin, Engine, Math, Music, Poli Sci,*
> *Pre-Law, Pre-Med/Pre-Dental, Psych*
> **SAN DIEGO** 1270/28
> *Amer St, Biochem, Bio, Chem, Comp Sci, Drama, Econ, Engine, Math, Music,*
> *Physics, Poli Sci, Pre-Law, Pre-Med/Pre-Dental, Psych*
> **SANTA BARBARA** 1182/26
> *Art, Art Hist, Bus Admin, Classics, Comp Sci, Ed, Engine, For Lang, Geog, Geol,*
> *Music, Philo, Physics, Poli Sci, Pre-Law, Reli Stu, Soc, Zoo*
> **SANTA CRUZ** 1145/25
> *Amer St, Anthro, Bio, Chem, Comp Sci, Math, Music, Physics, Pre-Med/Pre-*
> *Dental, Psych*

CALIFORNIA LUTHERAN UNIVERSITY (CA) 1020/22
Bus Admin, Ed, Psych

CALIFORNIA MARITIME ACADEMY (CA) 1100/24
Engine

CALIFORNIA POLYTECHNIC UNIVERSITY AT POMONA (CA) 1000/21
Ag, Arch, Bus Admin, Comp Sci, Engine, Zoo

CALIFORNIA POLYTECHNIC UNIVERSITY AT SAN LUIS OBISPO (CA) 1170/26
Ag, Arch, Comp Sci, Communic, Engine, English

CALIFORNIA STATE UNIVERSITY, AT:
> **BAKERSFIELD** 1000/21
> *Bus Admin, Ed, English, Geol, Nurs, Psych*
> **CHICO** 1040/22
> *Chem, Comp Sci, Geog, Geol, Nurs, Psych, Reli Stu*
> **DOMINGUEZ HILLS** 1000/21
> *Bus Admin, Nurs, Philo, Psych*
> **FRESNO** 1000/21
> *Ag, Art, Bus Admin, Chem, Ed, Home Ec, Music, Nurs, Philo, Soc*
> **FULLERTON** 1000/21
> *Anthro, Bus Admin, Communic, Hist, Music, Nurs, Pre-Med/Pre-Dental, Soc*
> **HAYWARD** 1000/21
> *Art, Bus Admin, Comp Sci, Geol, Music*
> **LONG BEACH** 1000/21
> *Art, Communic, Econ, Poli Sci, Pre-Law, Psych*
> **LOS ANGELES** 1000/21
> *Bus Admin, Ed, Nurs, Psych*
> **MONTEREY BAY** 1020/22
> *Art, Bio, Comp Sci, Ed, English, Math, Pre-Law, Pre-Med/Pre-Dental*

CALIFORNIA STATE UNIVERSITY, AT: *(Continued)*
    NORTHRIDGE 1000/21
        Communic, Econ, English, Geog, Music, Philo, Physics, Poli Sci, Pre-Law, Psych, Soc
    SACRAMENTO 1000/21
        Anthro, Bus Admin, Communic, Ed, English, Geol, Music, Poli Sci, Psych, Soc
    SAN BERNARDINO 1000/21
        Art, Bus Admin, Communic, Psych, Soc
    SAN JOSE 1060/23
        Art, Chem, Comp Sci, Math, Music, Nurs, Physics, Pre-Med/Pre-Dental, Zoo
    SAN MARCOS 1000/21
        Bus Admin, Comp Sci, Ed, Psych
    STANISLAUS 1000/21
        Bus Admin, Comp Sci, Ed, Psych

CALIFORNIA UNIVERSITY OF PENNSYLVANIA (PA) 1000/21
Ed

CALVIN COLLEGE (MI) 1140/25
Ed, Engine, English, For Lang, Hist, Pre-Law

CANISIUS COLLEGE 1100/24
Bio, Bus Admin, Communic, Ed, English, Hist, Pre-Med/Pre-Dental, Psych

CAPITAL UNIVERSITY (OH) 1100/24
Bus Admin, Ed, Hist, Music, Nurs

CARLETON COLLEGE (MN) 1345/30
*Bio, Chem, Drama, English, For Lang, Geol, Hist, Math, Physics, Pre-Law,
Pre-Med/Pre-Dental*

CARNEGIE MELLON UNIVERSITY (PA) 1350/30
Arch, Art, Bus Admin, Chem, Comp Sci, Drama, Engine, Music, Pre-Med/Pre-Dental, Psych

CARROLL COLLEGE (MT) 1080/23
Bio, Nurs, Pre-Med/Pre-Dental

CARROLL COLLEGE (WI) 1100/24
Chem, Ed, Nurs, Pre-Med/Pre-Dental, Psych

CARSON-NEWMAN COLLEGE (TN) 1080/23
Hist, Music, Nurs, Pre-Med/Pre-Dental, Psych

CARTHAGE COLLEGE (WI) 1099/24
Bus Admin, Psych

CASE WESTERN RESERVE UNIVERSITY (OH) 1320/30
*Anthro, Art Hist, Astro, Bus Admin, Chem, Comp Sci, Engine, Math, Music, Nurs, Physics,
Pre-Med/Pre-Dental, Psych*

CASTLETON STATE COLLEGE (VT) 1000/21
Bus Admin

CATAWBA COLLEGE (NC) 1000/21
Bus Admin, Comp Sci, Drama, Ed

CATHOLIC UNIVERSITY OF AMERICA (DC) 1170/26
Arch, Classics, Drama, Engine, For Lang, Music, Nurs, Poli Sci, Pre-Law, Reli Stu

CEDAR CREST COLLEGE (PA) **1070/23**
Nurs, Psych

CEDARVILLE COLLEGE (OH) **1099/24**
Bus Admin, Ed, Nurs

CENTENARY COLLEGE OF LOUISIANA (LA) **1125/24**
Bus Admin, Chem, Ed, Geol

CENTRAL ARKANSAS, UNIVERSITY OF (AR) **1070/23**
Bus Admin, Nurs

CENTRAL COLLEGE OF IOWA (IA) **1110/24**
Comp Sci, Ed, For Lang

CENTRAL CONNECTICUT STATE UNIVERSITY (CT) **1000/21**
Bus Admin, Ed, Engine, Geog, Hist, Music, Psych, Soc

CENTRAL FLORIDA, UNIVERSITY OF (FL) **1100/24**
Comp Sci, Communic, Engine, Psych

CENTRAL MICHIGAN UNIVERSITY (MI) **1000/21**
Ed, Home Ec

CENTRAL WASHINGTON UNIVERSITY **1000/21**
Music

CENTRE COLLEGE (KY) **1210/27**
Art, Chem, Econ, Ed, English, Hist, Physics, Poli Sci, Pre-Law, Pre-Med/Pre-Dental

CHAMPLAIN COLLEGE (VT) **1025/22**
Bus Admin

CHAPMAN UNIVERSITY (CA) **1150/25**
Bus Admin, Communic, Music, Pre-Law, Pre-Med/Pre-Dental, Psych

CHARLESTON, COLLEGE OF (SC) **1099/24**
Bio, Chem, Ed, Pre-Med/Pre-Dental

CHARLESTON, UNIVERSITY OF (WV) **1045/22**
Hist

CHATHAM COLLEGE (PA) **1080/23**
Art, Bio, Bus Admin, Communic, English, Hist, Poli Sci, Pre-Law

CHESTNUT HILL COLLEGE (PA) **1050/22**
English, Pre-Law

CHICAGO, UNIVERSITY OF (IL) **1360/31**
Anthro, Art Hist, Bio, Classics, Econ, English, For Lang, Geog, Geol, Hist, Math, Philo, Physics, Poli Sci, Pre-Law, Pre-Med/Pre-Dental, Psych, Reli Stu, Soc

CHOWAN COLLEGE (NC) **1000/21**
Art, Bus Admin, Comp Sci, English

CHRISTIAN BROTHERS UNIVERSITY (TN) **1100/24**
Bus Admin, Engine

CHRISTIANDOM COLLEGE (VA) 1175/26
Hist, Philo, Reli Stu

CINCINNATI, UNIVERSITY OF (OH) 1100/24
Arch, Classics, Engine, Math, Pharm, Psych

CLAREMONT MCKENNA COLLEGE (CA) 1380/31
Bio, Bus Admin, Econ, English, Hist, Philo, Poli Sci, Pre-Law, Pre-Med/Pre-Dental, Psych

CLARK UNIVERSITY (MA) 1140/25
Bus Admin, Communic, For Lang, Geog, Music, Pre-Law, Pre-Med/Pre-Dental, Psych

CLARKE COLLEGE (IA) 1115/24
Art, Art Hist, Bio, Chem, Comp Sci, Ed, Nurs, Philo

CLARKSON UNIVERSITY (NY) 1200/26
Bus Admin, Engine, Soc

CLEMSON UNIVERSITY (SC) 1140/25
Ag, Arch, Bus Admin, Chem, Comp Sci, Ed, Engine, Forest, Soc

CLEVELAND INSTITUTE OF MUSIC (OH) 1200/26
Music

COE COLLEGE (IA) 1150/25
Bus Admin, Classics, Ed, Hist, Music

COGSWELL POLYTECHNIC COLLEGE (CA) 1000/21
Comp Sci, Engine

COLBY COLLEGE (ME) 1310/29
Bio, Bus Admin, Econ, English, For Lang, Poli Sci, Pre-Law, Pre-Med/Pre-Dental, Psych, Soc

COLGATE UNIVERSITY (NY) 1310/29
Bio, Chem, English, Geog, Geol, Hist, Math, Philo, Poli Sci, Pre-Law, Pre-Med/Pre-Dental, Reli Stu

COLORADO COLLEGE (CO) 1270/28
Anthro, Bio, English, Geol, Hist, Philo, Poli Sci, Pre-Law, Pre-Med/Pre-Dental

COLORADO, UNIVERSITY OF (CO) 1180/26
Anthro, Astro, Biochem, Chem, Communic, Engine, Geog, Geol, Math, Music, Nurs, Physics, Pre-Med/Pre-Dental

COLORADO, UNIVERSITY OF (COLORADO SPRINGS) 1065/23
Bus Admin, Comp Sci, Engine, Geog, Physics, Psych

COLORADO, UNIVERSITY OF (DENVER) 1060/23
Comp Sci, Psych

COLORADO SCHOOL OF MINES (CO) 1240/28
Comp Sci, Engine, Geol, Physics, Pre-Med/Pre-Dental

COLORADO STATE UNIVERSITY (CO) 1125/25
Ag, Art, Art Hist, Bot, Bus Admin, Forest, Geol, Psych, Zoo

COLUMBIA COLLEGE (SC) 1050/22
Bio, Bus Admin, Drama, Ed, Pre-Law, Pre-Med/Pre-Dental, Psych

COLUMBIA UNIVERSITY/BARNARD COLLEGE (NY) **1350/30; 1325/30**
*Anthro, Arch, Art Hist, Biochem, Chem, Classics, Drama, Econ, Engine, English, For Lang,
Geol, Hist, Math, Music, Nurs, Philo, Physics, Poli Sci, Pre-Law, Psych, Reli Stu, Soc*

CONCORDIA COLLEGE-MOORHEAD (MN) **1120/24**
Bio, Bus Admin, Ed, Math, Music, Pre-Med/Pre-Dental, Psych, Soc

CONCORDIA COLLEGE (NE) **1050/22**
Bus Admin, Ed

CONCORDIA UNIVERSITY (CA) **1100/24**
Music, Reli Stu

CONNECTICUT, UNIVERSITY OF (CT) **1125/25**
Ag, Art, Bio, Bot, Ed, Pharm, Pre-Law, Pre-Med/Pre-Dental, Psych, Zoo

CONNECTICUT COLLEGE (CT) **1260/28**
Bot, Drama, Econ, Ed, English, Hist, Music, Philo, Poli Sci, Pre-Law, Psych

CONVERSE COLLEGE (SC) **1100/24**
Art, Drama, Ed, Music

THE COOPER UNION (NY) **1440/33**
Arch, Art, Engine

CORNELL COLLEGE (IA) **1150/25**
Bio, Ed, English, Geol, Philo, Pre-Law, Pre-Med/Pre-Dental, Psych, Soc

CORNELL UNIVERSITY (NY) **1350/30**
*Ag, Arch, Art, Astro, Biochem, Bio, Bot, Comp Sci, Drama, Econ, Engine, English, Hist,
Philo, Physics, Pre-Med/Pre-Dental, Zoo*

CORNISH COLLEGE OF THE ARTS (WA) **1100/24**
Art, Drama, Music

COVENANT COLLEGE (GA) **1150/25**
Hist, Soc

CREIGHTON UNIVERSITY (NB) **1140/25**
Bio, Communic, Nurs, Pharm, Poli Sci, Pre-Law, Pre-Med/Pre-Dental

CURTIS INSTITUTE OF MUSIC (PA) **1100/24**
Music

DAEMEN COLLEGE (NY) **1030/22**
Nurs

DALLAS, UNIVERSITY OF (TX) **1236/28**
*Art, Bio, Biochem, Classics, Comp Sci, Econ, Ed, English, For Lang, Hist, Pre-Law,
Pre-Med/Pre-Dental*

DANA COLLEGE (NB) **1040/22**
Drama, Ed, English

DARTMOUTH COLLEGE (NH) **1420/32**
*Anthro, Art, Bio, Chem, Comp Sci, Drama, Econ, Engine, English, For Lang, Geog, Geol,
Math, Physics, Poli Sci, Pre-Law, Pre-Med/Pre-Dental, Reli Stu, Soc*

DAVIDSON COLLEGE (NC) **1325/30**
Chem, English, Hist, Math, Philo, Pre-Law, Pre-Med/Pre-Dental, Reli Stu

DAYTON, UNIVERSITY OF (OH) **1170/26**
Bus Admin, Ed, Engine, Poli Sci

DELAWARE, UNIVERSITY OF (DE) **1140/25**
Art, Art Hist, Bio, Bot, Bus Admin, Chem, Communic, Ed, Engine, Nurs, Pre-Med/Pre-Dental

DELAWARE VALLEY COLLEGE (PA) **1030/22**
Ag, Bio, Bus Admin, Chem, Pre-Med/Pre-Dental

DENISON UNIVERSITY (OH) **1210/27**
Bio, Biochem, Econ, English, Geol, Hist, Philo, Poli Sci, Pre-Law, Pre-Med/Pre-Dental, Psych, Soc

DENVER, UNIVERSITY OF (CO) **1115/24**
Bio, Bus Admin, Chem, Communic, English, Music, Physics, Pre-Law, Pre-Med/Pre-Dental, Psych

DePAUL UNIVERSITY (IL) **1150/25**
Bus Admin, Communic, Comp Sci, Drama, Poli Sci, Pre-Law, Pre-Med/Pre-Dental

DePAUW UNIVERSITY (IN) **1200/26**
Bus Admin, Communic, Econ, Music, Nurs, Pre-Law

DETROIT MERCY, UNIVERSITY OF (MI) **1100/24**
Arch, Engine, Nurs

DICKINSON COLLEGE (PA) **1200/26**
Bio, Comp Sci, English, For Lang, Hist, Math, Physics, Poli Sci, Pre-Law, Pre-Med/Pre-Dental, Reli Stu

DILLARD UNIVERSITY (LA) **1000/21**
Bus Admin

DOANE COLLEGE (NE) **1070/23**
Bus Admin, Soc

DOMINICAN COLLEGE OF SAN RAFAEL (CA) **1030/22**
Ed, Nurs, Psych

DOMINICAN UNIVERSITY (IL) **1040/22**
Bus Admin, Psych

DORDT COLLEGE (IA) **1080/23**
Ag, Ed

DRAKE UNIVERSITY (IA) **1155/25**
Art, Astro, Bus Admin, Communic, Ed, For Lang, Music, Pharm, Poli Sci, Pre-Law

DREW UNIVERSITY (NJ) **1240/28**
Art, Chem, Classics, Drama, For Lang, Hist, Poli Sci, Pre-Law, Psych

DREXEL UNIVERSITY (PA) **1140/25**
Comp Sci, Engine

DRURY COLLEGE (MO) **1150/25**
Arch, Music

DUBUQUE, UNIVERSITY OF (IA) 1060/23
Ed

DUKE UNIVERSITY (NC) 1380/31
Anthro, Bio, Bot, Chem, Classics, Econ, Engine, English, Hist, Math, Nurs, Philo, Poli Sci, Pre-Law, Pre-Med/Pre-Dental, Psych, Reli Stu

DUQUESNE UNIVERSITY (PA) 1100/24
Bio, Chem, Communic, Music, Nurs, Pharm, Pre-Med/Pre-Dental

D'YOUVILLE COLLEGE (NY) 1050/22
Nurs, Soc

EARLHAM COLLEGE (IN) 1170/26
Anthro, Astro, Bio, Chem, Ed, English, For Lang, Geol, Math, Pre-Med/Pre-Dental, Psych, Soc

EAST CAROLINA UNIVERSITY (NC) 1030/22
Art, Ed, Engine, Music, Nurs, Pre-Med/Pre-Dental

EAST STROUDSBURG UNIVERSITY (PA) 1010/21
Bio, Comp Sci

EASTERN COLLEGE (PA) 1060/23
Bus Admin, Nurs, Soc

EASTERN CONNECTICUT STATE UNIVERSITY (CT) 1000/21
Bio, Bus Admin, Comp Sci, Ed, Math, Poli Sci, Psych, Soc

EASTERN ILLINOIS UNIVERSITY (IL) 1010/21
Art, Bot, Ed, Psych, Zoo

EASTERN KENTUCKY UNIVERSITY (KY) 1000/21
Ed, Nurs

EASTERN MICHIGAN UNIVERSITY (MI) 1000/21
Bus Admin, Ed, Psych

EASTERN NAZARENE COLLEGE (MA) 1030/22
Bus Admin, English

EASTERN OREGON UNIVERSITY (OR) 1000/21
Bio, Bus Admin, Ed

ECKERD COLLEGE (FL) 1180/26
Bio, Bus Admin, English, For Lang, Pre-Med/Pre-Dental, Reli Stu

EDGEWOOD COLLEGE (WI) 1050/22
Ed, Nurs

EDINBORO UNIVERSITY OF PENNSYLVANIA (PA) 1010/21
Art, Art Hist, Ed, English

ELIZABETHTOWN COLLEGE (PA) 1130/25
Bus Admin

ELMHURST COLLEGE (IL) 1000/21
Bio

ELMIRA COLLEGE (NY) 1120/24
Bus Admin, Ed, Psych

ELMS COLLEGE (MA) 1020/22
Nurs

ELON COLLEGE (NC) 1099/24
Bus Admin, Communic, Ed

EMERSON COLLEGE (MA) 1135/25
Drama, English, Pre-Law

EMMANUAL COLLEGE (MA) 1000/21
Art, Bio

EMORY & HENRY COLLEGE (VA) 1040/22
Bus Admin, For Lang

EMORY UNIVERSITY (GA) 1325/30
Bio, Bus Admin, Chem, English, For Lang, Hist, Nurs, Poli Sci, Pre-Law, Pre-Med/Pre-Dental, Psych, Reli Stu

ERSKINE COLLEGE (SC) 1110/24
Bio, Bus Admin, Ed, Hist, Pre-Med/Pre-Dental

EUREKA COLLEGE (IL) 1060/23
Bus Admin, Comp Sci

EVANSVILLE, UNIVERSITY OF (IN) 1150/25
Comp Sci, Drama, Nurs, Physics, Pre-Med/Pre-Dental

FAIRFIELD UNIVERSITY (CT) 1150/25
Bio, Bus Admin, Communic, Math, Nurs, Physics, Pre-Med/Pre-Dental, Psych

FAIRLEIGH DICKINSON (NJ) 1020/22
Art, Bus Admin, English, Pre-Law

FERRIS STATE UNIVERSITY (MI) 970/20
Bus Admin, Comp Sci, Nurs, Pharm

FISK UNIVERSITY (TN) 1030/22
Bus Admin, Math, Pre-Law, Soc

FITCHBURG STATE COLLEGE (MA) 1020/22
Communic, Nurs, Psych

FIVE TOWNS COLLEGE (NY) 1000/21
Music

FLAGLER COLLEGE (FL) 1100/24
Bus Admin, Communic, Ed, Pre-Law, Psych

FLORIDA, UNIVERSITY OF (FL) 1240/28
Ag, Anthro, Arch, Art, Astro, Bot, Bus Admin, Classics, Communic, English, Forest, Geol, Math, Nurs, Pharm, Philo, Physics, Pre-Law, Soc, Zoo

FLORIDA A&M (FL) 1000/21
Bus Admin, Ed, Pharm, Pre-Law, Pre-Med/Pre-Dental

FLORIDA ATLANTIC UNIVERSITY (FL) 1060/23
Bus Admin, Ed, Engine, Math

FLORIDA GULF COAST UNIVERSITY (FL) 1050/22
Bus Admin, Comp Sci, Ed, Nurs

FLORIDA INSTITUTE OF TECHNOLOGY (FL) 1145/25
Astro, Biochem, Bus Admin, Engine, Psych

FLORIDA INTERNATIONAL UNIVERSITY (FL) 1120/24
Bus Admin, Ed, Engine, Psych

FLORIDA SOUTHERN COLLEGE (FL) 1099/23
Communic, Pre-Med/Pre-Dental

FLORIDA STATE UNIVERSITY (FL) 1150/25
*Art, Art Hist, Bus Admin, Chem, Drama, Ed, Home Ec, Music, Philo, Pre-Med/Pre-Dental,
Psych, Reli Stu*

FONTBONNE COLLEGE (MO) 1035/22
Communic, Drama, Ed, Math

FORDHAM UNIVERSITY (NY) 1165/26
Classics, Communic, Drama, English, Philo, Pre-Law, Pre-Med/Pre-Dental, Reli Stu

FORT HAYS STATE UNIVERSITY (KS) 1050/22
Art, English, Music

FORT LEWIS COLLEGE (CO) 1025/22
Bio, English, Geol, Pre-Law

FRAMINGHAM STATE COLLEGE (MA) 1020/22
Bio, Bus Admin, Econ, Psych

FRANCISCAN UNIVERSITY OF STEUBENVILLE (OH) 1099/24
Nurs, Philo, Psych, Reli Stu

FRANKLIN COLLEGE OF INDIANA (IN) 1100/24
Communic, Drama, Ed

FRANKLIN & MARSHALL COLLEGE (PA) 1260/28
*Amer Stu, Bio, Bus Admin, Chem, English, Geol, Physics, Poli Sci, Pre-Law,
Pre-Med/Pre-Dental, Soc*

FREED-HARDEMAN UNIVERSITY (TN) 1050/22
Bus Admin, Ed, Pre-Med/Pre-Dental

FROSTBURG STATE UNIVERSITY (MD) 1000/21
Ed

FURMAN UNIVERSITY (SC) 1250/28
Art, Chem, Comp Sci, Geol, Music, Poli Sci, Pre-Law, Pre-Med/Pre-Dental, Psych, Reli Stu

GANNON UNIVERSITY (PA) 1050/22
Bus Admin, Engine, Nurs

GENEVA COLLEGE (PA) 1080/23
Ed, Engine

GEORGETOWN COLLEGE (KY) 1105/24
Bus Admin, Communic, English, Pre-Law

GEORGETOWN UNIVERSITY (DC) 1330/30
*Amer St, Bio, Bus Admin, Classics, Econ, For Lang, Hist, Nurs, Philo, Physics,
Poli Sci, Pre-Law, Pre-Med/Pre-Dental, Reli Stu*

GEORGE FOX UNIVERSITY (OR) 1065/23
Ed, Soc

GEORGE MASON UNIVERSITY (VA) 1100/24
Amer St, Bus Admin, Comp Sci, Drama, Econ, English, Nurs, Psych, Pre-Law

GEORGE WASHINGTON UNIVERSITY (DC) 1240/28
Amer St, Comp Sci, Geog, Hist, Philo, Poli Sci, Pre-Law, Psych

GEORGIA, UNIVERSITY OF (GA) 1195/26
*Ag, Astro, Bio, Chem, Communic, Ed, English, For Lang, Forest, Home Ec, Pharm,
Pre-Law, Pre-Med/Pre-Dental, Zoo*

GEORGIA INSTITUTE OF TECHNOLOGY (GA) 1305/29
Arch, Comp Sci, Econ, Engine, Physics

GEORGIA SOUTHERN UNIVERSITY (GA) 1040/22
Ed

GETTYSBURG COLLEGE (PA) 1200/26
Bio, Bus Admin, Communic, English, Hist, Pre-Law, Pre-Med/Pre-Dental, Psych, Soc

GONZAGA UNIVERSITY (WA) 1175/26
Bus Admin, Communic, Ed, Engine, English, Hist, Poli Sci, Pre-Law

GORDON COLLEGE (MA) 1180/26
Art, Ed, English, Music, Reli Stu

GOSHEN COLLEGE (IN) 1090/24
Nurs, Physics

GOUCHER COLLEGE (MD) 1180/26
Bus Admin, Chem, Comp Sci, Drama, Ed, English, Hist, Pre-Law

GRACELAND COLLEGE (IA) 1040/22
Bus Admin, Ed, Nurs

GRAMBLING UNIVERSITY (LA) 1000/21
Bus Admin, Nurs, Soc

GRAND VALLEY STATE UNIVERSITY (MI) 1100/24
Art, English, Pre-Law, Psych

GREEN MOUNTAIN COLLEGE (VT) 1040/22
Bus Admin

GRINNELL COLLEGE (IA) 1350/30
*Anthro, Bio, Chem, Comp Sci, Econ, English, For Lang, Hist, Physics, Poli Sci, Pre-Law,
Pre-Med/Pre-Dental, Psych, Soc*

GROVE CITY COLLEGE (PA) **1250/28**
Bio, Bus Admin, Ed, Engine

GUILFORD COLLEGE (NC) **1140/25**
Art, Bio, Bus Admin, Ed, English, Geol, Physics, Pre-Law, Pre-Med/Pre-Dental, Psych, Reli Stu

GUSTAVUS ADOLPHUS COLLEGE (MN) **1190/26**
Bus Admin, Ed, For Lang, Music, Nurs, Physics, Psych

GWYNEDD-MERCY COLLEGE (PA) **1040/22**
Nurs

HAMILTON COLLEGE (NY) **1250/28**
Bio, Chem, Econ, English, Hist, Philo, Poli Sci, Pre-Law, Pre-Med/Pre-Dental, Reli Stu

HAMLINE UNIVERSITY (MN) **1120/24**
Anthro, Art, Bio, Chem, English, Pre-Law, Pre-Med/Pre-Dental, Psych, Soc

HAMPDEN-SYDNEY COLLEGE (VA) **1120/24**
Bio, Classics, English, Hist, Pre-Law, Pre-Med/Pre-Dental

HAMPTON UNIVERSITY (VA) **1020/22**
Bus Admin

HANOVER COLLEGE (IN) **1145/25**
Bus Admin, Communic, Drama, Ed, Hist, Psych, Soc

HARDIN-SIMMONS UNIVERSITY (TX) **1020/22**
Communic, Ed, Music

HARDING UNIVERSITY (AR) **1110/24**
Ed, Reli Stu

HARTFORD, UNIVERSITY OF (CT) **1050/23**
Bus Admin, Engine, Music

HARTWICK COLLEGE (NY) **1099/23**
Bus Admin, Geol, Music, Nurs, Poli Sci, Pre-Law, Soc

HARVARD UNIVERSITY (MA) **1435/32**
*Amer St, Anthro, Art, Art Hist, Astro, Biochem, Bio, Chem, Classics, Comp Sci, Econ, English,
For Lang, Geol, Hist, Math, Music, Philo, Physics, Poli Sci, Pre-Law, Pre-Med/Pre-Dental, Psych*

HARVEY MUDD COLLEGE (CA) **1460/33**
Bio, Chem, Comp Sci, Engine, Math, Physics, Pre-Med/Pre-Dental

HASTINGS COLLEGE (NE) **1090/24**
Bus Admin, Ed

HAVERFORD COLLEGE (PA) **1380/31**
*Astro, Bio, Chem, Econ, English, Hist, Philo, Physics, Pre-Law, Pre-Med/Pre-Dental,
Psych, Reli Stu*

HAWAII, UNIVERSITY OF (HI) **1085/24**
Ag, Amer St, Anthro, Art, Astro, Bot, For Lang, Poli Sci, Pre-Law

HAWAII PACIFIC UNIVERSITY (HI) **1060/23**
Bus Admin, Communic, Comp Sci, Nurs

HEIDELBERG COLLEGE (OH) 1000/21
Bus Admin, Econ, Ed, Music, Pre-Law, Pre-Med/Pre-Dental

HENDERSON STATE UNIVERSITY (AR) 1020/22
Bus Admin, Ed, Nurs

HENDRIX COLLEGE (AR) 1230/27
Bio, Bus Admin, Chem, Comp Sci, Econ, Pre-Law, Pre-Med/Pre-Dental, Reli Stu, Soc

HIGH POINT UNIVERSITY (NC) 1020/22
Comp Sci

HILLSDALE COLLEGE (MI) 1140/25
Bus Admin, Ed, Hist

HIRAM COLLEGE (OH) 1150/25
Bio, Chem, Comp Sci, Ed, English, Hist, Math, Pre-Law, Pre-Med/Pre-Dental, Reli Stu

HOBART & WILLIAM SMITH COLLEGE (NY) 1190/26
Amer Stu, Bio, Chem, Econ, English, Hist, Poli Sci, Pre-Law, Pre-Med/Pre-Dental, Psych

HOFSTRA UNIVERSITY (NY) 1100/24
*Anthro, Art, Bus Admin, Communic, Drama, Music, Poli Sci, Pre-Law,
Pre-Med/Pre-Dental, Soc*

HOLLINS UNIVERSITY (VA) 1130/25
Amer St, Art, Art Hist, English, For Lang, Pre-Law, Psych

HOLY CROSS, COLLEGE OF THE (MA) 1250/28
Bio, Classics, Econ, English, Hist, Math, Philo, Pre-Law, Pre-Med/Pre-Dental

HOOD COLLEGE (MD) 1130/25
Bio, Bus Admin, Ed, Hist, Philo, Pre-Med/Pre-Dental, Psych

HOPE COLLEGE (MI) 1180/26
Bio, Chem, Geol, Music, Poli Sci, Pre-Law, Pre-Med/Pre-Dental, Psych

HOUGHTON COLLEGE (NY) 1180/26
Art, Bio, Chem, Ed, Music, Pre-Med/Pre-Dental, Psych, Reli Stu

HOUSTON BAPTIST UNIVERSITY (TX) 1060/23
Bio, Chem, Pre-Med/Pre-Dental

HOUSTON, UNIVERSITY OF (TX) 1060/23
Arch, Art, Bus Admin, Engine, Music, Psych

HOWARD UNIVERSITY (DC) 1020/22
Bus Admin, Communic, Nurs, Poli Sci, Pre-Law, Pre-Med/Pre-Dental, Soc, Zoo

HUMBOLDT STATE UNIVERSITY (CA) 1075/23
Anthro, Art, Bot, Drama, Forest, Geog, Geol, Music, Zoo

HUNTINGDON COLLEGE (AL) 1130/25
Chem, Ed, Pre-Med/Pre-Dental

HUNTINGTON COLLEGE (IN) 1060/23
Ed

HUSSON COLLEGE (ME) 1000/21
Bus Admin, Comp Sci, Ed, Nurs

IDAHO, UNIVERSITY OF (ID) 1095/24
Ag, Arch, Bus Admin, Communic, Engine, Forest

ILLINOIS, UNIVERSITY OF, AT:
    URBANA-CHAMPAIGN 1230/27
    Ag, Anthro, Arch, Astro, Bus Admin, Chem, Communic, Comp Sci, Ed, Engine, For
    Lang, Math, Music, Nurs, Pharm, Physics, Pre-Med/Pre-Dental, Psych, Soc
    CHICAGO 1110/24
    Arch, Art, Bio, Bus Admin, Classics, Econ, Engine, For Lang, Nurs, Pharm,
    Pre-Med/Pre-Dental, Psych

ILLINOIS COLLEGE (IL) 1100/24
Bio, Communic, Comp Sci, Econ, Ed, English, For Lang, Hist, Math, Pre-Law, Soc

ILLINOIS INSTITUTE OF TECHNOLOGY (IL) 1220/27
Arch, Engine, Math

ILLINOIS STATE UNIVERSITY (IL) 1040/22
Drama, Ed

ILLINOIS WESLEYAN UNIVERSITY (IL) 1245/28
Bio, Drama, English, Music, Nurs, Pre-Law, Pre-Med/Pre-Dental

IMMACULATA COLLEGE (PA) 1035/22
Bus Admin, Nurs

INDIANA STATE UNIVERSITY (IN) 1000/21
Art, Bus Admin, Ed

INDIANA UNIVERSITY (IN) 1100/24
Bio, Bus Admin, Chem, Communic, Drama, Ed, For Lang, Geog, Geol, Music,
Pre-Med/Pre-Dental, Psych, Zoo

INDIANA UNIVERSITY OF PENNSYLVANIA 1100/24
Bus Admin, Ed

INDIANA U./PURDUE U./INDIANAPOLIS (IN) 1000/21
Nurs

IONA UNIVERSITY (NY) 1000/21
Bus Admin

IOWA, UNIVERSITY OF 1150/25
Astro, Biochem, Bus Admin, Communic, Ed, Engine, English, For Lang, Music, Nurs,
Pre-Law, Pre-Med/Pre-Dental, Psych, Reli Stu

IOWA STATE UNIVERSITY (IA) 1160/25
Ag, Bio, Bus Admin, Comp Sci, Ed, Engine, Forest, Pre-Med/Pre-Dental, Soc, Zoo

ITHACA COLLEGE (NY) 1130/25
Chem, Music, Pre-Med/Pre-Dental

JACKSONVILLE STATE (AL) 1000/21
Ed

JACKSONVILLE UNIVERSITY (FL) 1050/22
Art, Bio, Bus Admin, Communic, Drama, Music, Nurs, Physics, Pre-Med/Pre-Dental

JAMES MADISON UNIVERSITY (VA) 1180/26
Art, Bus Admin, Ed, Communic, For Lang, Music

JOHN CARROLL UNIVERSITY (OH) 1110/24
Bus Admin, Communic, English

JOHNS HOPKINS UNIVERSITY (MD) 1385/31
Art Hist, Bio, Chem, Classics, Engine, Geog, Music, Philo, Poli Sci, Pre-Law, Pre-Med/Pre-Dental

JOHNSON C. SMITH (NC) 950/20
Communic, Soc

JOHNSON STATE COLLEGE (VT) 1000/21
Drama, Ed, English

JUDSON COLLEGE (AL) 1000/21
Music, Psych

JUILLIARD SCHOOL(NY) 1120/24
Drama, Music

JUNIATA COLLEGE (PA) 1150/25
Art, Bio, Bus Admin, Chem, Communic, Ed, Hist, Pre-Med/Pre-Dental

KALAMAZOO COLLEGE (MI) 1240/28
Amer St, Bio, Chem, Classics, Econ, English, For Lang, Hist, Physics, Pre-Law, Pre-Med/Pre-Dental, Soc

KANSAS NEWMAN COLLEGE (KS) 1100/24
Bus Admin, Philo

KANSAS, UNIVERSITY OF (KS) 1100/24
Anthro, Arch, Art, Art Hist, Astro, Chem, Communic, Drama, Engine, For Lang, Geog, Hist, Pharm, Pre-Med/Pre-Dental, Zoo

KANSAS STATE UNIVERSITY (KS) 1100/24
Ag, Arch, Bio, Biochem, Bus Admin, Communic, Ed, Engine, Home Ec, Math, Pre-Law, Pre-Med/Pre-Dental

KEAN UNIVERSITY (NJ) 1000/21
Ed, Psych, Soc

KEENE STATE COLLEGE (NH) 1000/21
Art, Communic, Drama, Ed, Geog, Music, Psych

KENNESAW STATE UNIVERSITY (GA) 1045/22
Bus Admin

KENT STATE UNIVERSITY (OH) 1010/21
Arch, Art, Communic, Ed, Music

KENTUCKY, UNIVERSITY OF (KY) 1130/25
Ag, Bio, Bus Admin, Communic, Ed, Engine, Hist, Pharm, Pre-Med/Pre-Dental, Psych, Zoo

KENTUCKY WESLEYAN (KY) **1060/23**
Bio, Bus Admin, Communic, Ed, English, Hist, Pre-Med/Pre-Dental, Psych

KENYON COLLEGE (OH) **1280/29**
Bio, Chem, Drama, Econ, English, Hist, Math, Philo, Poli Sci, Pre-Law, Pre-Med/Pre-Dental, Psych, Reli Stu

KETTERING UNIVERSITY (MI) **1220/27**
Engine

KING COLLEGE (TN) **1090/24**
Reli Stu

KING'S COLLEGE (PA) **1060/23**
Bus Admin

KNOX COLLEGE (IL) **1199/26**
Art, Chem, English, Hist, Math, Poli Sci, Pre-Law, Pre-Med/Pre-Dental, Soc

KUTZTOWN UNIVERSITY (PA) **1000/21**
Art, Ed

LAFAYETTE COLLEGE (PA) **1220/27**
Anthro, Art, Bio, Chem, Econ, Engine, English, Geol, Hist, Pre-Law, Pre-Med/Pre-Dental, Psych

LAKE FOREST COLLEGE (IL) **1140/25**
Art, Art Hist, Bio, Chem, Econ, English, Hist, Music, Pre-Law, Pre-Med/Pre-Dental, Psych, Soc

LAMAR UNIVERSITY (TX) **1000/21**
Ed, Engine, Geol, Soc

LA SALLE UNIVERSITY (PA) **1100/24**
Bus Admin, Comp Sci, English, Pre-Law

LASELL COLLEGE (MA) **1000/21**
Bus Admin, Ed

LA VERNE, UNIVERSITY OF (CA) **1000/21**
Bus Admin, Ed

LAWRENCE UNIVERSITY (WI) **1240/28**
Bio, Chem, Drama, English, For Lang, Hist, Music, Physics, Pre-Law, Pre-Med/Pre-Dental, Reli Stu

LEBANON VALLEY COLLEGE OF PENNSYLVANIA (PA) **1105/24**
Bus Admin, Math, Music, Nurs, Psych

LEHIGH UNIVERSITY (PA) **1250/28**
Bus Admin, Engine, Geol

LEMOYNE COLLEGE (NY) **1100/24**
Bus Admin, Communic, Drama, English, Psych

LENOIR-RHYNE COLLEGE (NC) **1000/21**
Bus Admin, Soc

LESLEY COLLEGE (MA) 1000/21
Bus Admin, Ed

LETOURNEAU COLLEGE (TX) 1110/24
Bus Admin, Ed, Engine

LEWIS & CLARK COLLEGE (OR) 1199/27
*Bio, Biochem, Bus Admin, Communic, Drama, English, For Lang, Physics,
Pre-Med/Pre-Dental, Soc*

LEWIS-CLARK STATE COLLEGE (ID) 1000/21
Bus Admin, Communic, Ed, Nurs

LINDENWOOD UNIVERSITY (MO) 1060/23
Psych

LINFIELD COLLEGE (OR) 1110/24
Bio, Bus Admin, Chem, Ed, For Lang

LOCK HAVEN UNIVERSITY (PA) 1060/23
Ed

LONG ISLAND UNIVERSITY (SOUTHAMPTON) (NY) 1050/22
Art, Bio, Bus Admin, Drama, English

LONGWOOD COLLEGE (VA) 1055/23
Bus Admin, Drama, Ed, English, Music, Pre-Law, Psych

LORAS COLLEGE (IA) 1110/24
Art, Bio, Bus Admin, Communic, Ed, English, Pre-Law, Psych

LOUISIANA STATE UNIVERSITY (LA 1095/24
*Ag, Arch, Art, Astro, Biochem, Bot, Chem, Communic, Geog, Geol, Math, Music, Physics,
Pre-Med/Pre-Dental, Psych, Zoo*

LOUISVILLE, UNIVERSITY OF (KY) 1000/21
Engine

LOWELL, UNIVERSITY OF MASSACHUSETTS AT (MA) 1050/22
Bus Admin, Engine, Music

LOYOLA COLLEGE (MD) 1190/26
Bio, Bus Admin, Communic, Engine, Pre-Law, Pre-Med/Pre-Dental

LOYOLA MARYMOUNT UNIVERSITY (CA) 1140/25
Art, Bus Admin, Communic, Engine

LOYOLA UNIVERSITY OF CHICAGO (IL) 1110/24
Bio, Communic, Drama, Music, Nurs, Physics, Pre-Med/Pre-Dental, Psych

LOYOLA UNIVERSITY OF NEW ORLEANS (LA) 1145/25
Bio, Bus Admin, Comp Sci, Communic, Music, Philo, Pre-Law, Pre-Med/Pre-Dental, Reli Stu

LUTHER COLLEGE (IA) 1155/22
Bus Admin, Ed, Music, Nurs, Psych

LYCOMING COLLEGE (PA) 1100/24
Astro, English, Philo, Psych, Reli Stu

LYNCHBURG COLLEGE (VA) 1045/22
Bio, Communic, Math, Pre-Law, Pre-Med/Pre-Dental, Soc

LYNDON STATE COLLEGE (VT) 1000/21
Communic

LYON COLLEGE (AR) 1170/26
Drama, Ed, Psych

MACALESTER COLLEGE (MN) 1300/29
Anthro, Art, Bio, Classics, Communic, Drama, Econ, English, Geog, Hist, Philo,
Physics, Poli Sci, Pre-Law, Pre-Med/Pre-Dental, Psych

MacMURRAY COLLEGE (IL) 1010/21
Nurs

MAINE, UNIVERSITY OF (ME) 1100/24
Ag, Bot, Bus Admin, Comp Sci, Drama, Engine, Forest, Music

MAINE, UNIVERSITY OF (FARMINGTON) (ME) 1020/22
Bus Admin, Ed, Geog, Psych

MALONE COLLEGE (OH) 1040/22
Bus Admin, Math

MANCHESTER COLLEGE (IN) 1045/22
Bus Admin, Psych

MANHATTAN COLLEGE (NY) 1100/24
Bus Admin, Ed, Engine, Poli Sci, Pre-Law

MANHATTAN SCHOOL OF MUSIC (NY) 1100/24
Music

MANHATTANVILLE COLLEGE (NY) 1150/25
Art, Art Hist, Bus Admin, Econ, Ed, Music, Psych, Soc

MANSFIELD UNIVERSITY OF PENNSYLVANIA (PA) 1040/22
Ed, English, For Lang, Geog, Philo

MARIETTA COLLEGE (OH) 1100/24
Art, Bus Admin, English, Pre-Law

MARIST COLLEGE (NY) 1140/25
Bio, Bus Admin, Comp Sci, Communic, Psych

MARQUETTE UNIVERSITY (WI) 1180/26
Bio, Bus Admin, Chem, Communic, Comp Sci, English, Engine, Hist, Nurs, Philo, Poli Sci,
Pre-Law, Pre-Med/Pre-Dental, Psych, Reli Stu

MARSHALL UNIVERSITY (WV) 1000/21
Bus Admin, Chem, Ed, Nurs

MARY BALDWIN COLLEGE (VA) 1040/22
Art, Bus Admin, Communic, Psych, Soc

MARYGROVE COLLEGE (MI) 1000/21
Comp Sci

MARYLAND INSTITUTE-COLLEGE OF ART (MD) 1130/25
Art

MARYLAND, UNIVERSITY OF (MD) 1195/26
Ag, Anthro, Arch, Astro, Bot, Bus Admin, Communic, Econ, Ed, Hist, Pharm, Pre-Law, Zoo

MARYLAND, UNIVERSITY OF (BALTIMORE COUNTY) (MD) 1200/26
Comp Sci, Drama, Nurs, Poli Sci, Pre-Law

MARYMOUNT COLLEGE - TARRYTOWN (NY) 1000/21
Drama

MARYMOUNT UNIVERSITY (VA) 1000/21
Nurs, Psych

MARYVILLE COLLEGE (TN) 1090/24
Bio, Psych

MARYVILLE UNIVERSITY-ST. LOUIS (MO) 1090/24
Art, Ed, Nurs

MARY WASHINGTON COLLEGE (VA) 1199/26
Amer St, Bio, Geog, Hist, Pre-Med/Pre-Dental, Psych

MASSACHUSETTS, UNIVERSITY OF (MA) 1140/25
*Astro, Bus Admin, Chem, Communic, Comp Sci, Engine, English, Hist, Nurs, Pre-Law,
Pre-Med/Pre-Dental, Zoo*

MASSACHUSETTS, UNIVERSITY OF (BOSTON) (MA) 1010/21
Bus Admin, Engine, Music, Nurs, Psych, Soc

MASSACHUSETTS, UNIVERSITY OF (DARTMOUTH) (MA) 1050/23
Art, Nurs, Psych, Soc

MASSACHUSETTS COLLEGE OF ART (MA) 1070/23
Art

MASSACHUSETTS COLLEGE OF LIBERAL ARTS (NO. ADAMS) (MA) 1050/22
Bus Admin, Communic, English, Soc

MASSACHUSETTS COLLEGE OF PHARMACY (MA) 1066/23
Pharm

MASSACHUSETTS INSTITUTE OF TECHNOLOGY (MA) 1450/32
*Arch, Astro, Biochem, Bio, Bus Admin, Chem, Comp Sci, Econ, Engine, Geol, Math,
Physics, Poli Sci, Pre-Law, Pre-Med/Pre-Dental*

MASSACHUSETTS MARITIME ACADEMY (MA) 1005/21
Engine

MASSACHUSETTS STATE COLLEGE SYSTEM (MA) 1005/21
Ed

MASTER'S COLLEGE, THE (CA) 1100/24
Bus Admin, Communic, English, Reli Stu

MCKENDREE COLLEGE (IL) 1075/23
Comp Sci, Nurs

MEMPHIS, UNIVERSITY OF (TN) 1040/22
Music

MERCER UNIVERSITY (GA) 1099/24
Bus Admin, Ed, Engine, Music, Pharm

MEREDITH COLLEGE (NC) 1060/23
Bio, Bus Admin, Music

MERCYHURST COLLEGE (PA) 1060/23
Art, Bus Admin

MERCY COLLEGE (NY) 1000/21
Nurs, Psych

MERRIMACK COLLEGE (MA) 1060/23
Bus Admin

MESSIAH COLLEGE (PA) 1150/25
Art, Ed

MIAMI UNIVERSITY (OH) 1170/26
Arch, Bot, Bus Admin, Ed, Zoo

MIAMI, UNIVERSITY OF (FL) 1185/26
Arch, Bio, Biochem, Communic, Drama, Ed, Hist, Music, Pre-Med/Pre-Dental

MICHIGAN, UNIVERSITY OF (MI) 1275/27
Amer St, Anthro, Arch, Art, Art Hist, Astro, Bot, Bus Admin, Classics, Communic, Comp Sci, Econ, Ed, Engine, Forest, For Lang, Geog, Music, Nurs, Pharm, Philo, Pre-Law, Pre-Med/Pre-Dental, Psych, Soc, Zoo

MICHIGAN, UNIVERSITY OF (DEARBORN) (MI) 1080/23
Bus Admin, Comp Sci, Engine

MICHIGAN STATE UNIVERSITY (MI) 1100/24
Ag, Biochem, Bio, Bot, Bus Admin, Chem, Communic, Econ, Ed, Engine, Forest, Geog, Home Ec, Math, Poli Sci, Pre-Law, Pre-Med/Pre-Dental, Psych, Soc

MICHIGAN TECHNOLOGICAL UNIVERSITY (MI) 1199/26
Bus Admin, Engine, Forest, Geol

MIDDLEBURY COLLEGE (VT) 1370/31
Art, Bio, Classics, Econ, English, For Lang, Geog, Hist, Poli Sci, Pre-Law, Pre-Med/Pre-Dental

MIDDLE TENNESSEE STATE UNIVERSITY (TN) 1000/21
Ed, Psych

MIDWESTERN STATE UNIVERSITY (TX) 1000/21
Nurs

MILLERSVILLE UNIVERSITY OF PENNSYLVANIA (PA) 1110/24
Bus Admin, Hist, Poli Sci, Pre-Law

MILLIGAN COLLEGE (TN) 1090/24
Bio, Bus Admin, Ed, Nurs, Philo, Psych, Reli Stu

MILLIKIN UNIVERSITY (IL) 1080/23
Art, Ed, Music

MILLS COLLEGE (CA) 1150/25
Art, Communic, Ed, For Lang, Music, Psych

MILLSAPS COLLEGE (MS) 1220/27
Bio, Bus Admin, Comp Sci, English, Geol, Math, Music, Pre-Law, Pre-Med/Pre-Dental

MILWAUKEE SCHOOL OF ENGINEERING (WI) 1175/26
Arch, Engine

MINNESOTA, UNIVERSITY OF (MN) 1150/25
Ag, Amer St, Art Hist, Bus Admin, Communic, Drama, Ed, Engine, Forest, Geog, Geol, Nurs, Pharm, Poli Sci, Pre-Law, Psych, Soc

MINNESOTA, UNIVERSITY OF (DULUTH) (MN) 1070/23
Bio, Communic

MINNESOTA, UNIVERSITY OF (MORRIS) (MN) 1199/26
Bio, Chem, Comp Sci, For Lang, Pre-Law, Pre Med/Pre-Dental

COLLEGE MISERICORDIA (PA) 1000/21
Biochem, Bio, Bus Admin, Chem, Communic, Ed, English, Hist, Nurs

MISSISSIPPI COLLEGE (MS) 1095/24
Bus Admin, Nurs, Reli Stu

MISSISSIPPI STATE UNIVERSITY (MS) 1070/23
Ag, Ed, Engine

MISSISSIPPI, UNIVERSITY OF (MS) 1099/24
Bus Admin, Communic, English, Pharm, Physics, Pre-Law

MISSISSIPPI UNIVERSITY FOR WOMEN (MS) 1115/24
Bus Admin, Nurs

MISSOURI, UNIVERSITY OF (MO) 1170/26
Ag, Art Hist, Bus Admin, Communic, English, Forest, Hist, Psych

MISSOURI, UNIVERSITY OF (KANSAS CITY) (MO) 1150/25
Art, Comp Sci, Music, Psych

MISSOURI, UNIVERSITY OF (ROLLA) (MO) 1260/28
Comp Sci, Engine, Nurs

MONMOUTH COLLEGE (IL) 1065/23
Bus Admin, Chem, Econ, Ed, Pre-Med/Pre-Dental

MONMOUTH UNIVERSITY (NJ) 1040/22
Art, Comp Sci, Music

MONTANA COLLEGE OF MINERAL SCIENCE & TECHNOLOGY (MT) 1120/24
Comp Sci, Engine

MONTANA, UNIVERSITY OF (MT) 1080/23
Astro, Bot, Classics, Communic, Comp Sci, Ed, Forest, Pharm, Zoo

MONTANA STATE UNIVERSITY (BILLINGS) (MT) 1000/21
Art, Ed

MONTANA STATE UNIVERSITY (MT) 1090/24
Ag, Arch, Art, Engine, For Lang, Forest

MONTCLAIR STATE (NJ) 1099/24
Art, Ed, English, Home Ec, Psych

MONTEVALLO, UNIVERSITY OF (AL) 1000/21
Art, Communic, Ed, English, Home Ec

MONTREAT COLLEGE (NC) 1070/23
Bus Admin

MOORE COLLEGE OF ART (PA) 1100/24
Art

MOORHEAD STATE UNIVERSITY (MN) 1000/21
Art, Music

MORAVIAN COLLEGE (PA) 1125/25
Art, Bus Admin, Communic, Comp Sci, Ed, Nurs, Soc

MOREHOUSE COLLEGE (GA) 1070/23
Bus Admin, Comp Sci

MORNINGSIDE COLLEGE (IA) 1060/23
Bio, Communic, Nurs, Pre-Med/Pre-Dental

MOUNT HOLYOKE COLLEGE (MA) 1250/28
Art Hist, Biochem, Bio, Chem, Drama, Econ, English, For Lang, Hist, Math, Poli Sci, Pre-Law, Pre-Med/Pre-Dental, Psych

MOUNT MERCY COLLEGE (IA) 1090/24
Bus Admin, Nurs

MOUNT ST. JOSEPH (OH) 1040/22
Art, Bus Admin, Ed, Nurs, Pre-Law, Pre-Med/Pre-Dental

MOUNT ST. MARY'S COLLEGE (CA) 1070/23
Bio, Bus Admin, Music, Nurs

MOUNT ST. MARY'S COLLEGE (MD) 1080/23
Bus Admin, Poli Sci, Pre-Law, Pre-Med/Pre-Dental

MOUNT ST. MARY'S COLLEGE (NY) 1040/22
Nurs

MOUNT UNION COLLEGE (OH) 1075/23
Bus Admin, Comp Sci

MUHLENBERG COLLEGE (PA) 1190/26
Art, Bio, Biochem, Bus Admin, Communic, Drama, English, Hist, Math, Philo, Pre-Law, Pre-Med/Pre-Dental, Psych

MUSKINGUM COLLEGE (OH) 1070/23
Bus Admin, Comp Sci, Ed, Hist

NAZARETH COLLEGE OF ROCHESTER (NY) 1135/25
Bio, Bus Admin, Ed, English, For Lang

NEBRASKA, UNIVERSITY OF (NE) 1095/24
Ag, Arch, Astro, Bus Admin, Communic, Econ, Music, Pre-Law

NEBRASKA WESLEYAN UNIVERSITY (NE) 1110/24
Bio, Pre-Med/Pre-Dental

NEVADA, UNIVERSITY OF, AT:
      LAS VEGAS 1010/21
      Arch, Art, Drama, Ed, Engine, Psych
      RENO 1040/22
      Ag, Bus Admin, Communic, Ed, Engine, Music, Pre-Med/Pre-Dental

NEW COLLEGE OF THE UNIVERSITY OF SOUTH FLORIDA (FL) 1310/29
Anthro, Bio, Chem, English, Math, Philo, Physics, Pre-Med/Pre-Dental, Psych

NEW ENGLAND CONSERVATORY (MA) 1100/24
Music

NEW HAMPSHIRE, UNIVERSITY OF (NH) 1120/24
Ag, Bio, Bus Admin, Chem, Communic, Ed, Engine, English, Hist, Music,
Pre-Med/Pre-Dental, Pre-Law, Psych

NEW JERSEY INSTITUTE OF TECHNOLOGY (NJ) 1145/25
Engine

NEW JERSEY, COLLEGE OF (NJ) 1220/27
Art, Ed, Engine, English, Math, Nurs, Pre-Law, Pre-Med/Pre-Dental, Psych

NEW MEXICO INSTITUTE OF MINING (NM) 1190/26
Engine, Geol, Physics

NEW MEXICO STATE UNIVERSITY (NM) 1040/22
Ag, Anthro, Engine

NEW MEXICO, UNIVERSITY OF (NM) 1050/22
Anthro, Art, Ed, For Lang, Hist, Pharm

NEW ORLEANS, UNIVERSITY OF (LA) 1000/21
Bus Admin, Engine

NEW YORK, CITY UNIVERSITY OF, AT
      BARUCH COLLEGE 1000/21
      Bus Admin
      BROOKLYN COLLEGE 1040/22
      Geol, Physics, Pre-Med/Pre-Dental
      CITY COLLEGE 1050/22
      Arch, Ed, Engine, Physics
      HERBERT LEHMAN COLLEGE 1000/21
      Ed, Psych
      HUNTER COLLEGE 1060/23
      Art, Art Hist, Communic, Comp Sci, Ed, English, Nurs, Pre-Law, Psych
      JOHN JAY COLLEGE OF CRIMINAL JUSTICE 1000/21
      Psych
      QUEENS COLLEGE 1010/22
      Anthro, Ed, Psych, Soc

NEW YORK, STATE UNIVERSITY OF, AT
    ALBANY **1140/25**
    Anthro, Bio, Bus Admin, English, Geol, Pre-Law, Pre-Med/Pre-Dental, Psych, Soc
    BINGHAMTON **1200/26**
    Biochem, Bus Admin, Math, Nurs, Philo, Physics, Pre-Law, Pre-Med/Pre-Dental, Psych
    BROCKPORT, COLLEGE AT **1050/22**
    Bus Admin, Communic, Comp Sci, Drama, Hist, Poli Sci, Psych
    BUFFALO **1150/25**
    Amer Stu, Anthro, Arch, Bus Admin, Ed, Engine, English, Geog, Pharm, Pre-Law,
    Pre-Med/Pre-Dental
    FREDONIA, COLLEGE AT **1110/24**
    Bus Admin, Communic, Ed, English, Music
    GENESEO, COLLEGE AT **1220/27**
    Bio, Biochem, Bus Admin, Ed, Geol, Music, Physics, Pre-Med/Pre-Dental
    NEW PALTZ, COLLEGE AT **1150/25**
    Bus Admin, Ed, Engine, English, For Lang, Psych
    ONEONTA, COLLEGE AT **1040/22**
    Econ, English, Home Ec, Music, Philo, Pre-Law
    OSWEGO, COLLEGE AT **1100/24**
    Bus Admin, Psych
    PLATTSBURGH, COLLEGE AT **1070/23**
    Bus Admin, Nurs
    POTSDAM, COLLEGE AT **1050/22**
    Bus Admin, Comp Sci, Ed, Math, Music
    PURCHASE, COLLEGE AT **1060/23**
    Drama, English, Music, Pre-Law, Psych
    STONY BROOK **1150/25**
    Astro, Biochem, Bio, Chem, Comp Sci, Engine, English, Geo, Philo, Physics,
    Pre-Law, Pre-Med/Pre-Dental, Psych, Reli Stu

NEW YORK UNIVERSITY (NY) **1340/30**
Art, Art Hist, Bus Admin, Classics, Drama, For Lang, Math, Music, Nurs, Philo,
Pre-Med/Pre-Dental, Psych

NIAGARA UNIVERSITY (NY) **1040/22**
Bus Admin, Drama, English, Pre-Law

NORTH CAROLINA SCHOOL OF THE ARTS (NC) **1075/23**
Drama

NORTH CAROLINA, UNIVERSITY OF, AT
    ASHEVILLE **1155/25**
    Ed, Hist, Psych, Soc
    CHAPEL HILL **1220/27**
    Amer St, Art Hist, Bus Admin, Chem, Classics, Communic, Drama, Ed,
    English, For Lang, Hist, Pharm, Pre-Law, Pre-Med/Pre-Dental, Soc
    CHARLOTTE **1025/22**
    Bus Admin, Nurs, Pre-Law, Pre-Med/Pre-Dental, Psych, Zoo
    GREENSBORO **1050/22**
    Art, Bus Admin, Communic, Drama, Music, Nurs
    WILMINGTON **1080/23**
    Bus Admin, English, Pre-Law, Psych, Soc

NORTH CAROLINA STATE UNIVERSITY (NC) **1175/26**
Ag, Arch, Bot, Econ, Engine, Forest, Math, Pre-Law, Zoo

NORTH CENTRAL COLLEGE (IL) **1140/25**
Bio, Communic, Comp Sci, Poli Sci, Pre-Law, Pre-Med/Pre-Dental

NORTH DAKOTA STATE UNIVERSITY (ND) 1100/24
Ag, Engine, Pharm

NORTH DAKOTA, UNIVERSITY OF (ND) 1100/24
Art, Bus Admin, Ed, Nurs

NORTH FLORIDA, UNIVERSITY OF (FL) 1120/24
Bus Admin, Comp Sci, Ed, Music

NORTH GEORGIA COLLEGE (GA) 1000/21
Bus Admin

NORTH TEXAS, UNIVERSITY OF (TX) 1070/23
Music

NORTHEASTERN UNIVERSITY (MA) 1150/25
Bus Admin, Comp Sci, Engine, English, Hist, Pharm, Philo

NORTHEAST LOUISIANA UNIVERSITY (LA) 1000/21
Bus Admin, Nurs, Pharm

NORTHERN ARIZONA (AZ) 1025/22
Astro, Bot, Ed, Forest, Psych

NORTHERN COLORADO UNIVERSITY 1030/22
Bus Admin, Music, Soc

NORTHERN ILLINOIS UNIVERSITY (IL) 1050/22
Bus Admin, Ed, Engine, Home Ec, Nurs

NORTHERN IOWA, UNIVERSITY OF (IA) 1080/23
Art, Bus Admin, Ed

NORTHLAND COLLEGE (WI) 1080/23
Bio

NORTHWESTERN COLLEGE (IA) 1095/24
Bio, Chem, Drama, Ed, Hist, Music, Physics, Reli Stu

NORTHWESTERN COLLEGE (MN) 1080/23
Ed, Psych, Reli Stu

NORTHWESTERN UNIVERSITY (IL) 1360/31
Amer Stu, Anthro, Astro, Chem, Classics, Communic, Drama, Econ, Engine, English, Hist, Math, Music, Poli Sci, Pre-Law, Pre-Med/Pre-Dental, Reli Stu, Soc

NORTHWOOD UNIVERSITY (MI) 1000/21
Bus Admin

NOTRE DAME, UNIVERSITY OF (IN) 1310/29
Arch, Bus Admin, Chem, Engine, Hist, Poli Sci, Pre-Med/Pre-Dental, Pre-Law, Psych, Reli Stu

NOVA SOUTHEASTERN UNIVERSITY (FL) 1090/24
Bus Admin, Pre-Med/Pre-Dental

NYACK COLLEGE (NY) 1000/21
Bus Admin, Ed, Music, Psych, Reli Stu

OAKLAND UNIVERSITY (MI) **1040/22**
Communic, Comp Sci, Engine, Nurs

OBERLIN COLLEGE (OH) **1300/29**
Art Hist, Chem, English, Hist, Music, Philo, Pre-Law, Pre-Med/Pre-Dental, Reli Stu, Soc

OCCIDENTAL COLLEGE (CA) **1200/26**
Bio, Chem, Econ, Ed, Math, Physics, Poli Sci, Pre-Law, Pre-Med/Pre-Dental, Psych, Reli Stu

OGLETHORPE UNIVERSITY (GA) **1199/26**
Bus Admin, Poli Sci, Pre-Law

OHIO NORTHERN UNIVERSITY (OH) **1125/24**
Bio, Biochem, Chem, Engine, Pharm

OHIO STATE UNIVERSITY (OH) **1140/25**
Ag, Arch, Art, Bus Admin, Drama, Ed, Engine, Geog, Nurs, Pharm, Physics, Pre-Med/Pre-Dental

OHIO UNIVERSITY (OH) **1100/24**
*Art, Bot, Bus Admin, Communic, Drama, Ed, Engine, English, Hist, Math, Music,
Physics, Pre-Law, Psych, Zoo*

OHIO WESLEYAN UNIVERSITY (OH) **1195/26**
Bio, Bot, Chem, Communic, Econ, Poli Sci, Pre-Med/Pre-Dental, Pre-Law, Psych

OKLAHOMA BAPTIST UNIVERSITY (OK) **1080/23**
Ed, Music, Nurs, Psych, Reli Stu

OKLAHOMA CITY UNIVERSITY (OK) **1100/24**
Bio, Bus Admin, Communic, Comp Sci, Drama, English, Music, Poli Sci, Pre-Law, Psych

OKLAHOMA, UNIVERSITY OF (OK) **1135/25**
*Arch, Astro, Bus Admin, Chem, Classics, Communic, Engine, English, Geog, Geol, Hist,
Poli Sci, Pre-Law, Psych, Zoo*

OKLAHOMA STATE UNIVERSITY (OK) **1110/24**
Ag, Bio, Bus Admin, Drama, Ed, Engine, Forest, Geog, Geol, Physics, Poli Sci, Soc, Zoo

OLD DOMINION UNIVERSITY (VA) **1050/22**
Art, Bus Admin

OLIN COLLEGE OF ENGINEERING (MA) **1380/31**
Engine

OREGON, UNIVERSITY OF (OR) **1120/24**
Anthro, Arch, Art Hist, Bus Admin, Chem, Communic, Comp Sci, Ed, Geog, Math, Music, Psych

OREGON INSTITUTE OF TECHNOLOGY (OR) **1020/22**
Bus Admin, Engine

OREGON STATE UNIVERSITY (OR) **1075/23**
Ag, Biochem, Bot, Forest, Home Ec, Physics, Zoo

OTIS ART INSTITUTE/PARSONS (CA) **1000/21**
Art

OTTERBEIN COLLEGE (OH) **1120/24**
Drama, Psych

OZARKS, COLLEGE OF THE (MO) 1050/22
Ag, Bus Admin, Ed, Psych

PACE UNIVERSITY (NY) 1140/25
Bus Admin, Comp Sci, Nurs, Psych, Soc

PACIFIC LUTHERAN UNIVERSITY (WA) 1105/24
Bus Admin, Comp Sci, Nurs, Pre-Med/Pre-Dental

PACIFIC UNIVERSITY (OR) 1110/24
Bus Admin, For Lang

PACIFIC, UNIVERSITY OF THE (CA) 1120/24
Art, Engine, Music, Pharm

PALM BEACH ATLANTIC COLLEGE (FL) 1070/23
Psych

PARSONS SCHOOL OF DESIGN (NY) 1070/23
Art

PENNSYLVANIA, UNIVERSITY OF (PA) 1360/31
Amer St, Anthro, Art, Art Hist, Astro, Biochem, Bus Admin, Classics, Econ, Engine, English, For Lang, Geol, Hist, Nurs, Philo, Poli Sci, Pre-Law, Psych, Soc

PENNSYLVANIA STATE UNIVERSITY (PA) 1199/26
Ag, Arch, Astro, Biochem, Bot, Bus Admin, Chem, Comp Sci, Ed, Engine, Forest, Geog, Nurs, Pre-Med/Pre-Dental, Zoo

PEPPERDINE UNIVERSITY (CA) 1190/26
Bus Admin, Communic, Comp Sci, For Lang

PERU STATE COLLEGE (NE) 1000/21
Ed

PHILADELPHIA COLLEGE OF ART (PA) 1000/21
Art

PHILADELPHIA COLLEGE OF TEXTILES AND SCIENCE (PA) 1050/22
Bus Admin

PHILLIPS UNIVERSITY (OK) 1070/23
Bus Admin

PINE MANOR COLLEGE (MA) 960/20
Amer St, Art Hist, Bio, Bus Admin, Communic, Poli Sci, Psych

PITTSBURGH, UNIVERSITY OF (PA) 1160/25
Anthro, Astro, Bio Chem, Bus Admin, Engine, English, Nurs, Pharm, Philo, Pre-Law, Pre-Med/Pre-Dental, Psych

PITTSBURGH, UNIVERSITY OF (BRADFORD) (PA) 1060/23
Comp Sci

PITTSBURGH, UNIVERSITY OF (JOHNSTOWN) (PA) 1100/24
Comp Sci, Engine

PITZER COLLEGE (CA) 1190/26
Anthro, Bio, Pre-Med/Pre-Dental, Psych, Soc

POINT LOMA (CA) 1040/22
Bus Admin, Ed, Home Ec, Nurs

POINT PARK COLLEGE (PA) 1000/21
Drama

POLYTECHNIC UNIVERSITY OF NEW YORK (NY) 1199/26
Engine

POMONA COLLEGE (CA) 1430/32
*Amer St, Anthro, Bio, Chem, Econ, English, For Lang, Geol, Hist, Math, Philo,
Poli Sci, Pre-Law, Pre-Med/Pre-Dental, Reli Stu*

PORTLAND, UNIVERSITY OF (OR) 1126/25
Bus Admin, Engine, Nurs

PRATT INSTITUTE (NY) 1040/22
Arch

PRESBYTERIAN COLLEGE (SC) 1130/25
Bio, Bus Admin, English, Poli Sci, Pre-Law, Pre-Med/Pre-Dental,

PRINCETON UNIVERSITY (NJ) 1430/32
*Arch, Art Hist, Bio, Biochem, Chem, Classics, Drama, Econ, Engine, English, For Lang,
Geol, Hist, Math, Music, Philo, Physics, Poli Sci, Pre-Law, Pre-Med/Pre-Dental, Reli Stu*

PRINCIPIA COLLEGE (IL) 1100/24
Art, Bus Admin, Ed, English, Pre-Law, Soc

PROVIDENCE COLLEGE (RI) 1150/25
Bus Admin, Poli Sci, Pre-Law

PUERTO RICO, UNIVERSITY OF (PR) 1100/24
Bus Admin, Ed

PUERTO RICO, UNIVERSITY OF (CAYEY) (PR) 1000/21
Bio, Bus Admin, Ed

PUERTO RICO, UNIVERSITY OF (MAYAGUEZ) (PR) 1150/25
Engine

PUGET SOUND, UNIVERSITY OF (WA) 1220/27
Bio, Bus Admin, English, Pre-Law, Pre-Med/Pre-Dental. Soc

PURDUE UNIVERSITY (IN) 1120/24
Ag, Biochem, Bot, Bus Admin, Chem, Engine, Forest, Geol, Pharm

QUEENS COLLEGE (NC) 1140/25
Bus Admin, English, Hist, Music, Pre-Law

QUINCY UNIVERSITY (IL) 1080/23
Bus Admin, Soc

QUINNIPIAC UNIVERSITY (CT) 1099/24
Bus Admin, Comp Sci

RADFORD UNIVERSITY (VA) 1000/21
Bus Admin, Ed, Geog, Poli Sci, Pre-Law

RANDOLPH-MACON COLLEGE (VA) 1120/24
Bio, Bus Admin, Econ, English, Poli Sci, Pre-Law, Pre-Med/Pre-Dental, Psych

RANDOLPH-MACON WOMAN'S COLLEGE (VA) 1185/26
Art, Bio, Classics, Communic, English, Pre-Law, Pre-Med/Pre-Dental, Psych

REDLANDS, UNIVERSITY OF (CA) 1120/24
Art, Bus Admin, Ed, English, Music, Poli Sci, Pre-Law, Pre-Med/Pre-Dental

REED COLLEGE (OR) 1335/30
Bio, Chem, English, Hist, Philo, Physics, Pre-Law, Pre-Med/Pre-Dental, Psych

REGIS COLLEGE (MA) 1000/21
Communic, English

REGIS UNIVERSITY (CO) 1100/24
*Bio Chem, Bus Admin, Communic, Comp Sci, Ed, Philo, Pre-Med/Pre-Dental, Psych,
Reli Stu, Soc*

REINHARDT COLLEGE (GA) 1000/21
Bio, Bus Admin, Communic

RENSSELAER POLYTECHNIC INSTITUTE (NY) 1270/28
Arch, Bus Admin, Comp Sci, Engine, Math, Physics

RHODE ISLAND SCHOOL OF DESIGN (RI) 1100/24
Arch, Art

RHODE ISLAND, UNIVERSITY OF (RI) 1080/23
Anthro, Comp Sci, Engine, English, Nurs, Pharm, Poli Sci, Pre-Law

RHODES COLLEGE (TN) 1270/28
*Bio, Bus Admin, Econ, English, Hist, Music, Physics, Poli Sci, Pre-Law, Pre-Med/Pre-
Dental, Psych*

RICE UNIVERSITY (TX) 1400/31
*Anthro, Arch, Biochem, Bio, Chem, Comp Sci, Engine, Hist, Math, Music, Physics, Pre-
Law, Pre-Med/Pre-Dental*

RICHMOND, UNIVERSITY OF (VA) 1270/28
Bus Admin, English, Poli Sci, Pre-Law

RIDER UNIVERSITY (NJ) 1010/21
Bus Admin, Comp Sci, Music

RIPON COLLEGE (WI) 1130/25
Bio, Biochem, Bus Admin, Chem, Econ, English, Hist, Poli Sci, Pre-Law, Pre-Med/Pre-Dental

ROANOKE COLLEGE (VA) 1110/24
Art, Bio, Bus Admin, English, Pre-Law, Psych, Reli Stu, Soc

ROBERT MORRIS COLLEGE (PA) 1000/21
Bus Admin, Comp Sci, Communic

ROCHESTER, UNIVERSITY OF (NY) 1320/30
*Art, Art Hist, Biochem, Bio, Chem, Comp Sci, Econ, Engine, English, For Lang,
Geol, Music, Nurs, Philo, Poli Sci, Pre-Law, Pre-Med/Pre-Dental, Psych*

ROCHESTER INSTITUTE OF TECHNOLOGY (NY) 1160/25
Comp Sci, Engine, Math

ROCKFORD COLLEGE (IL) 1040/22
Art, Drama, English, Pre-Law

ROCKHURST COLLEGE (MO) 1100/24
Bus Admin, Chem

ROGER WILLIAMS UNIVERSITY (RI) 1065/23
Arch, Ed, Engine, Psych

ROLLINS COLLEGE (FL) 1160/25
Chem, Classics, Drama, English, Physics, Psych, Reli Stu

ROOSEVELT UNIVERSITY (IL) 1000/21
Bus Admin, Music

ROSE-HULMAN INSTITUTE OF TECHNOLOGY 1360/31
Comp Sci, Econ, Engine

ROSEMONT COLLEGE (PA) 1100/24
Art, Art Hist, English, For Lang, Hist, Pre-Law, Psych

ROWAN UNIVERSITY OF NEW JERSEY (NJ) 1140/25
Bus Admin, Communic, Ed, Engine, Music

RUSSELL SAGE COLLEGE (THE SAGE COLLEGES) (NY) 1065/23
Nurs

RUTGERS UNIVERSITY (NJ) 1200/26
*Ag, Biochem, Bio, Chem, Drama, Ed, Engine, English, For Lang, Pharm, Pre-Law,
Pre-Med/Pre-Dental*

RUTGERS UNIVERSITY (CAMDEN) (NJ) 1160/25
Comp Sci, English, Hist, Pre-Law, Soc

SACRED HEART UNIVERSITY (CT) 1060/23
Biochem, Bus Admin, Psych

ST. AMBROSE COLLEGE (IA) 1030/22
Communic, Comp Sci

ST. ANDREWS PRESBYTERIAN COLLEGE (NC) 1030/22
Biochem, Bus Admin, Philo

ST. ANSELM COLLEGE (NH) 1110/24
Classics, Econ, English, For Lang, Nurs, Pre-Law, Psych, Soc,

ST. BONAVENTURE UNIVERSITY (NY) 1100/24
Bus Admin, Communic, Ed, Philo, Poli Sci, Pre-Law, Reli Stu

ST. CATHERINE, COLLEGE OF (MN) 1060/23
Bus Admin, Music, Nurs, Reli Stu, Soc

ST. FRANCIS COLLEGE (NY) 1000/21
Bus Admin, Psych

ST. JOHN FISHER COLLEGE (NY) 1065/23
Bus Admin, Communic

ST. JOHN'S UNIVERSITY (NY) 1040/22
Bus Admin, Pharm

SAINT JOHN'S UNIVERSITY/COLLEGE OF SAINT BENEDICT (MN) 1170/26
Bio, Bus Admin, Chem, Comp Sci, Econ, Physics, Poli Sci, Pre-Law, Pre-Med/Pre-Dental

SAINT JOSEPH'S COLLEGE (CT) 1000/21
Ed

ST. JOSEPH'S COLLEGE (IN) 1040/22
Bus Admin, Ed, Psych

ST. JOSEPH'S COLLEGE (ME) 1050/22
Ed, Nurs

ST, JOSEPH'S COLLEGE (NY) 1050/22
Bus Admin, Comp Sci, Ed, Hist, Math, Psych

SAINT JOSEPH'S UNIVERSITY (PA) 1185/26
Bus Admin, English, Pre-Med/Pre-Dental

ST. LAWRENCE UNIVERSITY (NY) 1160/25
Econ, English, Geol, Poli Sci, Pre-Law, Psych, Soc

ST. LOUIS COLLEGE OF PHARMACY (MO) 1115/24
Pharm, Pre-Med/Pre-Dental

SAINT LOUIS UNIVERSITY (MO) 1150/25
Bio, Chem, Communic, Ed, Nurs, Philo, Pre-Med/Pre-Dental

SAINT MARY COLLEGE (KS) 1030/22
English

SAINT MARY'S COLLEGE (IN) 1110/24
Art, Bus Admin, Communic, Ed, English, Nurs, Pre-Law

SAINT MARY'S COLLEGE OF CALIFORNIA (CA) 1150/25
Bus Admin, Ed, Soc

ST. MARY'S COLLEGE OF MARYLAND (MD) 1250/28
Anthro, Bio, Econ, Math, Music, Pre-Med/Pre-Dental, Psych

ST. MARY'S UNIVERSITY OF MINNESOTA (MN) 1070/23
Bus Admin, Chem, Communic, Comp Sci, Drama, Ed, Hist

ST. MARY'S UNIVERSITY OF SAN ANTONIO (TX) 1070/23
Bus Admin, Poli Sci, Pre-Law, Pre-Med/Pre-Dental, Soc

SAINT MICHAEL'S COLLEGE (VT) 1120/24
Bus Admin, Chem, Communic, Ed

ST. NORBERT COLLEGE (WI) 1120/24
Bus Admin

ST. OLAF COLLEGE (MN) 1225/27
*Amer St, Art, Bio, Chem, Econ, English, Math, Music, Nurs, Philo, Physics,
Pre-Law, Pre-Med/Pre-Dental, Psych*

SAINT ROSE, COLLEGE OF (NY) 1060/23
Art, Bus Admin, Ed, Soc

SAINT SCHOLASTICA, COLLEGE OF (MN) 1070/23
Nurs, Psych

SAINT THOMAS AQUINAS COLLEGE (NY) 1060/23
Ed, Psych

SAINT THOMAS, UNIVERSITY OF (MN) 1099/24
Bus Admin, Geol, Philo

SAINT THOMAS, UNIVERSITY OF (TX) 1160/25
Pre-Med/Pre-Dental, Psych

ST. VINCENT COLLEGE (PA) 1080/23
Bio, Pre-Med/Pre-Dental, Psych

SALEM COLLEGE (NC) 1120/24
Art, Art Hist, Bus Admin, Econ, English, Pre-Law, Soc

SALEM STATE COLLEGE (MA) 1000/21
Chem, Communic, Drama, Geog

SALISBURY STATE UNIVERSITY (MD) 1125/24
Ed, English, Geog, Philo, Pre-Law, Psych

SAMFORD UNIVERSITY (AL) 1115/24
Bus Admin, Communic, Nurs, Pharm

SAN DIEGO STATE UNIVERSITY (CA) 1060/23
Art, Astro, Bus Admin, Communic, Ed, Engine, English, Hist, Nurs, Soc

SAN DIEGO, UNIVERSITY OF (CA) 1115/24
Bus Admin, Nurs, Pre-Law, Pre-Med/Pre-Dental, Reli Stu

SAN FRANCISCO CONSERVATORY OF MUSIC (CA) 1150/25
Music

SAN FRANCISCO, UNIVERSITY OF (CA) 1100/24
Bus Admin, Econ, Nurs, Pre-Law, Pre-Med/Pre-Dental, Psych

SAN FRANCISCO STATE UNIVERSITY (CA) 1000/21
Anthro, Astro, Communic, Drama, English, Hist, Pre-Law, Soc

SANTA CLARA UNIVERSITY (CA) 1185/26
Bus Admin, Communic, Comp Sci, Engine, Music, Pre-Law, Psych

SANTA FE, COLLEGE OF (NM) 1100/24
Art, Communic, Drama

SARAH LAWRENCE COLLEGE (NY) 1230/27
Amer St, Drama, English, Pre-Law

SCHOOL OF THE ART INSTITUTE OF CHICAGO (IL) 1120/24
Art

SCHREINER COLLEGE (TX) 1050/22
Bus Admin

SCIENCES IN PHILADELPHIA, UNIVERSITY OF THE (PA) 1145/25
Pharm

SCRANTON, UNIVERSITY OF (PA) 1170/26
Bio, Bus Admin, Communic, Pre-Med/Pre-Dental

SCRIPPS COLLEGE (CA) 1250/28
Art, Bio, Drama, English, For Lang, Pre-Law, Pre-Med/Pre-Dental

SEATTLE PACIFIC UNIVERSITY (WA) 1100/24
Engine, Nurs

SEATTLE UNIVERSITY (WA) 1086/24
Bus Admin, Drama, Engine, English, Nurs, Pre-Law

SETON HALL UNIVERSITY (NJ) 1060/23
Bus Admin, Communic, Ed, Nurs, Psych

SETON HILL COLLEGE (PA) 1040/22
Art, Drama, Music

SHAW UNIVERSITY (NC) 1010/21
Bus Admin, Soc

SHENANDOAH UNIVERSITY (VA) 1010/21
Music, Nurs

SHEPHERD COLLEGE (WV) 1170/26
Art, Bus Admin, Chem, Ed, Hist, Music, Psych

SHIPPENSBURG UNIVERSITY (PA) 1050/22
Bus Admin, Ed, Physics, Psych, Soc

SIENA COLLEGE (NY) 1115/24
Bus Admin, Poli Sci, Pre-Law, Pre-Med/Pre-Dental, Psych

SIENA HEIGHTS UNIVERSITY (MI) 1000/21
Art, Psych

SIMMONS COLLEGE (MA) 1100/24
Bus Admin, Communic, Math, Nurs, Psych, Soc

SIMPSON COLLEGE (IA) 1099/24
Bus Admin, Ed, Math, Music

SKIDMORE COLLEGE (NY) 1240/28
Amer St, Anthro, Art, Art Hist, Bio, Biochem, Bus Admin, Chem, Classics, Drama, Ed, English, For Lang, Geol, Music, Philo, Poli Sci, Pre-Law, Pre-Med/Pre-Dental

SMITH COLLEGE (MA) 1300/27
Amer St, Anthro, Art, Art Hist, Bio, Econ, Engine, English, For Lang, Geol, Hist,
Music, Philo, Physics, Poli Sci, Pre-Law, Pre-Med/Pre-Dental, Psych

SONOMA STATE UNIVERSITY (CA) 1020/22
Anthro, Bus Admin, Chem, Geog, Nurs, Physics, Psych

SOUTH, UNIVERSITY OF THE (TN) 1220/27
Amer St, Anthro, Bio, Econ, English, Forest, For Lang, Hist, Poli Sci, Pre-Law, Pre-Med/
Pre-Dental, Reli Stu

SOUTH ALABAMA, UNIVERSITY OF (AL) 1070/23
Bus Admin, Nurs

SOUTH CAROLINA, UNIVERSITY OF (SC) 1095/24
Bus Admin, Communic, Comp Sci, Ed, Engine, Phar

SOUTH DAKOTA, UNIVERSITY OF (SD) 1050/22
Art, Bus Admin, Nurs

SOUTH DAKOTA SCHOOL OF MINES (SD) 1135/25
Engine, Geol

SOUTH DAKOTA STATE UNIVERSITY (SD) 1060/23
Engine, Nurs, Soc

SOUTHERN CALIFORNIA, UNIVERSITY OF (CA) 1199/26
Astro, Arch, Bus Admin, Communic, Drama, Engine, Math, Music, Pharm, Psych

SOUTHERN CONNECTICUT STATE UNIVERSITY (CT) 1000/21
Chem, Communic, Ed, Physics, Psych, Soc

SOUTHERN ILLINOIS UNIVERSITY (CARBONDALE) (IL) 1040/22
Bot, Bus Admin, Zoo

SOUTHERN MAINE, UNIVERSITY OF (ME) 1050/22
Art, Bus Admin, Communic, Comp Sci, Drama, Engine, Music, Nurs

SOUTHERN METHODIST UNIVERSITY (TX) 1180/26
Art, Art Hist, Bus Admin, Communic, Drama, Reli Stu

SOUTHERN MISSISSIPPI, UNIVERSITY OF (MS) 1040/22
Bus Admin

SOUTHERN OREGON STATE UNIVERSITY (OR) 1040/22
Bus Admin, Ed, For Lang, Soc

SOUTHERN UTAH UNIVERSITY (UT) 1015/22
Drama, Ed

SOUTH FLORIDA, UNIVERSITY OF (FL) 1075/24
Amer St, Bus Admin, Drama, Ed, For Lang, Nurs

SOUTHWEST BAPTIST UNIVERSITY (MO) 1040/22
Ed, Music, Reli Stu

SOUTHWEST MISSOURI STATE UNIVERSITY (MO) 1070/23
Ed, Math

SOUTHWEST TEXAS STATE UNIVERSITY (TX) 1010/21
Bus Admin, Ed, Math

SOUTHWESTERN OKLAHOMA STATE UNIVERSITY (OK) 1000/21
Ed, Pharm

SOUTHWESTERN UNIVERSITY (TX) 1235/28
Art, Bio, Bus Admin, Chem, Communic, Drama, Econ, English, For Lang, Hist, Music, Philo, Poli Sci, Pre-Law, Pre-Med/Pre-Dental, Psych, Reli Stu, Soc

SPELMAN COLLEGE (GA) 1080/24
Bio, Chem, Comp Sci, English, Poli Sci, Pre-Law, Pre-Med/Pre-Dental, Soc

SPRING HILL COLLEGE (AL) 1100/24
Bio, Bus Admin, Chem, Communic, English, Hist, Poli Sci, Pre-Law, Pre-Med/Pre-Dental

SPRINGFIELD COLLEGE (MA) 1000/21
Psych

STANFORD UNIVERSITY (CA) 1430/32
Amer St, Anthro, Bio, Chem, Classics, Communic, Comp Sci, Econ, Engine, English, Math, Music, Physics, Poli Sci, Pre-Law, Pre-Med/Pre-Dental, Psych, Reli Stu, Soc

STEPHEN F. AUSTIN STATE UNIVERSITY (TX) 1000/21
Forest

STEPHENS (MO) 1000/21
Drama

STETSON UNIVERSITY (FL) 1130/25
Bus Admin, Chem, Comp Sci, Ed, English, Hist, Math, Music, Pre-Law, Pre-Med/Pre-Dental, Psych, Reli Stu

STEVENS INSTITUTE OF TECHNOLOGY (NJ) 1290/29
Comp Sci, Engine

STOCKTON STATE (RICHARD STOCKTON COLLEGE OF NEW JERSEY) (NJ) . 1140/25
Bus Admin, Physics

STONEHILL COLLEGE (MA) 1140/25
Bus Admin, Poli Sci, Pre-Law, Psych

SUFFOLK UNIVERSITY (MA) 1000/21
Bus Admin, Soc

SUNY COLLEGE OF ENVIRONMENTAL SCIENCE & FORESTRY (NY) 1200/26
Forest

SUSQUEHANNA UNIVERSITY (PA) 1140/25
Biochem, Bus Admin, Communic, Drama, Psych

SWARTHMORE COLLEGE (PA) 1400/31
Art Hist, Biochem, Bio, Classics, Econ, Ed, Engine, English, Hist, Philo, Physics, Poli Sci, Pre-Law, Pre-Med/Pre-Dental, Psych

SWEET BRIAR COLLEGE (VA) 1120/24
Art Hist, For Lang, Math, Psych

SYRACUSE UNIVERSITY (NY) **1180/26**
Arch, Art, Bus Admin, Communic, Comp Sci, Drama, Forest, Music, Poli Sci,
Pre-Law, Psych, Soc

TAMPA, UNIVERSITY OF (FL) **1045/22**
Bus Admin, Communic, Music

TAYLOR UNIVERSITY (IN) **1099/24**
Psych, Reli Stu

TEMPLE UNIVERSITY (PA) **1060/23**
Art, Biochem, Bio, Chem, Communic, Comp Sci, Drama, English, For Lang, Music,
Pharm, Pre-Law, Pre-Med/Pre-Dental, Soc

TENNESSEE, UNIVERSITY OF (TN) **1110/24**
Ag, Anthro, Art, Bot, Bus Admin, Ed, Engine, English, Forest, Hist, Pre-Law,
Pre-Med/Pre-Dental, Zoo

TEXAS, UNIVERSITY OF, AT
       ARLINGTON... **1030/22**
       Arch, Bus Admin, Engine, Poli Sci
       AUSTIN **1199/26**
       Amer St, Arch, Astro, Bot, Bus Admin, Communic, Comp Sci, Drama, Ed,
       Engine, For Lang, Geog, Geol, Hist, Math, Pharm, Physics, Pre-Med/Pre-Dental,
       Psych, Zoo
       SAN ANTONIO **1000/21**
       Art, Bio, Bus Admin, Pre-Med/Pre-Dental

TEXAS A&M (TX) **1170/26**
Ag, Arch, Bus Admin, Chem, Econ, Ed, Engine, Forest, Geol, Pre-Med/Pre-Dental, Zoo

TEXAS A&M AT GALVESTON (TX) **1130/25**
Bus Admin

TEXAS CHRISTIAN UNIVERSITY (TX) **1130/25**
Bus Admin, Communic, Drama, Geol, Hist, Nurs, Reli Stu

TEXAS LUTHERAN UNIVERSITY (TX) **1040/22**
Bio, Chem

TEXAS TECH UNIVERSITY (TX) **1060/23**
Ag, Art, Ed, Home Ec, Math

TEXAS WESLEYAN COLLEGE (TX) **1000/21**
Bus Admin, Communic, Ed

THOMAS MORE COLLEGE (KY) **1080/23**
Bio, Bus Admin, Pre-Med/Pre-Dental

TOLEDO, UNIVERSITY OF (OH) **1040/22**
Bus Admin, Econ, Hist, Pharm

TOUGALOO COLLEGE (MS) **1000/21**
Bio, Ed

TOWSON UNIVERSITY (MD) **1080/23**
Bus Admin

TRANSYLVANIA UNIVERSITY (KY) **1170/26**
Bus Admin, Comp Sci, Pre-Med/Pre-Dental, Psych

TRINITY COLLEGE (CT) **1255/28**
Bio, Bus Admin, Econ, Engine, Math, Philo, Pre-Law, Pre-Med/Pre-Dental, Reli Stu

TRINITY COLLEGE (DC) **1100/24**
Bus Admin, For Lang, Math, Poli Sci, Pre-Law, Soc

TRINITY UNIVERSITY (TX) **1270/28**
*Art, Art Hist, Bus Admin, Chem, Classics, Communic, Econ, Ed, English, For Lang,
Hist, Philo, Poli Sci, Pre-Law, Pre-Med/Pre-Dental*

TRI-STATE UNIVERSITY (IN) **1060/23**
Engine

TRUMAN STATE UNIVERSITY (MO) **1190/26**
Bio, Bus Admin, Chem, Ed, For Lang, Nurs, Pre-Med/Pre-Dental

TUFTS UNIVERSITY (MA) **1300/29**
*Bio, Chem, Classics, Drama, Ed, Engine, English, Hist, Poli Sci, Pre-Law,
Pre-Med/Pre-Dental, Psych*

TULANE UNIVERSITY (LA) **1300/29**
*Amer St, Arch, Art, Bio, Biochem, Bus Admin, Drama, Engine, For Lang, Hist,
Math, Philo, Pre-Med/Pre-Dental, Psych*

TULSA, UNIVERSITY OF (OK) **1180/26**
Anthro, Communic, Engine, Geol, Psych

TUSKEGEE INSTITUTE (AL) **1000/21**
Ag, Arch, Engine, Nurs

UNION COLLEGE (NY) **1250/28**
Bio, Chem, Engine, Hist, Math, Poli Sci, Pre-Law, Pre-Med/Pre-Dental, Psych

UNION UNIVERSITY (TN) **1100/24**
Nurs, Reli Stu

U. S. AIR FORCE ACADEMY (CO) **1270/28**
Bus Admin, Engine

U. S. COAST GUARD ACADEMY (CT) **1260/28**
Engine

U. S. MILITARY ACADEMY (NY) **1265/28**
Engine

U. S. NAVAL ACADEMY (MD) **1300/29**
Engine, Poli Sci

URSINUS COLLEGE (PA) **1170/26**
Bio, Bus Admin, Chem, Econ, Ed, Physics, Poli Sci, Pre-Law, Pre-Med/Pre-Dental

UTAH, UNIVERSITY OF (UT) **1115/24**
Comp Sci, Drama, Engine, English, For Lang, Pharm, Pre-Law, Pre-Med/Pre-Dental

UTAH STATE UNIVERSITY (UT) **1040/22**
Ag, Ed, Forest, Home Ec

UTICA COLLEGE OF SYRACUSE UNIVERSITY (NY) **1070/23**
Bus Admin

VALPARAISO UNIVERSITY (IN) **1180/26**
Bus Admin, Ed, Engine, Math, Music, Nurs

VANDERBILT UNIVERSITY (TN) **1310/29**
Anthro, Bio, Econ, Ed, Engine, English, Geol, Hist, Music, Nurs, Philo, Poli Sci, Pre-Law, Pre-Med/Pre-Dental, Psych

VASSAR COLLEGE (NY) **1320/30**
Art Hist, Astro, Bio, Drama, English, Hist, Music, Pre-Law, Psych

VERMONT, UNIVERSITY OF (VT) **1150/25**
Ag, Bio, Bot, Bus Admin, Chem, Econ, For Lang, Geog, Geol, Hist, Physics, Poli Sci, Pre-Law, Pre-Med/Pre-Dental, Zoo

VILLANOVA UNIVERSITY (PA) **1215/27**
Astro, Bio, Bus Admin, Communic, Econ, Engine, Math, Nurs, Poli Sci, Pre-Law, Pre-Med/Pre-Dental

VIRGINIA, UNIVERSITY OF (VA) **1285/29**
Amer St, Arch, Art, Astro, Bio, Bus Admin, Chem, Econ, Engine, English, Hist, Nurs, Pre-Law, Pre-Med/Pre-Dental, Reli Stu, Soc

VIRGINIA COMMONWEALTH UNIVERSITY (VA) **1040/22**
Art, Drama, Pharm, Pre-Med/Pre-Dental, Pre-Law, Psych, Reli Stu

VIRGINIA MILITARY INSTITUTE (VA) **1120/24**
Bus Admin, Econ, Engine, Pre-Law

VIRGINIA POLYTECHNIC INSTITUTE (VA) **1165/26**
Ag, Arch, Biochem, Bus Admin, Engine, Forest, Psych

VIRGINIA WESLEYAN UNIVERSITY (VA) **1010/21**
Bio, Bus Admin, Poli Sci, Pre-Law, Pre-Med/Pre-Dental, Psych, Soc

VITERBO COLLEGE (WI) **1100/24**
Nurs

WABASH COLLEGE (IN) **1180/26**
Bio, Econ, Hist, Math, Poli Sci, Pre-Law, Pre-Med/Pre-Dental, Psych

WAGNER COLLEGE (NY) **1090/24**
Amer St, Bus Admin, Drama, Ed, Soc

WAKE FOREST UNIVERSITY (NC) **1310/29**
Bio, Bus Admin, Econ, English, For Lang, Hist, Physics, Poli Sci, Pre-Law, Pre-Med/Pre-Dental, Psych, Reli Stu

WALLA WALLA COLLEGE (WA) **1000/21**
Engine, Nurs, Pre-Med/Pre-Dental

WARREN WILSON COLLEGE (NC) **1135/25**
English, Hist, Pre-Law

WARTBURG COLLEGE (IA) 1120/24
Bio, Communic, Ed, English, Hist, Music, Pre-Med/Pre-Dental, Reli Stu

WASHINGTON COLLEGE (MD) 1150/25
Amer St, Bio, Bus Admin, Hist, Pre-Med/Pre-Dental, Psych

WASHINGTON & JEFFERSON COLLEGE (PA) 1120/24
Art, Bio, Bus Admin, Chem, Econ, Ed, English, Poli Sci, Pre-Law, Pre-Med/Pre-Dental, Psych

WASHINGTON & LEE UNIVERSITY (VA) 1325/30
Bus Admin, Econ, English, For Lang, Geol, Hist, Poli Sci, Pre-Law

WASHINGTON UNIVERSITY (MO) 1320/30
Anthro, Arch, Art, Art Hist, Bio, Bus Admin, Comp Sci, Engine, English, For Lang, Geol, Math, Philo, Physics, Pre-Law, Pre-Med/Pre-Dental

WASHINGTON STATE UNIVERSITY (WA) 1060/23
Ag, Anthro, Bus Admin, Econ, Ed, Engine, Home Ec, Pharm, Zoo

WASHINGTON, UNIVERSITY OF (WA) 1145/25
Anthro, Arch, Art, Astro, Bot, Bus Admin, Chem, Comp Sci, Drama, Econ, Ed, Engine, Forest, Geol, Math, Nurs, Pre-Law, Pre-Med/Pre-Dental, Psych, Zoo

WAYNE STATE UNIVERSITY (MI) 1000/21
Engine, For Lang, Nurs, Pharm, Pre-Med/Pre-Dental

WEBSTER UNIVERSITY (MO) 1100/24
Drama, Nurs, Psych

WELLESLEY COLLEGE (MA) 1350/30
Art, Art Hist, Bio, Chem, Econ, Ed, English, For Lang, Hist, Math, Physics, Poli Sci, Pre-Law, Pre-Med/Pre-Dental, Reli Stu

WELLS COLLEGE (NY) 1150/25
Amer St, Bus Admin, Ed, English, For Lang, Hist, Pre-Law, Pre-Med/Pre-Dental, Psych, Soc

WESLEYAN COLLEGE (GA) 1100/24
Amer St, Art, Bus Admin

WESLEYAN UNIVERSITY (CT) 1380/31
Amer St, Art, Astro, Bio, Chem, Drama, Econ, English, Hist, Math, Poli Sci, Pre-Law, Pre-Med/Pre-Dental, Psych, Reli Stu

WEST CHESTER UNIVERSITY (PA) 1040/22
Bus Admin, Music

WEST FLORIDA, UNIVERSITY OF (FL) 1099/24
Bus Admin, Comp Sci, Ed

WESTERN CONNECTICUT STATE UNIVERSITY (CT) 1000/21
Art, Bus Admin, English, Music, Nurs, Soc

WESTERN KENTUCKY (KY) 1000/21
Ed, Nurs, Soc

WESTERN MARYLAND COLLEGE (MD) 1150/25
Bio, Bus Admin, Ed, Pre-Med/Pre-Dental, Soc

WESTERN MICHIGAN UNIVERSITY (MI) 1100/24
Art, Bus Admin, Communic, Drama, Ed, English, Engine, Hist, Music, Nurs, Psych

WESTERN NEW ENGLAND COLLEGE (MA) 1060/23
Bus Admin, Comp Sci, Ed, Engine, Psych

WESTERN STATE COLLEGE OF COLORADO 1020/22
Drama, English, Hist, Geol, Music

WESTERN WASHINGTON UNIVERSITY (WA) 1120/24
Art, Communic, Ed, English, Geog, Pre-Law, Soc

WESTFIELD STATE COLLEGE (MA) 1020/22
Ed, Music, Poli Sci, Psych

WESTMINSTER COLLEGE (MO) 1140/25
Econ, Pre-Law, Psych

WESTMINSTER COLLEGE (PA) 1130/25
Bio, Comp Sci, Pre-Med/Pre-Dental, Soc

WESTMINSTER COLLEGE OF SALT LAKE CITY (UT) 1080/23
Bus Admin, Nurs

WESTMONT COLLEGE (CA) 1170/26
Econ, Pre-Law, Pre-Med/Pre-Dental, Psych, Reli Stu

WEST VIRGINIA UNIVERSITY (WV) 1040/22
Art, Bus Admin, Communic, Drama, Engine, Forest, Music

WEST VIRGINIA WESLEYAN COLLEGE (WV) 1060/23
Art, Comp Sci, Ed

WHEATON COLLEGE (IL) 1300/29
*Art, Bio, Chem, Communic, Ed, English, Math, Music, Philo, Physics, Pre-Law,
Pre-Med/Pre-Dental, Reli Stu, Soc*

WHEATON COLLEGE (MA) 1190/26
*Art, Art Hist, Bio, Drama, Econ, English, For Lang, Hist, Math, Poli Sci, Pre-Law,
Pre-Med/Pre-Dental, Psych, Soc*

WHEELING JESUIT (WV) 1000/21
Bio, Bus Admin, Chem, Hist, Nurs, Philo, Psych, Reli Stu

WHEELOCK COLLEGE (MA) 1000/21
Ed

WHITMAN COLLEGE (WA) 1300/29
*Astro, Bio, Chem, Drama, Econ, English, For Lang, Geol, Hist, Math, Music, Philo,
Physics, Poli Sci, Pre-Law, Pre-Med/Pre-Dental, Psych, Soc*

WHITTIER COLLEGE (CA) 1090/24
Bus Admin, Chem, Econ, Ed, English, Poli Sci, Pre-Law

WHITWORTH COLLEGE (WA) 1130/25
Art, Communic, Ed, English, Music, Physics, Psych, Reli Stu

WICHITA STATE UNIVERSITY (KS) 1000/21
Bus Admin, Communic, English

WIDENER UNIVERSITY (PA) 1060/23
Bus Admin, Ed, Engine, Nurs

WILBERFORCE UNIVERSITY (OH) 1000/21
Bus Admin, Poli Sci, Pre-Law

WILKES UNIVERSITY (PA) 1050/23
Bio, Comp Sci, English, Hist, Nurs, Pre-Med/Pre-Dental, Psych

WILLAMETTE UNIVERSITY (OR) 1230/27
Art Hist, Bio, Chem, Econ, English, Hist, Math, Music, Poli Sci, Pre-Law,
Pre-Med/Pre-Dental, Psych, Soc

WILLIAM JEWELL COLLEGE (MO) 1130/25
Bus Admin, Ed, Music, Nurs

WILLIAM & MARY, COLLEGE OF (VA) 1340/30
Amer St, Bio, Bus Admin, Comp Sci, Drama, Ed, Geol, Hist, Physics, Pre-Med/Pre-Dental,
Reli Stu

WILLIAM PATERSON UNIVERSITY (NJ) 1050/22
Comp Sci, English, Music, Psych, Soc

WILLIAMS COLLEGE (MA) 1400/32
Amer St, Art, Art Hist, Astro, Bio, Chem, Classics, Comp Sci, Econ, English, Hist,
Poli Sci, Pre-Law, Pre-Med/Pre-Dental, Psych

WILMINGTON COLLEGE (OH) 1000/21
Ag, Ed

WILSON COLLEGE (PA) 1055/23
Econ, Pre-Law, Soc

WINONA STATE UNIVERSITY (MN) 1050/22
Bio, Communic, English, Pre-Med/Pre-Dental, Soc

WISCONSIN, UNIVERSITY OF, AT
       EAU CLAIRE 1080/23
       Bio, Math, Nurs
       GREEN BAY 1030/22
       Bus Admin, Hist, Psych
       LA CROSSE 1080/23
       Astro, Comp Sci
       MADISON 1199/26
       Ag, Anthro, Art, Astro, Biochem, Bot, Bus Admin, Communic, Comp Sci,
       Ed, Engine, English, For Lang, Forest, Geog, Geol, Hist, Home Ec, Math,
       Nurs, Pharm, Physics, Pre-Law, Pre-Med/Pre-Dental, Psych, Soc, Zoo
       MILWAUKEE 1065/23
       Anthro, Ed, English, Nurs, Pre-Law
       PLATTEVILLE 1050/23
       Ag, Engine, Ed
       STEVENS POINT 1110/24
       Art, Bio, Bus Admin, Communic, Ed, Home Ec, Soc
       STOUT 1000/21
       Bus Admin, Home Ec

WITTENBERG UNIVERSITY (OH) 1180/26
Art, Bio, Bus Admin, Chem, Ed, English, Geog, Hist, Music, Poli Sci, Pre-Law, Pre-Med/
Pre-Dental, Psych

WOFFORD COLLEGE (SC) 1195/26
Bio, Chem, Comp Sci, Econ, Ed, English, For Lang, Hist, Math, Philo, Pre-Law,
Pre-Med/Pre-Dental, Psych, Soc

WOODBURY UNIVERSITY (CA) 1000/21
Arch, Bus Admin

WOOSTER, COLLEGE OF (OH) 1170/26
Art Hist, Bio, Chem, Drama, Econ, Geol, Hist, Math, Music, Pre-Law, Pre-Med/Pre-Dental,
Reli Stu, Soc

WORCESTER POLYTECHNIC INSTITUTE (MA) 1285/29
Comp Sci, Engine, Physics, Pre-Law

WORCESTER STATE COLLEGE (MA) 1000/21
Bus Admin, Chem, Communic, Ed, Math, Nurs, Psych

WYOMING, UNIVERSITY OF (WY) 1090/24
Ag, Amer St, Astro, Bio, Bot, Bus Admin, Chem, Econ, Ed, Engine, Geog, Geol, Pharm,
Pre-Law, Pre-Med/Pre-Dental, Psych, Zoo

XAVIER UNIVERSITY (OH) 1140/25
Bus Admin, Communic

XAVIER UNIVERSITY OF LOUISIANA (LA) 1080/23
Bio, Bus Admin, Chem, Ed, Music, Pharm, Pre-Med/Pre-Dental, Psych

YALE UNIVERSITY (CT) 1450/32
Amer St, Anthro, Arch, Art, Art Hist, Bio, Biochem, Classics, Drama, Econ, English, For
Lang, Math, Music, Philo, Poli Sci, Pre-Law, Pre-Med/Pre-Dental, Psych, Reli Stu, Soc

YESHIVA UNIVERSITY (NY) 1220/27
Bio, Bus Admin, Comp Sci, Hist, Physics, Poli Sci, Pre-Med/Pre-Dental, Psych

YORK COLLEGE OF PENNSYLVANIA (PA) 1110/24
Ed, Nurs

SECTION FOUR

APPENDICES

APPENDIX A
The 900 Colleges Used In This Study

A **Abilene Christian University**
Abilene, Texas 79699

Adelphi University
Garden City, NY 11530

Adrian College
Adrian, Michigan 49221

◆ **Agnes Scott College**
Decatur, Georgia 30030

◆ **Alabama, University of**
Tuscaloosa, Alabama 35487

Alaska Pacific University
Anchorage, Alaska 99508

Alaska, University of
Anchorage, Alaska 99508

Alaska, University of
Fairbanks, Alaska 99775

Albany College of Pharmacy
Albany, New York 12208

Albertson College
Caldwell, Idaho 83605

◆ **Albion College**
Albion, Michigan 49224

Albright College
Reading, Pennsylvania 19612

Alderson-Broaddus College
Phillipi, West Virginia 26416

Alfred University
Alfred, New York 14802

◆ **Allegheny College**
Meadville, Pennsylvania 16335

Allentown College of St. Francis De Sales
Center Valley, Pennsylvania 18034

◆ **Alma College**
Alma, Michigan 48801

Alverno College
Milwaukee, Wisconsin 53234

American Academy of Dramatic Arts
New York, New York 10016

American International College
Springfield, Massachusetts 01109

◆ **American University**
Washington, DC 20016

◆ **Amherst College**
Amherst, Massachusetts 01002

Anna Maria College
Paxton, Massachusetts 01612

Appalachian State University
Boone, North Carolina 28608

Aquinas College
Grand Rapids, Michigan 49506

◆ **Arizona, University of**
Tucson, Arizona 85721

◆ **Arizona State University**
Tempe, Arizona 85287

◆ **Arkansas, University of**
Fayetteville, Arkansas 72701

Art Center College of Design
Pasadena, California 91103

Art Institute of Chicago, School of the
Chicago, Illinois 60603

Arts, University of the
Philadelphia, Pennsylvania 19102

Asbury College
Wilmore, Kentucky 40390

Auburn University
Auburn University, Alabama 36849

Augsburg College
Minneapolis, Minnesota 55454

◆ **Augustana College**
Rock Island, Illinois 61201

Augustana College
Sioux Falls, South Dakota 57197

Austin College
Sherman, Texas 75091

Avila College
Kansas City, Missouri 64145

Averett College
Danville, Virginia 24541

B **Babson College**
Wellesley, Massachusetts 02157

Baker University
Baldwin City, Kansas 66006

Baldwin-Wallace College
Berea, Ohio 44017

Ball State University
Muncie, Indiana 47306

Bard College,
Annandale-on-Hudson
New York 12504

Barry University
Miami Shores, Florida 33161

◆ Phi Beta Kappa Schools   ▮ Predominantly African-American Institutions

◆ **Bates College**
Lewiston, Maine 04240

◆ **Baylor University**
Waco, Texas 76798

Beaver College
Glenside, Pennsylvania 19038

Belhaven College
Jackson, Mississippi 39202

Bellarmine College
Louisville, Kentucky 40205

Belmont Abbey College
Belmont, North Carolina 28012

Belmont University
Nashville, Tennessee 37212

◆ **Beloit College**
Beloit, Wisconsin 53511

Bemidji State University
Bemidji, Minnesota 56601

Benedictine College
Atchison, Kansas 66002

Benedictine University
Lisle, Illinois 60532

◆ **Bennett College**
Greensboro, North Carolina 27401

Bennington College
Bennington, Vermont 05201

Bentley College
Waltham, Massachusetts 02154

Berea College
Berea, Kentucky 40404

Berklee College of Music
Boston, Massachusetts 02215

Berry College
Rome, Georgia 30149

Bethany College
Bethany, West Virginia 26032

Bethel College
St. Paul, Minnesota 55112

Biola University
La Mirada, California 90639

◆ **Birmingham-Southern College**
Birmingham, Alabama 35254

Bloomsburg University
Bloomsburg, Pennsylvania 17815

Bluffton College
Bluffton, Ohio 45817

◆ **Boston College**
Chestnut Hill, Massachusetts 02167

Boston Conservatory
Boston, Massachusetts 02215

◆ **Boston University**
Boston, Massachusetts 02215

◆ **Bowdoin College**
Brunswick, Maine 04011

◆ **Bowling Green State University**
Bowling Green, Ohio 43403

Bradley University
Peoria, Illinois 61625

◆ **Brandeis University**
Waltham, Massachusetts 02254

Brescia University
Owensboro, Kentucky 42301

Bridgewater College
Bridgewater, Virginia 22812

Bridgewater State College
Bridgewater, Massachusetts 02325

Brigham Young University
Provo, Utah 84602

◆ **Brown University**
Providence, Rhode Island 02912

Bryant College
Smithfield, Rhode Island 02917

Bryn Mawr College
Bryn Mawr, Pennsylvania 19010

◆ **Bucknell University**
Lewisburg, Pennsylvania 17837

Buena Vista University
Storm Lake, Iowa 50588

Butler University
Indianapolis, Indiana 46208

C **Caldwell College**
Caldwell, New Jersey 07006

California Institute of the Arts
Valencia, California 91355

California Institute of Technology
Pasadena, California 91125

California, University of, at
◆ **Berkeley,** California 94720
◆ **Davis,** California 95616
◆ **Irvine,** California 92717
◆ **Los Angeles,** California 90024
◆ **Riverside,** California 92521
◆ **San Diego,** California 92093
◆ **Santa Barbara,** California 93106
◆ **Santa Cruz,** California 95064

California Lutheran University
Thousand Oaks, California 91360

California Maritime Academy
Vallejo, California 94590

California Polytechnic State University
Pomona, California 91768

California Polytechnic State University
San Luis Obispo, California 93407

California, State University of, at
Bakersfield, California 93311
◆ **Chico,** California 95929
Dominguez Hills, Carson, California 90747
Fresno, California 93740
Fullerton, California 92834
Hayward, California 94542
Long Beach, California 90840
Los Angeles, California 90032
Monterey Bay, California 93955
Northridge, California 91330
Sacramento, California 95819
San Bernardino, California 92407
San Jose, California 95192
San Marcos, California 92096
Stanislaus, California 95382

Calvin College
Grand Rapids, Michigan 49456

Capital University
Columbus, Ohio 43209

◆ **Carleton College**
Northfield, Minnesota 55057

◆ **Carnegie Mellon University**
Pittsburgh, Pennsylvania 15213

Carroll College
Helena, Montana 59601

Carroll College
Waukesha, Wisconsin 53186

Carson-Newman College
Jefferson City, Tennessee 37760

Carthage College
Kenosha, Wisconsin 53140

◆ **Case Western Reserve University**
Cleveland, Ohio 44106

Catawba College
Salisbury, North Carolina 28144

Catholic University of America
Washington, DC 20064

Cedar Crest College
Allentown, Pennsylvania 18104

Cedarville College
Cedarville, Ohio 45314

Centenary College of Louisiana
Shreveport, Louisiana 71104

Central Arkansas, University of
Conway, Arkansas 72035

Central College
Pella, Iowa 50219

Central Connecticut State University
New Britain, Connecticut 06050

Central Florida, University of
Orlando, Florida 32816

Central Michigan University
Mount Pleasant, Michigan 48859

Centre College
Danville, Kentucky 40422

Champlain College
Burlington, Vermont 05402

Chapman College
Orange, California 92866

College of Charleston
Charleston, South Carolina 29424

Charleston, University of
Charleston, West Virginia 25304

◆ **Chatham College**
Pittsburgh, Pennsylvania 15232

Chestnut Hill College
Philadelphia, Pennsylvania 19118

◆ **Chicago, University of**
Chicago, Illinois 60637

Chowan College
Murfreesboro, North Carolina 27855

Christian Brothers College
Memphis, Tennessee 38104

Christiandom College
Front Royal, Virginia 22630

◆ **Cincinnati, University of**
Cincinnati, Ohio 45221

◆ **Claremont McKenna College**
Claremont, California 91711

◆ **Clark University**
Worcester, Massachusetts 01610

Clarke College
Dubuque, Iowa 52001

Clarkson University
Potsdam, New York 13676

Clemson University
Clemson, South Carolina 29634

Cleveland Institute of Music
Cleveland, Ohio 44106

◆ **Coe College**
Cedar Rapids, Iowa 52402

◆ Phi Beta Kappa Schools   ■ Predominantly African-American Institutions

Cogswell Polytechnic College
Sunnyvale, California 94089

◆ **Colby College**
Waterville, Maine 04901

◆ **Colgate University**
Hamilton, New York 13346

◆ **Colorado College**
Colorado Springs, Colorado 80903

◆ **Colorado, University of**
Boulder, Colorado 80309

Colorado, University of
Colorado Springs, Colorado 80933

Colorado, University of
Denver, Colorado 80217

Colorado School of Mines
Golden, Colorado 80401

◆ **Colorado State University**
Fort Collins, Colorado 80523

Columbia College
Columbia, South Carolina 29203

◆ **Columbia University**
New York, New York 10027
  ◆ **Barnard College,** New York, NY 10027

Concordia University
Irvine, California 92612

Concordia College
Moorhead, Minnesota 56560

Concordia College
Seward, Nebraska 68434

◆ **Connecticut, University of**
Storrs, Connecticut 06269

◆ **Connecticut College**
New London, Connecticut 06320

Converse College
Spartanburg, South Carolina 29302

Cooper Union College, The
New York, New York 10003

◆ **Cornell College**
Mount Vernon, Iowa 52314

◆ **Cornell University**
Ithaca, New York 14853

Cornish College of the Arts
Seattle, Washington 98102

Covenant College
Lookout Mountain, Georgia 30750

Creighton University
Omaha, Nebraska 68178

Curtis Institute of Music
Philadelphia, Pennsylvania 19103

D **Daemen College**
Amherst, New York 14226

◆ **Dallas, University of**
Irving, Texas 75062

Dana College
Blair, Nebraska 68088

◆ **Dartmouth College**
Hanover, New Hampshire 03755

◆ **Davidson College**
Davidson, North Carolina 28036

Dayton, University of
Dayton, Ohio 45469

◆ **Delaware, University of**
Newark, Delaware 19716

Delaware Valley College of Pennsylvania
Doylestown, Pennsylvania 18901

◆ **Denison University**
Granville, Ohio 43023

◆ **Denver, University of**
Denver, Colorado 80208

DePaul University
Chicago, Illinois 60604

◆ **DePauw University**
Greencastle, Indiana 46135

Detroit Mercy, University of
Detroit, Michigan 48221

◆ **Dickinson College**
Carlisle, Pennsylvania 17013

❚ **Dillard University**
New Orleans, Louisiana 70122

Doane College
Crete, Nebraska 68333

Dordt College
Sioux Center, Iowa 51250

◆ **Drake University**
Des Moines, Iowa 50311

◆ **Drew University**
Madison, New Jersey 07940

Drexel University
Philadelphia, Pennsylvania 19104

Drury College
Springfield, Missouri 65802

◆ **Duke University**
Durham, North Carolina 27706

Duquesne University
Pittsburgh, Pennsylvania 15282

D'Youville College
Buffalo, New York 14201

E ◆ Earlham College
Richmond, Indiana 47374

East Carolina University
Greenville, North Carolina 27858

East Stroudsburg University
East Stroudsburg, Pennsylvania 18301

Eastern College
St. Davids, Pennsylvania 19087

Eastern Connecticut State University
Willimantic, Connecticut 06226

Eastern Kentucky University
Richmond, Kentucky 40475

Eastern Michigan University
Ypsilanti, Michigan 48197

Eastern Nazarene College
Quincy, Massachusetts 02170

Eastern Oregon University
La Grande, Oregon 97850

Eckerd College
St. Petersburg, Florida 33733

Edgewood College
Madison, Wisconsin 53711

Edinboro University of Pennsylvania
Edinboro, Pennsylvania 16444

Elizabethtown College
Elizabethtown, Pennsylvania 17022

Elon College
Elon College, North Carolina 27244

◆ Elmira College
Elmira, New York 14901

Elms College
Chicopee, Massachusetts 01013

Emerson College
Boston, Massachusetts 02116

Emmanuel College
Boston, Massachusetts 02115

Emory and Henry College
Emory, Virginia 24327

◆ Emory University
Atlanta, Georgia 30322

Erskine College
Due West, South Carolina 29639

Eureka College
Eureka, Illinois 61530

Evansville, University of
Evansville, Indiana 47722

F ◆ Fairfield University
Fairfield, Connecticut 06430

Fairleigh Dickinson University
Teaneck, New Jersey 07666

Ferris State University
Big Rapids, Michigan 49307

◆▮ Fisk University
Nashville, Tennessee 37208

Fitchburg State College
Fitchburg, Massachusetts 01420

Five Towns College
Dix Hills, New York 11746

Flagler College
St. Augustine, Florida 32085

◆ Florida, University of
Gainesville, Florida 32611

◆ Florida A&M University
Tallahassee, FL 32307

Florida Atlantic University
Boca Raton, Florida 33431

Florida Gulf Coast University
Fort Myers, Georgia 33965

Florida Institute of Technology
Melbourne, Florida 32901

Florida International University
Miami, Florida 33199

Florida Southern College
Lakeland, Florida 33801

◆ Florida State University
Tallahassee, Florida 32306

Fontbonne College
St. Louis, Missouri 63105

◆ Fordham University
Bronx, New York 10458

Fort Hays State University
Hays, Kansas 67601

Fort Lewis College
Durango, Colorado 81301

Framingham State College
Framingham, Massachusetts 01701

Franciscan University of Steubenville
Steubenville, Ohio 43952

Franklin College of Indiana
Franklin, Indiana 46131

◆ Phi Beta Kappa Schools ▮ Predominantly African-American Institutions

◆ **Franklin & Marshall College**
Lancaster, Pennsylvania 17604

Freed-Hardeman University
Henderson, Tennessee 38340

Frostburg State University
Frostburg, Maryland 21532

◆ **Furman University**
Greenville, South Carolina 29613

G **Gannon University**
Erie, Pennsylvania 16541

Geneva College
Beaver Falls, Pennsylvania 15010

Georgetown College
Georgetown, Kentucky 40324

◆ **Georgetown University**
Washington, DC 20057

George Fox University
Newberg, Oregon 97132

George Mason University
Fairfax, Virginia 22030

◆ **George Washington University**
Washington, DC 20052

◆ **Georgia, University of**
Athens, Georgia 30602

Georgia Institute of Technology
Atlanta, Georgia 30332

Georgia Southern University
Statesboro, Georgia 30460

◆ **Gettysburg College**
Gettysburg, Pennsylvania 17325

Gonzaga University
Spokane, Washington 99258

Gordon College
Wenham, Massachusetts 01984

Goshen College
Goshen, Indiana 46526

◆ **Goucher College**
Towson, Maryland 21204

Graceland College
Lamoni, Iowa 50140

Grambling University
Grambling, Louisiana 71245

Grand Valley State University
Allendale, Michigan 49401

◆ **Grinnell College**
Grinnell, Iowa 50112

Grove City College
Grove City, Pennsylvania 16127

Guilford College
Greensboro, North Carolina 27410

◆ **Gustavus Adolphus College**
St. Peter, Minnesota 56082

H ◆ **Hamilton College**
Clinton, New York 13323

◆ **Hamline University**
St. Paul, Minnesota 55104

◆ **Hampden-Sydney College**
Hampden-Sydney, Virginia 23943

◆ **Hampton University**
Hampton, Virginia 23668

Hanover College
Hanover, Indiana 47243

Harding University
Searcy, Arkansas 72149

Hardin-Simmons University
Abilene, Texas 79698

Hartford, University of
Hartford, Connecticut 06117

Hartwick College
Oneonta, New York 13820

◆ **Harvard University**
Cambridge, Massachusetts 02138

Harvey Mudd College
Claremont, California 91711

Hastings College
Hastings, Nebraska 68901

◆ **Haverford College**
Haverford, Pennsylvania 19041

Hawaii Pacific University
Honolulu, Hawaii 96813

◆ **Hawaii, University of**
Manoa, Honolulu, Hawaii 96822

Heidelberg College
Tiffin, Ohio 44883

Henderson State University
Arkadelphia, Arkansas 71999

◆ **Hendrix College**
Conway, Arkansas 72032

High Point University
High Point, North Carolina 27262

Hillsdale College
Hillsdale, Michigan 49242

◆ **Hiram College**
Hiram, Ohio 44234

◆ Phi Beta Kappa Schools   ▮ Predominantly African-American Institutions

◆ **Hobart & William Smith Colleges**
Geneva, New York 14456

◆ **Hofstra University**
Hempstead, New York 11550

◆ **Hollins University**
Roanoke, Virginia 24020

◆ **Holy Cross, College of the**
Worcester, Massachusetts 01610

Hood College
Frederick, Maryland 21701

◆ **Hope College**
Holland, Michigan 49423

Houghton College
Houghton, New York 14744

Houston Baptist University
Houston, Texas 77074

Houston, University of
Houston, Texas 77004

◆▮ **Howard University**
Washington, DC 20059

Humboldt State University
Arcata, California 95521

Huntingdon College
Montgomery, Alabama 36106

Husson College
Bangor, Maine 04401

I ◆ **Idaho, University of**
Moscow, Idaho 83844

Illinois, University of, at
◆ **Urbana-Champaign,** Illinois 61801
◆ **Chicago,** Illinois 60680

◆ **Illinois College**
Jacksonville, Illinois 62650

Illinois Institute of Technology
Chicago, Illinois 60616

Illinois State University
Normal, Illinois 61761

Illinois Wesleyan University
Bloomington, Illinois 61702

Indiana State University
Terre Haute, Indiana 47809

◆ **Indiana University**
Bloomington, Indiana 47405

Indiana University of Pennsylvania
Indiana, Pennsylvania 15705

I.U. - P.U. - Indianapolis University
Indianapolis, Indiana 46202

Iona College
New Rochelle, New York 10801

◆ **Iowa, University of**
Iowa City, Iowa 52242

◆ **Iowa State University of Science
& Technology**
Ames, Iowa 50011

Ithaca College
Ithaca, New York 14850

J **Jacksonville State University**
Jacksonville, Alabama 36265

Jacksonville University
Jacksonville, Florida 32211

James Madison University
Harrisonburg, Virginia 22807

John Carroll University
Cleveland, Ohio 44118

◆ **Johns Hopkins University**
Baltimore, Maryland 21218

Johnson State College
Johnson, Vermont 05656

Johnson C. Smith University
Charlotte, North Carolina 28216

Judson College
Marion, Alabama 36756

Juilliard School
New York, New York 10023

Juniata College
Huntingdon, Pennsylvania 16652

K ◆ **Kalamazoo College**
Kalamazoo, Michigan 49006

Kansas Newman College
Wichita, Kansas 67213

◆ **Kansas, University of**
Lawrence, Kansas 66045

◆ **Kansas State University**
Manhattan, Kansas 66506

Kean University of New Jersey
Union, New Jersey 07083

Keene State College
Keene, New Hampshire 03435

Kennesaw State College
Marietta, Georgia 30144

◆ **Kent State University**
Kent, Ohio 44242

◆ **Kentucky, University of**
Lexington, Kentucky 40506

◆ Phi Beta Kappa Schools   ▮ Predominantly African-American Institutions

Kentucky Wesleyan College
Owensboro, Kentucky 42301

◆ **Kenyon College**
Gambier, Ohio 43022

Kettering University
Flint, Michigan 48504

King College
Bristol, Tennessee 37620

King's College
Wilkes-Barre, Pennsylvania 18711

◆ **Knox College**
Galesburg, Illinois 61401

Kutztown University
Kutztown, Pennsylvania 19530

L ◆ **Lafayette College**
Easton, Pennsylvania 18042

◆ **Lake Forest College**
Lake Forest, Illinois 60045

Lamar University
Beaumont, Texas 77710

LaSalle University
Philadelphia, Pennsylvania 19141

LaSell College
Newton, Massachusetts 02466

La Verne, University of
La Verne, California 91750

◆ **Lawrence University**
Appleton, Wisconsin 54912

Lebanon Valley College
Annville, Pennsylvania 17003

◆ **Lehigh University**
Bethlehem, Pennsylvania 18015

LeMoyne College
Syracuse, New York 13214

Lenoir Rhyne College
Hickory, North Carolina 28603

Lesley College
Cambridge, Massachusetts 02138

Letourneau College
Longview, Texas 75607

◆ **Lewis & Clark College**
Portland, Oregon 97219

Lewis-Clark State College
Lewiston, Idaho 83501

Lindenwood University
St. Charles, Missouri 63301

Linfield College
McMinnville, Oregon 97128

Lock Haven University of Pennsylvania
Lock Haven, Pennsylvania 17745

Long Island University-Southampton College
Southampton, New York 11968

Longwood College
Farmville, Virginia 23909

Loras College
Dubuque, Iowa 52001

◆ **Louisiana State University**
Baton Rouge, Louisiana 70803

Louisville, University of
Louisville, Kentucky 40292

Lowell, University of
Lowell, Massachusetts 01854

◆ **Loyola College**
Baltimore, Maryland 21210

◆ **Loyola Marymount University**
Los Angeles, California 90045

◆ **Loyola University of Chicago**
Chicago, Illinois 60611

Loyola University
New Orleans, Louisiana 70118

◆ **Luther College**
Decorah, Iowa 52101

Lycoming College
Williamsport, Pennsylvania 17701

Lynchburg College
Lynchburg, Virginia 24501

Lyon College
Batesville, Arkansas 72503

M ◆ **Macalester College**
St. Paul, Minnesota 55105

MacMurray College
Jacksonville, Illinois 62650

Maine, University of
Farmington, Maine 04938

◆ **Maine, University of**
Orono, Maine 04469

Malone College
Canton, Ohio 44709

Manchester College
Manchester, Indiana 46962

◆ **Manhattan College**
Riverdale, New York 10471

◆ Phi Beta Kappa Schools ▪ Predominantly African-American Institutions

Manhattan School of Music
New York, New York 10027

Manhattanville College
Purchase, New York 10577

Mansfield University of Pennsylvania
Mansfield, Pennsylvania 16933

◆ **Marietta College**
Marietta, Ohio 45750

Marist College
Poughkeepsie, NY 12601

◆ **Marquette University**
Milwaukee, Wisconsin 53201

Marshall University
Huntington, West Virginia 25755

◆ **Mary Baldwin College**
Staunton, Virginia 24401

∎ **Marygrove College**
Detroit, Michigan 48221

Maryland Institute-College of Art
Baltimore, Maryland 21217

◆ **Maryland, University of Baltimore County**
Baltimore, Maryland 21250

◆ **Maryland, University of**
College Park, Maryland 20742

Marymount College - Tarrytown
Tarrytown, New York 10591

Marymount University
Arlington, Virginia 22207

Maryville College
Maryville, Tennessee 37804

Maryville University-Saint Louis
St. Louis, Missouri 63141

◆ **Mary Washington College**
Fredericksburg, Virginia 22401

Massachusetts College of Art
Boston Massachusetts 02215

Massachusetts College of Liberal Arts
North Adams, Massachusetts 01247

◆ **Massachusetts, University of**
Amherst, Massachusetts 01003

Massachusetts, University of
Boston, Massachusetts 02125

Massachusetts, University of
Lowell, Massachusetts 01854

Massachusetts, University of
North Dartmouth, Massachusetts 02747

◆ **Massachusetts Institute of Technology**
Cambridge, Massachusetts 02139

Massachusetts Maritime Academy
Buzzards Bay, Massachusetts 02532

Master's College, The
Santa Clarita, California 91321

Memphis, University of
Memphis, Tennessee 38152

Mercer University
Macon, Georgia 31207

Mercy College
Dobbs Ferry, New York 10522

Mercyhurst College
Erie, Pennsylvania 16546

Meredith College
Raleigh, North Carolina 27607

Merrimack College
No. Andover, Massachusetts 01845

Messiah College
Grantham, Pennsylvania 17027

◆ **Miami University**
Oxford, Ohio 45056

◆ **Miami, University of**
Coral Gables, Florida 33124

◆ **Michigan, University of**
Ann Arbor, Michigan 48109

Michigan, University of
Dearborn, Michigan 48128

◆ **Michigan State University**
East Lansing, Michigan 48824

Michigan Technological University
Houghton, Michigan 49931

◆ **Middlebury College**
Middlebury, Vermont 05753

Middle Tennessee State
Murfreesboro, Tennessee 37132

Midwestern State University
Wichita Falls, Texas 76308

Millersville University of Pennsylvania
Millersville, Pennsylvania 17551

Milligan College
Milligan College, Tennessee 37682

Millikin University
Decatur, Illinois 62522

◆ **Mills College**
Oakland, California 94613

◆ **Millsaps College**
Jackson, Mississippi 39210

◆ Phi Beta Kappa Schools   ∎ Predominantly African-American Institutions

Milwaukee School of Engineering
Milwaukee, Wisconsin 53201

Minnesota, University of
Duluth, Minnesota 55812

◆ **Minnesota, University of**
Minneapolis, Minnesota 55455

Minnesota, University of
Morris, Minnesota 56267

Misericordia, College
Dallas, Pennsylvania 18612

Mississippi College
Clinton, Mississippi 39058

Mississippi State University
Mississippi State, Mississippi 39762

Mississippi, University of
University, Mississippi 38677

Mississippi University for Women
Columbus, Mississippi 39701

◆ **Missouri, University of**
Columbia, Missouri 65211

Missouri, University of
Kansas City, Missouri 64110

Missouri, University of
Rolla, Missouri 65401

Monmouth College
Monmouth, Illinois 61462

Monmouth University
West Long Branch, New Jersey 07764

Montana College of Mineral Science & Technology
Butte, Montana 59701

Montana, University of
Missoula, Montana 59812

Montana State University
Billings, Montana 59101

Montana State University
Bozeman, Montana 59717

Montevallo, University of
Montevallo, Alabama 35115

Montclair State College
Upper Montclair, New Jersey 07043

Montreat College
Montreat, North Carolina 28757

Moore College of Art
Philadelphia, Pennsylvania 19103

Moorhead State University
Moorhead, Minnesota 56563

Moravian College
Bethlehem, Pennsylvania 18018

◆ ∎**Morehouse College**
Atlanta, Georgia 30314

Morningside College
Sioux City, Iowa 51106

◆ **Mount Holyoke College**
South Hadley, Massachusetts 01075

Mount Mercy College
Cedar Rapids, Iowa 52402

Mount St. Joseph
Cincinnati, Ohio 45233

Mount St. Mary's College
Emmitsburg, Maryland 21727

Mount St. Mary's College
Los Angeles, California 90049

Mount St. Mary's College
Newburgh, New York, 12550

Mount Union College
Alliance, Ohio 44601

◆ **Muhlenberg College**
Allentown, Pennsylvania 18104

Muskingum College
New Concord, Ohio 43762

N **Nazareth College of Rochester**
Rochester, New York 14618

◆ **Nebraska, University of**
Lincoln, Nebraska 68588

Nebraska Wesleyan University
Lincoln, Nebraska 68504

Nevada, University of, at
Las Vegas, Nevada 89154
Reno, Nevada 89557

New College of U.S.F.
Sarasota, Florida 34243

New England Conservatory of Music
Boston, Massachusetts 02115

◆ **New Hampshire, University of**
Durham, New Hampshire 03824

New Jersey, College of
Ewing, New Jersey 08628

New Jersey Institute of Technology
Newark, New Jersey 07102

New Mexico Institute of Mining and Technology
Socorro, New Mexico 87801

New Mexico State University
Las Cruces, New Mexico 88003

◆ **New Mexico, University of**
Albuquerque, New Mexico 87131

New Orleans, University of
New Orleans, Louisiana 70148

New York, City University of, at
◆ **Baruch College,** New York, NY 10010
◆ **Brooklyn College,** Brooklyn, NY 11210
◆ **City College,** New York, New York 10031
◆ **Herbert H. Lehman Coll.,** Bronx, NY 10468
◆ **Hunter College,** New York, NY 10021
  John Jay College, New York, NY 10019
◆ **Queens College,** Flushing, NY 11367

New York, State University of, at
◆ **Albany,** New York 12222
◆ **Binghamton,** New York 13902
  Brockport, New York 14420
◆ **Buffalo,** New York 14214
  Fredonia, New York 14063
  Geneseo, New York 14454
  New Paltz, New York 12561
  Oneonta, New York 13820
  Oswego, New York 13126
  Plattsburgh, New York 12901
  Potsdam, New York 13676
  Purchase, New York 10577
◆ **Stony Brook,** New York 11794

◆ **New York University**
New York, New York 10011

Niagara University
Niagara Falls, New York, 14109

North Carolina School of the Arts
Winston-Salem, North Carolina 27117

North Carolina, University of, at
  Asheville, North Carolina 28804
◆ **Chapel Hill,** North Carolina 27599
  Charlotte, North Carolina 28223
◆ **Greensboro,** North Carolina 27412
  Wilmington, North Carolina 28403

◆ **North Carolina State University**
Raleigh, North Carolina 27695

North Central College
Naperville, Illinois 60566

North Dakota State University
Fargo, North Dakota 58105

◆ **North Dakota, University of**
Grand Forks, North Dakota 58202

North Florida, University of
Jacksonville, Florida 32216

North Georgia College
Dahlonega, Georgia 30597

North Texas, University of
Denton, Texas 76203

Northeastern University
Boston, Massachusetts 02115

Northern Arizona University
Flagstaff, Arizona 86011

Northern Colorado University
Greeley, Colorado 80639

Northern Illinois University
DeKalb, Illinois 60115

Northern Iowa, University of
Cedar Falls, Iowa 50614

Northern Michigan
Marquette, Michigan 49855

Northwestern College
Orange City, Iowa 51041

Northwestern College
St. Paul, Minnesota 55113

◆ **Northwestern University**
Evanston, Illinois 60204

Northwood University
Midland, Michigan 48640

◆ **Notre Dame, University of**
Notre Dame, Indiana 46556

Nova Southeastern University
Ft. Lauderdale, Florida 33314

Nyack College
Nyack, New York 10960

O **Oakland University**
Rochester, Michigan 48309

◆ **Oberlin College**
Oberlin, Ohio 44074

◆ **Occidental College**
Los Angeles, California 90041

Oglethorpe University
Atlanta, Georgia 30319

Ohio Northern University
Ada, Ohio 45810

◆ **Ohio State University**
Columbus, Ohio 43210

◆ **Ohio University**
Athens, Ohio 45701

◆ **Ohio Wesleyan University**
Delaware, Ohio 43015

Oklahoma Baptist University
Shawnee, Oklahoma 74801

Oklahoma City University
Oklahoma City, Oklahoma 73106

◆ Phi Beta Kappa Schools ∎ Predominantly African-American Institutions

◆ **Oklahoma, University of**
Norman, Oklahoma 73069

Oklahoma State University
Stillwater, Oklahoma 74078

Old Dominion University
Norfolk, Virginia 23529

Olin College of Engineering
Needham, Massachusetts 02492

Oregon Institute of Technology
Klamath Falls, Oregon 97601

◆ **Oregon, University of**
Eugene, Oregon 97403

Oregon State University
Corvallis, Oregon 97331

Otis College of Art and Design
Los Angeles, California 90057

Otterbein College
Westerville, Ohio 43081

Ozarks, College of the
Point Lookout, Missouri 65726

P **Pace University**
New York, New York 10038

Pacific Lutheran University
Tacoma, Washington 98447

Pacific, U. of the
Stockton, California 95211

Pacific University
Forest Grove, Oregon 97116

Palm Beach Atlantic College
West Palm Beach, Florida 33416

Parsons School of Design
New York, New York 10011

◆ **Pennsylvania State University**
University Park, Pennsylvania 16802

◆ **Pennsylvania, University of**
Philadelphia, Pennsylvania 19104

Pepperdine University
Malibu, California 90263

Philadelphia College of Pharmacy and Science
Philadelphia, Pennsylvania 19104

Philadelphia College of Textiles and Sciences
Philadelphia, Pennsylvania 19144

Phillips University
Enid, Oklahoma 73701

Pine Manor College
Chestnut Hill, Massachusetts 02167

Pittsburg State University
Pittsburg, Kansas 66762

Pittsburgh, University of
Johnstown, Pennsylvania 15904

Pittsburgh, University of
Bradford, Pennsylvania 16701

◆ **Pittsburgh, University of**
Pittsburgh, Pennsylvania 15260

Pitzer College
Claremont, California 91711

Point Loma Nazarene College
San Diego, California 92106

Point Park College
Pittsburgh, Pennsylvania 15222

Polytechnic Institute of New York
Brooklyn, New York 11201

◆ **Pomona College**
Claremont, California 91711

Portland, University of
Portland, Oregon 97203

Pratt Institute
Brooklyn, New York 11205

Presbyterian College
Clinton, South Carolina 29325

◆ **Princeton University**
Princeton, New Jersey 08544

Principia College
Elsah, Illinois 62028

Providence College
Providence, Rhode Island 02918

Puerto Rico, University of
Cayey, Puerto Rico 00736

Puerto Rico, University of
Mayaguez, Puerto Rico 00680

Puerto Rico, University of
Rio Piedras, Puerto Rico 00931

◆ **Puget Sound, University of**
Tacoma, Washington 98416

◆ **Purdue University**
W. Lafayette, Indiana 47907

Q **Queens College**
Charlotte, North Carolina 28274

Quincy University
Quincy, Illinois 62301

Quinnipiac University
Hamden, Connecticut 06518

◆ Phi Beta Kappa Schools ▮ Predominantly African-American Institutions

R

Radford University
Radford, Virginia 24142

◆ **Randolph-Macon College**
Ashland, Virginia 23005

◆ **Randolph-Macon Woman's College**
Lynchburg, Virginia 24503

◆ **Redlands, University of**
Redlands, California 92373

◆ **Reed College**
Portland, Oregon 97202

Regis College
Weston, Massachusetts 02193

Regis University
Denver, Colorado 80221

Reinhardt College
Waleska, Georgia 30183

Rensselaer Polytechnic Institute
Troy, New York 12180

Rhode Island School of Design
Providence, Rhode Island 02903

◆ **Rhode Island, University of**
Kingston, Rhode Island 02881

◆ **Rhodes College**
Memphis, Tennessee 38112

◆ **Rice University**
Houston, Texas 77251

◆ **Richmond, University of**
Richmond, Virginia 23173

Rider University
Lawrenceville, New Jersey 08648

◆ **Ripon College**
Ripon, Wisconsin 54971

Roanoke College
Salem, Virginia 24153

Robert Morris College
Moon Township, Pennsylvania 15108

◆ **Rochester, University of**
Rochester, New York 14627

Rochester Institute of Technology
Rochester, New York 14623

◆ **Rockford College**
Rockford, Illinois 61108

Rockhurst College
Kansas City, Missouri 64110

Roger Williams University
Bristol, Rhode Island 02809

Rollins College
Winter Park, Florida 32789

Roosevelt University
Chicago, Illinois 60605

Rose-Hulman Institute of Technology
Terre Haute, Indiana 47803

Rosemont College
Rosemont, Pennsylvania 19010

Rowan University of New Jersey
Mahwah, New Jersey 08028

◆ **Rutgers University**
New Brunswick, New Jersey 08854

Rutgers University
Camden, New Jersey 08101

S

Sacred Heart University
Fairfield, Connecticut 06432

Sage Colleges
Troy, New York 12180

St. Ambrose University
Davenport, Iowa 52803

St. Andrews Presbyterian College
Laurinburg, North Carolina 28352

St. Anselm College
Manchester, New Hampshire 03102

St. Bonaventure University
St. Bonaventure, New York 14778

◆ **St. Catherine, College of**
St. Paul, Minnesota 55105

St. Francis College
Brooklyn, New York 11201

St. John Fisher College
Rochester, New, York 14618

St. John's University
Jamaica, New York 11439

Saint John's University/College of Saint Benedict
Collegeville, Minnesota 56321

Saint Joseph's College
W. Hartford, Connecticut 06117

St. Joseph's College
Rensselaer, Indiana 47978

St. Joseph's College
Standish, Maine 04084

St. Joseph's College
Patchogue, New York 11772

Saint Joseph's University
Philadelphia, Pennsylvania 19131

◆ **St. Lawrence University**
Canton, New York 13617

◆ Phi Beta Kappa Schools   ■ Predominantly African-American Institutions

St. Louis College of Pharmacy
St. Louis, Missouri 63110

◆ **Saint Louis University**
St. Louis, Missouri 63103

Saint Mary's College
Notre Dame, Indiana 46556

Saint Mary's College of California
Moraga, California 94575

◆ **St. Mary's College of Maryland**
St. Mary's City, Maryland 20686

St. Mary's University of Minnesota
Winona, Minnesota 55987

St. Mary's University of San Antonio
San Antonio, Texas 78228

Saint Michael's College
Winooski Park, Colchester, Vermont 05439

St. Norbert College
DePere, Wisconsin 54115

◆ **St. Olaf College**
Northfield, Minnesota 55057

Saint Rose, College of
Albany, New York 12203

Saint Scholastica, College of
Duluth, Minnesota 55811

St. Thomas Aquinas College
Sparkhill, New York 10976

Saint Thomas, University of
St. Paul, Minnesota 55105

St. Thomas, University of
Houston, Texas 77006

St. Vincent College
Latrobe, Pennsylvania 15650

Salem College
Winston-Salem, North Carolina 27108

Salem State College
Salem, Massachusetts 01970

Salisbury State University
Salisbury, Maryland 21801

Samford University
Birmingham, Alabama 35229

◆ **San Diego State University**
San Diego, California 92182

San Diego, University of
San Diego, California 92110

San Francisco Conservatory of Music
San Francisco, California 94122

San Francisco, University of
San Francisco, California 94117

◆ **San Francisco State University**
San Francisco, California 94132

San Jose State University
San Jose, California 95192

◆ **Santa Clara University**
Santa Clara, California 95053

Santa Fe, College of
Santa Fe, New Mexico 87501

Sarah Lawrence College
Bronxville, New York 10708

School of the Art Institute of Chicago
Chicago, Illinois 60603

Schreiner College
Kerrville, Texas 78028

Scranton, University of
Scranton, Pennsylvania 18510

◆ **Scripps College**
Claremont, California 91711

Seattle Pacific University
Seattle, Washington 98119

Seattle University
Seattle, Washington 98122

Seton Hall University
South Orange, New Jersey 07079

Seton Hill College
Greensburg, Pennsylvania 15601

■ **Shaw University**
Raleigh, North Carolina 27601

Shenandoah University
Winchester, Virginia 22601

Shepherd College
Shepherdstown, West Virginia 25443

Shippensburg University
Shippensburg, Pennsylvania 17257

Siena College
Loudonville, New York 12211

Siena Heights University
Adrian, Michigan 49221

Simmons College
Boston, Massachusetts 02115

Simpson College
Indianola, Iowa 50125

◆ **Skidmore College**
Saratoga Springs, New York 12866

Slippery Rock University
Slippery Rock, Pennsylvania 16057

◆ Phi Beta Kappa Schools   ■ Predominantly African-American Institutions

◆ **Smith College**
Northampton, Massachusetts 01063

◆ **South, University of the**
Sewanee, Tennessee 37383

South Alabama, University of
Mobile, Alabama 36688

◆ **South Carolina, University of**
Columbia, South Carolina 29208

◆ **South Dakota, University of**
Vermillion, South Dakota 57069

South Dakota School of Mines
Rapid City, South Dakota 57701

South Dakota State University
Brookings, South Dakota 57006

South Florida, University of
Tampa, Florida 33620

◆ **Southern California, University of**
Los Angeles, California 90089

Southern Connecticut State University
New Haven, Connecticut 06515

Southern Illinois University
Carbondale, Illinois 62901

Southern Maine, University of
Portland, Maine 04103

◆ **Southern Methodist University**
Dallas, Texas 75275

Southern Oregon State University
Ashland, Oregon 97520

Southern Utah University
Cedar City, Utah 84720

Southwest Baptist University
Bolivar, Missouri 65613

Southwest Texas State University
San Marcos, Texas 78666

◆ **Southwestern University**
Georgetown, Texas 78626

◆∎ **Spelman College**
Atlanta, Georgia 30314

Spring Hill College
Mobile, Alabama 36608

◆ **Stanford University**
Stanford, California 94305

Stephen F. Austin State University
Nagogdoches, Texas 75962

◆ **Stetson University**
Deland, Florida 32720

Stevens Institute of Technology
Hoboken, New Jersey 07030

Stockton State
Pomona, New Jersey 08240

Stonehill College
North Easton, Massachusetts 02357

Suffolk University
Boston, Massachusetts 02108

Susquehanna University
Selinsgrove, Pennsylvania 17870

◆ **Swarthmore College**
Swarthmore, Pennsylvania 19081

◆ **Sweet Briar College**
Sweet Briar, Virginia 24595

◆ **Syracuse University**
Syracuse, New York 13210

T **Tampa, University of**
Tampa, Florida 33606

Taylor University
Upland, Indiana 46989

◆ **Temple University**
Philadelphia, Pennsylvania 19122

◆ **Tennessee, University of**
Knoxville, Tennessee 37996

Texas, University of, at
  Arlington, Texas 76019
◆ **Austin,** Texas 78712
  San Antonio, Texas 78249

Texas A & M
College Station, Texas 77843

Texas A & M at Galveston
Galveston, Texas 77553

◆ **Texas Christian University**
Fort Worth, Texas 76129

Texas Lutheran University
Seguin, Texas 78155

Texas Tech University
Lubbock, Texas 79409

Texas Wesleyan College
Fort Worth, Texas 76105

Thomas More College
Crestview Hills, Kentucky 41017

Toledo, University of
Toledo, Ohio 43606

∎ **Tougaloo College**
Tougaloo, Mississippi 39174

Towson University
Towson, Maryland 21204

◆ Phi Beta Kappa Schools   ∎ Predominantly African-American Institutions

Transylvania University
Lexington, Kentucky 40508

◆ **Trinity College**
Hartford, Connecticut 06106

◆ **Trinity College**
Washington, DC 20017

◆ **Trinity University**
San Antonio, Texas 78212

Tri-State University
Angola, Indiana 46703

Truman State University
Kirksville, Missouri 63501

◆ **Tufts University**
Medford, Massachusetts 02155

◆ **Tulane University**
New Orleans, Louisiana 70118

◆ **Tulsa, University of**
Tulsa, Oklahoma 74104

▮ **Tuskegee University**
Tuskegee, Alabama 36088

U ◆ **Union College**
Schenectady, New York 12308

Union University
Jackson, Tennessee 38305

U.S. Air Force Academy
Colorado Springs, Colorado 80840

U.S. Coast Guard Academy
New London, Connecticut 06320

U.S. Military Academy
West Point, New York 10996

U.S. Naval Academy
Annapolis, Maryland 21402

◆ **Ursinus College**
Collegeville, Pennsylvania 19426

◆ **Utah, University of**
Salt Lake City, Utah 84112

Utah State University
Logan, Utah 84322

Utica College of Syracuse University
Utica, New York 13502

V **Valparaiso University**
Valparaiso, Indiana 46383

◆ **Vanderbilt University**
Nashville, Tennessee 37240

◆ **Vassar College**
Poughkeepsie, New York 12601

◆ **Vermont, University of**
Burlington, Vermont 05401

◆ **Villanova University**
Villanova, Pennsylvania 19085

◆ **Virginia, University of**
Charlottesville, Virginia 22903

Virginia Commonwealth University
Richmond, Virginia 23284

Virginia Military Institute
Lexington, Virginia 24450

◆ **Virginia Polytechnic Institute**
Blacksburg, Virginia 24061

Virginia Wesleyan College
Norfolk, Virginia 23502

Viterbo College
La Crosse, Wisconsin 54601

W ◆ **Wabash College**
Crawfordsville, Indiana 47933

Wagner College
Staten Island, New York 10301

◆ **Wake Forest University**
Winston-Salem, North Carolina 27109

Walla Walla College
College Place, Washington 99324

Warren Wilson College
Asheville, North Carolina 28815

Wartburg College
Waverly, Iowa 50677

Washington College
Chestertown, Maryland 21620

◆ **Washington & Jefferson College**
Washington, Pennsylvania 15301

◆ **Washington & Lee University**
Lexington, Virginia 24450

◆ **Washington University**
St. Louis, Missouri 63130

◆ **Washington, University of**
Seattle, Washington 98195

◆ **Washington State University**
Pullman, Washington 99164

◆ **Wayne State University**
Detroit, Michigan 48202

Webster University
Lows, Missouri 63119

◆ **Wellesley College**
Wellesley, Massachusetts 02481

◆ **Wells College**
Aurora, New York 13026

◆ Phi Beta Kappa Schools ▮ Predominantly African-American Institutions

Wesleyan College
Macon, Georgia 31210

◆ **Wesleyan University**
Middletown, Connecticut 06457

West Chester University
West Chester, Pennsylvania 19383

Western Connecticut State University
Danbury, Connecticut 06810

Western Kentucky University
Bowling Green, Kentucky 42101

◆ **Western Maryland College**
Westminster, Maryland 21157

◆ **Western Michigan University**
Kalamazoo, Michigan 49008

Western New England College
Springfield, Massachusetts 01119

Western Washington University
Bellingham, Washington 98225

Westfield State College
Westfield, Massachusetts 01086

West Florida, University of
Pensacola, FL 32514

Westminster College
Fulton, Missouri 65251

Westminster College
Wilmington, Pennsylvania 16172

Westminster College of Salt Lake City
Salt Lake City, Utah 84105

Westmont College
Santa Barbara, California 93108

◆ **West Virginia University**
Morgantown, West Virginia 26506

West Virginia Wesleyan
Buckhannon, West Virginia 26201

Wheaton College
Wheaton, Illinois 60187

◆ **Wheaton College**
Norton, Massachusetts 02766

Wheeling Jesuit University
Wheeling, West Virginia 26003

Wheelock College
Boston, Massachusetts 02215

◆ **Whitman College**
Walla Walla, Washington 99362

Whittier College
Whittier, California 90608

Whitworth College
Spokane, Washington 99251

Wichita State University
Wichita, Kansas 67260

Widener University
Chester, Pennsylvania 19013

▋ **Wilberforce University**
Wilberforce, Ohio 45384

Wilkes University
Wilkes-Barre, Pennsylvania 18766

◆ **Willamette University**
Salem, Oregon 97301

William Jewell College
Liberty, Missouri 64068

◆ **William & Mary, College of**
Williamsburg, Virginia 23187

William Paterson University
Wayne, New Jersey 07470

◆ **Williams College**
Williamstown, Massachusetts 01267

Wilmington College
Wilmington, Ohio 45177

◆ **Wilson College**
Chambersburg, Pennsylvania 17201

Winona State University
Winona, Minnesota 55987

◆ **Wisconsin, University of,** at
    Eau Claire, Wisconsin 54701
    Green Bay, Wisconsin 54311
    LaCrosse, Wisconsin 5460
  ◆ **Madison,** Wisconsin 53706
  ◆ **Milwaukee,** Wisconsin 53201
    Platteville, Wisconsin 53818
    Stevens Point, Wisconsin 54481
    Stout, Menomonie, Wisconsin 54751

◆ **Wittenberg University**
Springfield, Ohio 45501

◆ **Wofford College**
Spartanburg, South Carolina 29303

Woodbury University
Burbank, California 91510

◆ **Wooster, College of**
Wooster, Ohio 44691

Worcester Polytechnic Institute
Worcester, Massachusetts 01609

Worcester State College
Worcester, Massachusetts 01602

◆ **Wyoming, University of**
Laramie, Wyoming 82071

Xavier University
Cincinnati, Ohio 45207

◆ Phi Beta Kappa Schools   ▋ Predominantly African-American Institutions

■ **Xavier University of Louisiana**
New Orleans, Louisiana 70125

✿ **Yeshiva University**
New York, New York 10033

◆ **Yale University**
New Haven, Connecticut 06520

York College of Pennsylvania
York, Pennsylvania 17403

◆ Phi Beta Kappa Schools   ■ Predominantly African-American Institutions   ✿ Predominantly Jewish Institutions

APPENDIX B
The Miscellaneous Majors Colleges Used In This Study

Antioch College
Yellow Springs, OH 45387

Arkansas, U. of
Pine Bluff, Arkansas 71601

Assumption College
Worcester, MA 01609

Atlantic, College of the
Bar Harbor, ME 04609

Aurora University
Aurora, Il 60506

Black Hills State University
Spearfish, SD 57799

Bluefield College
Bluefield, VA 24605

Bluffton College
Bluffton, OH 45817

Boise State University
Boise, ID 83725

Bradford College
Haverhill, MA 01835

Brooks Institute of Photography
Santa Barbara, CA 93108

Cabrini College
Radnor, Pennsylvania 79087

California Institute of the Arts
Valencia, CA 91355

California University of Pennsylvania
California, PA 15419

Carlow College
Pittsburgh, PA 15213

Centenary College
Hackettstown, NJ 07840

Cheyney University of Pennsylvania
Cheyney, PA 19319

Cleveland State University
Cleveland, OH 44115

Colby-Sawyer College
New London, NH 03257

Cortland State College
Cortland, NY 13045

Curry College
Milton, MA 02186

Daemen College
Amherst, NY 14226

David Lipscomb University
Nashville TN 37204

Davis & Elkins College
Elkins, WV 26241

Deep Springs College
Deep Springs Via Dyer, NV 89010

Eastern Montana College
Billings, MT 59101

Eugene Lang College
(New School Social Research)
New York, NY 11743

Fashion Institute of Technology
New York, NY 10001

Findlay, University of
Findlay, OH 45840

Georgia State University
Atlanta, GA 30303

Hampshire College
Amherst, MA 01002

Kansas City Art Institute
Kansas City, MO 64111

Kendall College of Art and Design
Grand Rapids, MI 49503

Lake Erie College
Painesville, OH 44077

Landmark College
Putney, VT 05346

Lees-McRae College
Banner Elk, NC 28604

Lesley College
Cambridge, MA 02138

Long Island University
Southampton Center, NY 11968

Lourdes College
Sylvania, OH 43560

Lyndon State College
Lyndonville, VT 05851

Madonna University
Livonia, MI 48150

Marian College of Fond du Lac
Fond du Lac, WI 54935

Marist College
Poughkeepsie, NY 12601

Memphis College of Art
Memphis, TN 38112

Mesa State College
Grand Junction, CO 81502

Metropolitan State College
Denver, CO 80204

University of New England
Biddeford, ME 04005

New Hampshire College
Manchester, NH 03104

New Haven, University of
New Haven, CT 06516

New School for Social Research
New York, NY 11743

North Carolina Wesleyan College
Rocky Mount, NC 27804

North Dakota State University
Fargo, ND 58105

Northeastern Louisiana University
Monroe, LA 71209

Norwich University
Northfield, VT 05663

Park College of St. Louis University
Cahokia, IL 62206

Pfeiffer College
Misenheimer, NC 28109

Portland State University
Portland, OR 97207

Prescott College
Prescott, Arizona 86301

Ramapo College of New Jersey
Mahwah, NJ 07430

Rhode Island College
Providence, RI 02908

Ringling School of Art & Design
Sarasota, FL 34234

Robert Morris College
Coraopolis, PA 15108

Rowan College of New Jersey
Glassboro, NJ, 08028

St. Edward's University
Austin, TX 78704

St. Elizabeth, College of
Convent Station, NJ 07960

Saint John's College
Annapolis, MD 21404

Saint Leo College
Saint Leo, FL 33574

Saint Peter's College
Jersey City, NJ 07306

Saint Thomas University
Miami, FL 33054

Salem Teikyo University
Salem, WV 26426

Salve Regina-The Newport College
Newport, RI 02840

Sam Houston State University
Huntsville, Texas 77341

Simon's Rock College of Bard
Great Barrington, MA 01230

Slippery Rock University
Slippery Rock, PA 16057

Spring Arbor College
Spring Arbor, MI 49283

SUNY-Maritime College
Throg's Neck, NY 10465

Texas Woman's University
Denton, TX 76204

Thomas Aquinas College
Santa Paula, CA 93060

Tusculum College
Greenville, TN 37743

United States Merchant Marine Academy
Kings Point, NY 11024

Virginia Intermont College
Bristol, Virginia 24201

Webb Institute
Glen Cove, NY 11542

Weber State University
Ogden, Utah 84408

William Woods University
Fulton, MO 65251

Wingate College
Wingate, NC 28174

Wisconsin, University of
Oshkosh, WI 54901

Wright State University
Dayton, OH 45435

Youngstown State University
Youngstown, OH 44555

APPENDIX C

Single Sex Colleges Included In This Study

WOMEN'S COLLEGES

Agnes Scott College (GA)
Alverno (WI)
Bennett College (NC)
Alverno Collee (WI)
Bryn Mawr College (PA)
Cedar Crest College (PA)
Chatham College (PA)
Chestnut Hill (PA)
Converse College(SC)
Hollins College (VA)
Hood College (MD)
Immaculata (PA)
Judson College (AL)
Lesley (MA)

Mary Baldwin College (VA)
Meredith College (NC)
Mills College (CA)
Mount Holyoke College (MA)
Randolph-Macon Woman's Coll. (VA)
Regis (MA)
Rosemont College (PA)
St. Catherine, College of (MN)
Saint Joseph's (CT)
Saint Mary's College (IN)
Salem College (NC)
Scripps College (CA)
Seton Hill (PA)
Simmons College (MA)

Smith College (MA)
Spelman College (GA)
Sweet Briar College (VA)
Texas Woman's College
Trinity College (DC)
Wellesley College (MA)
Wesleyan College (GA)

MEN'S COLLEGES

Hampden-Sydney College (VA)
Morehouse College (GA)
Wabash College (IN)

APPENDIX D

Anyone who has been touched by the problem of alcohol or substance abuse, or who has worked with those struggling in recovery, knows that higher education will increasingly have to meet the needs of these persons. The colleges listed below are trying to address the needs of these students. The Wellness Institute at Ball State has published this list of wellness dorms. I cannot vouch personally for the level or quality of services here. I can only state that they do exist and that parents requiring such services would do well to contact colleges on their selection lists to determine the availability of such accommodations. More may indeed exist.

Respectfully submitted,
Joseph W. Streit
Secondary School Counselor in New Jersey

INSTITUTIONS OFFERING WELLNESS RESIDENCE HALLS

ALABAMA

University of Alabama/Tuscaloosa	Yoland Reese, Health Educator	205/348-3878
University of Montevallo	Freida Shivers, Director or Housing	205/665-2988

ARIZONA

Arizona State University	Tamra Summers, Asst. Director, Student Services	602/965-8900

ARKANSAS

John Brown University	G. Robert Burns, Chair, Health Promotion	501/524-2000
University of Arkansas	Jim Conneeley, Director, Residence Life	501/575-5000

CALIFORNIA

California Poly State Univ./Pomona	Ali Mossares-Rahmani, Director of Housing	909/869-3306
University of California/Irvine	E. Ellen Thomas, Director, Health Education	714/824-5806
University of California/Los Angeles	Alan Hanson, Director, Residence Life	310/825-3066
University of California/Santa Barbara	Wilfred Brown, Director of Housing	805/893-4155

COLORADO
Fort Lewis College	Bill Bolden, Director, Residence Life	970/247-7503
Regis University	Diane Cooper, Asst. Director, Residence Life	303/458-3505
University of Northern Colorado	Andy Blank, Director of Housing	970/351-2721

CONNECTICUT
Wesleyan University	Patricia Houmiel, Director, Residential Life	860/865-2222

DELAWARE
University of Delaware	Dave Buttler, Executive Director, Housing	302/831-6573

FLORIDA
Florida State University	Dr. Rita Moser, Director, University Housing	904/644-2860
Stetson University	Michelle Espinosa, Director, Residence Life	904/822-7201
University of Miami	Loreto Jackson, Director of Wellness	305/284-3253
University of North Florida	Doreen Perez, Director, Student Health	904/646-2900
University of Tampa	Monnie Huston, Director, Residence Life	813/253-6239

GEORGIA
Georgia Institute of Technology	Terry Sichta, Director of Housing	404/894-2486

ILLINOIS
Illinois State University	Linda Sorrells, Director, Wellness Program	309/438-7003
Northern Illinois University	Chika Nnamani, Exec. Director, Student Housing	815/753-9607
Northwestern University	Bill Tempelmeyer, Director, University Housing	708/491-7564
University of Illinois/Urbana-Champaign	Rosanne Proite, Assoc. Director of Housing	217/333-0770

INDIANA
Ball State University	Neil Schmottlach, Director, Fisher Institute	765/285-8259
Indiana University	Bruce Jacobs, Director, Residence Life	812/855-1764
Manchester College	Charlie Mackey, Director, Residence Life	219/982-5000
Purdue University	Tom Paczolt, Manager, Shreve Hall	317/494-2569
Valparaiso University	Christopher Rasmussen, Asst. Dean of Students	219/464-5413

IOWA
Iowa State University	Charles Frederiksen, Director, Residence Life	515/294-5636
University of Northern Iowa	Bob Hartman, Director, Dept. of Residence	319/273-2333

KENTUCKY
Centre College	Sherry Raitiere, Nurse, Wellness Center	606/238-5330
Northern Kentucky University	Patty Hayden, Director, Residence Life	606/572-5448
University of Kentucky	Melanie Tyner-Wilson, Director, Residence Life	606/257-4783

MAINE
University of Maine/Machias	Peter Schmidt, Coordinator, Residential Life	207/255-3313
University of Maine/Farmington	Wendy Young, Residential Life	207/778-7050

MARYLAND
Coppin State College	Linda Dark, Director, Health Promotion	410/383-5859
Loyola College	Kathy Clark-Petersen, Director, Student Life	410/617-2488

MASSACHUSETTS
Boston University	Celine McNelis-Kline, Director, Wellness Center	617/353-3698
Dean College	Admissions Office	508/528-9100
Framingham State College	Joe Onofrietto, Director, Residence Life	508/626-4632

MICHIGAN
Oakland University	Eleanor Reynolds, Director, Residence Halls	810/370-3570
Northern Michigan University	Mary McDonald, RD, Director, Residence Life	906/227-2396
Western Michigan University	Julie Gerard, Director, Residence Hall Life	616/387-4460

MINNESOTA
Augsburg College	Denise Anderson-Diffenbach, Hall Director	612/330-1109 Bemidji
State University	Dale Ladig, Director, Residence Life	218/755-3750
Macalester College	Ann Bolger, Director, Residence Life	612/696-6215
University of Minnesota	David Golden, Director, Health Education	612/626-6738

MISSOURI
Central Missouri State University	Lisa Schulte, Director of Housing	816/543-4515, 4164
University of Missouri	Janet Snook, Coordinator for Fitwell	314/882-2066
Webster University	Sandra Henkes, Director, Residence Life	314/968-7030

MONTANA
Montana State University/Billings	Gina Swartz, Director of Housing	406/657-2376

NEW HAMPSHIRE
Plymouth State College	Tim Keefe, Director, Residential Life	603/535-2260

NEW JERSEY
Rutgers University	Roselle Wilson, Vice President, Student Affairs	908/932-7255

NEW YORK
Binghamton University	Jeanne Mathias, Wellness Coordinator	607/777-2594
SUNY/Coll. of Tech./Delhi	John Leddy, Director, Residence Life	607/746-4632
SUNY/Cortland	Michael Holland, Director, Residential Services	607/753-2095
SUNY/Oswego	Marie Driscoll, Assistant Director, Housing	315/341-3039
SUNY/Potsdam	John Horan, Director, Residence Halls	315/267-2305
SUNY/Stony Brook	Andre Serrano, Residence Hall Director	516/632-2910

NORTH CAROLINA
Elon College	Alice Ledford, Director, Residential Life	910/584-2218
Univ. of North Carolina/Chapel Hill	Wayne T. Kunel, Director of Housing	919/962-5405

OHIO
Capital University	Ronald Bell, Director, Residence Life	614/236-6811
Miami University	Kim Rovansek, Director, Student Housing	513/529-5000

PENNSYLVANIA

Bucknell University	Kari Conrad, Director, Residence Life	717/524-1195
Dickinson College	Tom Matoua, Director of Housing	717/245-1555
Duquesne University	Sharon Goedert, Director, Residence Life	412/396-5028
Muhlenberg College	Scott Salsberry, Director, Residence Life	610/821-3167
Pennsylvania State University	Gail Hurley, Director, Residence Life	814/863-1710
Susquehanna University	Donald Hamum, Athletic Director	717/372-4271
University of Scranton	Fr. Reusseau, Assistant Director, Residence Life	717/941-6226

RHODE ISLAND

Bryant College	Doris Helmich, Health Educator	401/232-6703
Roger Williams University	Richard Stegman, Director, Student Life	401/254-3161
University of Rhode Island	Lester Yuesan, Director, Residential Life	401/874-5374

TENNESSEE

David Lipscomb University	Donna White, Director of Housing	615/269-1000 X2218

TEXAS

St. Mary's University	Lisa McDouglas, Director, Residence Life	210/436-3714
Southern Methodist University	Dr. Michael Lawrence, Director of Housing	214/768-2422
Texas Tech University	Carl Andersen, Director	806/742-2011
West Texas A&M University	John Davis, Director, Residence Life	806/656-3000

UTAH

Brigham Young University	David Hunt, Housing Services Director	801/378-2611

VERMONT

Green Mountain College	Admissions Office	802/776-6675
Lyndon State College	Lorraine Matteis, Director, Health Services	802/626-6440

WASHINGTON

The Evergreen State College	Mike Segawa, Housing Director	360/866-6000 X6132
Washington State University	Health and Wellness Services	509/335-3528
Western Washington University	Kay Rich, Director, University Residence	360/650-2960

WISCONSIN

Cardinal Stritch College	Janet Callender, Director, Residence Life	414/352-5400 X471
University of Wisconsin/Oshkosh	Jim Chitwood, Director, Residence Life	414/424-3212
University of Wisconsin/Stevens Point	John Munson, Assoc. Dean, Professional Studies	719/346-4614

CANADA

University of Calgary	Kelly Weltanffee, Director of Housing	403/220-5312

INSTITUTIONS REQUIRING UNDERGRADUATE WELLNESS COURSES

Albertson College	Dennis Freeburn, Dean of Student Affairs	208/459-5508
The American University	Stephanie F. Franchi, President	202/885-6282
Anderson University	Rebecca A. Hull, Department Chair	317/649-9071
Ball State University	Dr. Neil Schmottlach, Director	765/285-8259
Bellin College Nursing	Vicki A. Moss, Associate Professor	414/433-3409
Black Hills State University	Dr. Rob L. Schurrer, Assistant Professor	605/642-6169
Brigham Young University	Dr. Larry A. Tucker, Director of Health	801/378-4927
Bucks County Community College	Dr. Barry Sysler, Professor	215/968-8455
California State University	Sam J. Gitchel, Health Educator	209/278-2734
California State University	Nancy E. Shanfeld, Health Promotion Coordinator	818/885-3693
Capital University	Barbara A. Nash, Co-Director	614/236-6114
University of **Central Arkansas**	Dr. Arvil Burks, Department Chair	501/450-3191
Coastal Carolina College	Dr. Marshall E. Parker, Assistant Dean	803/349-2810
University of **Dayton**	Dr. Lloyd. L. Laubach, Wellness Program Director	513/229-4205
University of **Delaware**	Joyce L. Walter, Coordinator	302/457-8992
Delgado Community College	Jimmie R. Singleton, Director of Fitness Center	504/483-4255
Delta College	Sandy L. Wright, Health Service Director	504/483-4255
Dickinson College	Dr. Judith M. Vorio, Director, Truly Living Program	717/245-1525
East Los Angeles College	Dr. Sharon Deny, WPE Department Chair	213/265-8917
Eastern Montana College	Kamette C. Butterfield, Program Technician	406/657-2214
Elon College	Robert D. Pelley, Assistant Dean of Student Affairs	919/584-2218
Emporia State University	Dr. Darrell A. Lang, Director, Health Promotion	316/343-5929
Essex Community College	Thomas D. Kemp, Director, Health Fitness Lab	301/522-1415
Fayetteville State University	Dr. Nosa O'Bannor, Assistant Professor	919/486-1524, 1115
Fort Valley State College	Gwendolyn D. Reeves, Wellness Coordinator	912/825-9207
Gateway Community College	Sue Butler, Fitness Coordinator	Phoenix, AZ 85034
Georgia Insitute of Technology	Jami L. Fraze, Director, Wellness Center	404/853-0074
Georgia Southern University	Dr. Jerry E. Lafferty, Dean, Health & Prof. Stu.	912/681-5322
University of **Georgia**	Dr. Harry P. Duval, Associate Professor	404/542-4395
Gordon College	Dr. Peter W. Iltis, Associate Professor	508/927-2300, 4324
Goshen College	Willard S. Krabill, Director of Student Health	219/535-7474
Goucher College	Sally J. Baum, Assoc. Dir., Phys. Ed. Wellness Co.	301/337-6383
Hanover College	William D. Tereshko, Department Chairman	812/866-7375
Henderson University	Dr. Tom E. Ward, Associate Professor	501/246-5511, 3552
Hope College	Donna S. Eaton, Director, Health Dynamics	616/394-7693
Jacksonville State University	Dr. John B. Hammett, Coordinator, Wellness Center	205/782-5114
James Madison University	Nancy O. Grembi, Assistant Director	703/568-6177
Kalamazoo Valley Community Coll.	Allan R. Thompson, Department Chair	616/372-5392
Kennesaw State College	Susan O. Bulter, Wellness Coordinator	401/423-6394
Lake Michigan College	Donald E. Alsbro, Instructor	616/927-3571, X330
Lane Community College	Sandra L. Ing, Director, Special Student Svcs	503/747-4501, 2666
University of **Maine** - Farmington	Wendy Young, Head Housing	207/778-7050
University of **Maine**	Donna L. Duley, P.E. Lecturer, Women's Coach	207/255-3313, X352

Memphis State University	Dr. David J. Anspaugh, Professor, Division Head	901/678-2323
Millersville University	Dr. William V. Kahler, Chairperson	717/872-3674
Missouri Southern State College	Charles M. Conklin, Faculty Wellness Coordinator	417/625-9713
Montana State University	Dr. Gary F. Evans, Director of Employee Wellness	406/994-4001
University of **Montevallo**	Dr. J. W. Tishler, Professor of Health & P. E.	205/665-6587
Montgomery College	Karen M. Thomas, Assistant Professor	301/251-7582
Muhlenberg College	Connie R. Kunda, Wellness Director	215/821-3393
Murray State University	Dr. Pamela L Rice, Associate Professor	502/762-6826
Northeast Louisiana University	Dr. Luke E. Thomas, Professor	318/342-1310
University of **Northern Iowa**	Kathy M. Gulick, Director, Wellness Promo. Prog.	319/273-6921
Northern Kentucky University	Wiley T. Piazza, Wellness Coordinator	606/572-5684
Northern Michigan University	Dr. Harvey A. Wallace, CHES, Coor. HL Ed.	906/227-1135
Northwestern College	Ev Otten, Director of Health Services	712/737-7288
University of **Richmond**	Carol Johnson, Director of Wellness	804/289-8404
Rockford College	Cecil Bristol, Director of Health	815/226-4118
Ursuline College	Denise Keary, Program Coordinator	216/646-8315
Western New Mexico University	Dr. Mary Cowan, Department Chair	505/538-6216
University of **Wisconsin**/Superior	Dr. Barbara P. Hamann, Program Coord., Health	715/394-8273
University of **Wyoming**	Annette K. Tommerdahl, Director, Cardiac Rehab	307/766-5423

APPENDIX E

A Simplified Timetable and Checklist for Seniors Planning on College*

SEPTEMBER - OCTOBER	Write for college catalogs, applications, financial aid information and pick up a financial aid booklet.
SEPTEMBER - OCTOBER	Inquire at your high school Guidance Office about upcoming college nights.
SEPTEMBER - NOVEMBER	Continue campus visits as senior year academic commitments permit.
SEPTEMBER	Deadline for mailing in the late October or early November National College Exam Forms.
OCTOBER	Think about which two teachers you will ask to write college recommendations for you.
LATE OCTOBER	Deadline for mailing in the December National College Exam Forms.
NOVEMBER	Prepare a final list of colleges. Talk to your counselor about need-based funds. And look into merit-based money awarded by the colleges themselves. Talk to your counselor and/or a favorite teacher - show them your completed college essay, if your colleges require one.
NOVEMBER 1-15	Many early applications due.
NOVEMBER OR DECEMBER	Attend, with your parents, a local financial aid night given by an area high school.
NOVEMBER - DECEMBER	Apply to colleges.
EARLY DECEMBER	Last call for mailing in the National College Exam Forms (SAT/ACT).
DECEMBER 15	Profile of Financial Aid Form (Step 1) due to College Scholarship Service (CSS).
JANUARY	Fill out the Financial Aid Form (FAF/FAFSA/PROFILE) or Family Financial Statement. Your counselor has it. This form will probably help you get a good deal of your total scholarships, jobs, and loans. It is the big one.
JANUARY - FEBRUARY	Send mid-year reports to colleges.
FEBRUARY 1	Profile application (Step 2) to College Scholarship Service (CSS).
MARCH	Local scholarship forms available in the guidance office.
EARLY APRIL	All colleges will notify you by this time if they will accept you or not. The more competitive colleges usually deliberate longer and many of these top schools wait until the first week of April to notify you.
MID-APRIL	If unhappy with the financial aid package at any of the colleges where you have been accepted, call that office and discuss it.
LATE APRIL	Send deposit to selected college.
MAY 1	Inform all colleges which accepted you whether or not you plan to attend.
MAY 1	Notify Guidance Office of your choice of college.
MAY - JUNE	Apply for summer jobs so that you can meet summer earnings expectations. Don't forget to graduate from high school!
SUMMER	Attend college orientation.

*NOTE: Before your senior year, prepare preliminary list of colleges you're interested in and those you would like to visit. Spring visits in the junior year are advised.

APPENDIX F

The Get-Going Form

A simple, useful form to use with the college-bound to get them started applying to colleges.
The student and/or counselor and/or parent should fill in four colleges below,
complete with address and zip codes.

Dear Student:

Within the next two weeks, please write to the Director of Admissions at the schools listed below, requesting information. A sample letter is included at the bottom of the page.

1. _____
   _____
   _____

2. _____
   _____
   _____

3. _____
   _____
   _____

4. _____
   _____
   _____

SAMPLE LETTER

Date

Director of Admissions
Name of College
Address of College and Zip Code

Dear Director:

I am a student of Easthampton High School in Easthampton, Massachusetts and expect to graduate in June, 2001.

I am interested in your school and would appreciate your sending me an application for admission and information concerning your financial aid program, and your _____ program of studies. Thank you.

Very truly yours,

Your signature
Your Name
Your Address and Zip Code

COUNSELOR'S NOTES

COUNSELOR'S NOTES

COUNSELOR'S NOTES

COUNSELOR'S NOTES

ABOUT THE AUTHOR

Fred E. Rugg

FRED E. RUGG has travelled down more paths and paid more dues than any other college guidebook author. He is a writer, speaker, workshop presenter, and conducts executive and counselor searches for secondary schools. Unlike virtually all other college guidebook people, Rugg is one of the *true* professionals, having directed secondary college counseling programs for 20 years in all types of communities. A 1967 Applied Math graduate from Brown, Rugg is the holder of advanced degrees in secondary school guidance and administration. Early in his career he was employed as a statistician for two New England companies and worked his way through Ivy League Brown - the only member of his class to enter public school teaching. Offering dozens of workshops yearly from coast to coast, Fred is an often animated, charismatic and humorous speaker, and is the only one giving monthly seminars who draws a crowd. In addition, he is a consultant to dozens of secondary schools and his evening speaking engagements for parents and students are popular and fun. He has lived and worked just about everywhere in America, has been married for 30 years, and has two daughters. Rugg is also a volunteer basketball coach in his town, and he's taught courses at four colleges. A native of New England, he has been based in Colorado and Florida, and now resides in California. As always, he is totally independent of the colleges.

RUGG'S PROMISE TO PARENTS

Prepare one to five questions on the colleges and/or the admission process that you really need the answers to. Send the questions with a check for $100.⁰⁰ made out to "Rugg's Promise to Parents". Mail it to the address below and include your telephone numbers. Within 24 hours of receipt, Fred Rugg will personally call you and answer your questions. That's a promise. As a parent in Tempe, Arizona says, "As always, your wise advice is priceless!"

✂ **PLEASE CLIP AND MAIL TO:** ✂

Rugg's Recommendations • Box 417 • Fallbrook, CA 92088

Please send me _____ copies of *Rugg's Recommendations on the Colleges* at $21.95 (plus shipping/see page 188) each.

I have enclosed my check in the amount of $_____

Name _____   _____

Address _____

City _____ State _____ Zip _____

For additional information call 760-728-4467 or 760-728-4558.
Other products and resources from Rugg's appear on pages 186-187.

FROM RUGG'S RECOMMENDATIONS...

INFORMATION THAT IS TO THE POINT, THAT YOU CAN USE IMMEDIATELY

Saving the college counselor enormous time with lists and answers found nowhere else - presented from the secondary school point of view!

FROM RUGG, YOU ALWAYS GET A NEW SLANT ON THE COLLEGES

---

1. THE NEW BOOK: *RUGG'S RECOMMENDATIONS ON THE COLLEGES 18th Ed.*
Locating Quality Undergraduate Colleges For Counselors, Parents & Students.
ISBN #1-883062-38-1 • LC89-062896 • $21.95 • © 2001 by Frederick E. Rugg
★ Over 1000 Entry Changes in the New GRAY Book★

Rugg's Recommendations on the Colleges enters its 3rd decade recommending quality departments at quality colleges. It is the primary brainstorming source for secondary public school counselors in creating a student's initial college list. Rugg's 18th edition is available listing 7000 quality departments at 900 quality colleges. The guidebook has been designated nationally as "a revered staple, the book parents and students must start with" in the search for a college to attend. The 18th edition is the accumulation of 30 years of work in the undergraduate college admissions process, and as always, *Rugg's* is independent of the colleges. There are over 1000 entry changes since the 17th edition, 87 majors, 118 recommended departments per major.

"A Revered Staple."
—West Coast Library Reviewer

"Your book is the foundation for my college counseling practice"
—George Gibbs, Gibbs & Wall Educational Consultants, Allentown, PA

"A gem."
—College Bound, Evanston, Illinois

"As always, your wise advice is priceless!"
—Pat Foster, parent Tempe, AZ

---

2. THE SPECIAL REPORT: *TWENTY MORE TIPS ON THE COLLEGES, Revised*
Twenty new behind the scenes tips. Ideal for counselors, parents, and students. 7th Edition.
ISBN #1-883062-43-8 • $8.95 • © 2001

Brutally honest information about colleges and the application process. This Special Report, *Twenty More Tips on the Colleges*, offers insights into assessing a college or university from the first "hello." Author Rugg succinctly presents 20 key tips to assist counselors, parents and students in selecting the best college for a student. Rugg honestly assesses the value of several college rating and reference books. Tips include colleges with high success rates for medical school acceptance, and what to consider before deciding to attend a military school. Overlooked state institutions, as well as other important and helpful comments, are included. The college search and selection process is incomplete without reading the valuable information contained within this Special Report.

"Brutally honest."
—The College Choice Report

"I can talk to some students and parents until I'm blue in the face, and they don't seem to listen. But if it's written by Fred Rugg, they accept it. And that's only one reason why I buy his special reports."
—Guidance Counselor, State College, PA

"I have used your information for years. It is a wonderful resource."
—Harriet Gershman, Academic Counseling Services, Evanston, IL

---

3. *FORTY TIPS ON THE COLLEGES :* THE REVISED SPECIAL REPORT *7th edition*
For all college bound students, parents, and their counselors. 20 pages. Over 35 college entry changes for 2001.
ISBN # 1-883062-40-3 • $9.95 (money back guarantee) • Revised 2001

Get the "insider's" advice on college admissions. In *Forty Tips on the Colleges*, author Rugg shares with the reader 40 key tips on the college admissions process. Rugg spent in excess of 2000 hours visiting with over 6000 secondary school counselors in 42 states, to compile the information contained in this transcript. These insightful suggestions provide the reader with some of the unwritten do's and don'ts in the college admissions process. Rugg presents his 40 tips, accompanied by his personal observations of the campuses, with honesty and a sense of humor. *Forty Tips on the Colleges* offers straight talk about selecting a college and gaining admission. The transcript contains helpful advice for the student, parent and school counselor alike. Topics include previously unpublished tips on which colleges really care about their students; colleges with good learning disabilities programs; and how to choose a college where the student "fits in." The tips also contain helpful information concerning financial aid, college applications and SAT/ACT scores. Throughout this transcript, Rugg cites several helpful reference books. This ***must read*** is our most popular special report.

"After attending Fred's workshop in Bar Harbor, Maine, I was very eager to buy his special report, 40 Tips on the Colleges. This report is as 'on-target' as his workshop. I've used the report in English classes with juniors, in parent meetings, and in faculty meetings. Each time the response has been overwhelmingly positive. 'Finally, someone is telling it as it is!' is a common response. No glossy advertising or slick words, just honest, accurate information".
—Beulah J. Grant, Dean of Students, George Stevens Academy, Blue Hill, ME

---

4. THE SPECIAL REPORT: *THIRTY QUESTIONS ON THE COLLEGES, Revised 7th Edition*
For all college bound students, parents and their counselors. 27 pages.
ISBN # 1-883062-41-1 • $9.95 • Revised 2001 • Over 35 college entry changes

Thirty frequently asked questions with some answers even Deans of Admissions can't give you. This Special Report includes: The state university all others should visit and copy • 125 recommended colleges where black youngsters will maximize their education • What makes individuals happy at college? • Community college graduates – how do top colleges really view them at transfer time? • The best of the best journalism schools • Understanding student body make-up • Engineering schools – how to choose them and the best bets around the USA. And 22 other topics based on over 150 counselor meetings across the country. Counselors and parents find this transcript form extremely useful (yes, it's O.K. to copy it with appropriate acknowledgement).

""When I attended the college admissions institute this past summer, all of the private H.S. counselors and Ivy School directors of admission said that Rugg's work was the best."
—Colorado Public Secondary School Counselor

5. **SPECIAL REPORT:** *FINANCIAL AID IN LESS THAN 3000 WORDS, REVISED*
ISBN #1-883062-42-X • $6.95 • **Completely Revised 2001** • **7th Edition**

From his 30 years studying the college admissions process, Rugg has boiled down the financial aid game in this special 5-page report. Find out why several U.S. publishers offered big money to buy this transcript outright. Takes the counselor and parent step-by-step through the aid process, with authentic examples of awards and family situations of present college frosh. This special report closes with 12 revised tips on financial aid for counselors, parents, and students that Rugg has put together from hundreds of meetings with counselors and parents around the country.

Especially for parents and counselors— gets Financial Aid off the Counselor's back.

"Rugg is the only critic who has been in the trenches, worked the cities, lived all over, and has the network and the contacts in place."
—Vern Vargas, College Counselor, Moreau H.S., Hayward, CA.

6. *THIRTY SEMINAR SHEETS* $25

Our most popular lists are now available separately. Includes all of the rankings in #7 below, plus colleges where the following youngsters maximize their education: Jewish (125), Hispanic (125), Asian (70), and Black (150). *Call us for a sample—5 sheets for $5.*

"I use Rugg's material and wit all over the place."
—Dr. John Dromgoole, College Search, Concord, MA

7. *THE COLLEGE SEMINAR SUBSTITUTE*
For Secondary School Counselors, public and private • *$55 (lists updated monthly)*

Can't make it to a college seminar? Do the next best thing: Order this special package. *The College Seminar Substitute* provides you with 96% of the 60 items covered in our seminar agenda. In this package you receive Rugg's four Special Reports, *Twenty More Tips on the Colleges, Forty Tips on the Colleges, Thirty Questions and Answers, Financial Aid In Less Than 3000 Words,* plus 30 seminar handouts. These handouts contain over 1400 entries—a wealth of information. Topics covered include: a listing of safe campuses, college guidebook ratings, up-and-coming colleges; snob schools; prestigious school rankings; underrated schools, the top 160 schools for the learning disabled, the most generous schools, new information on financial aid; advice on school recommendations; a listing of intense (rigorous) schools; big colleges that play small; rated Catholic colleges; and four minority lists. This package gives the counselor a foundation in understanding and navigating the admission game. See why over 6000 secondary school counselors have attended Rugg's College Admission Seminars.

"It is the best single source of information that we have. It answers the questions most frequently asked by parents. Your college materials help both the beginning and experienced counselor. The various ratings and lists inspire both students and their parents to further research the college scene. When parents and students are clueless, your information provides direction and humor in beginning the college selection process."
—Ira Lipton, Counselor, East Hampton (NY) High School

8. **SPECIAL!** *SEND IT ALL!* $70

Includes 1 book, 4 special reports, 30 seminar sheets—all our products.

"What a wonderful surprise to get the mail today and find your most valuable update. Believe me, I study them and treasure them."
—Fran Fisher, Educational Consultant, Muskegon, MI

➡ **ORDER FORM ON REVERSE**

THE 2001 RUGG COLLEGE ADMISSION SEMINAR SCHEDULE (Most seminars are on Fridays)	La Jolla, CA March 2, 2001	Boston, MA May 11, 2001	Chicago, IL September 28, 2001
	San Francisco, CA March 23, 2001	New York (Rye), NY June 28, 2001	E. Hanover, N.J. October 26, 2001
	Philadelphia, PA April 27, 2001	Columbus, OH August 9, 2001	

For more information: Call or write for a brochure; e-mail us at frugg@thegrid.net; or visit our Website at http://www.thegrid.net/frugg

2001 PRODUCT ORDER FORM

ITEM #	TITLE OR DESCRIPTION	PRICE	QTY	AMOUNT
1	*Rugg's Recommendations on the Colleges:* The Book (18th ed.)	$21.95		
2	*20 More Tips on the Colleges:* Revised Special Report (7th ed.)	$ 8.95		
3	*Forty Tips on the Colleges:* Revised Special Report (7th ed.)	$ 9.95		
4	*Thirty Questions & Answers:* Revised Special Report (7th ed.)	$ 9.95		
5	*Financial Aid in Less Than 3000 Words:* Revised Special Report (7th ed.)	$ 6.95		
6	*Thirty Seminar Sheets: Colleges*	$25.00		
7	*College Seminar Substitute:* Includes 2 thru 6	$55.00		
8	SEND IT ALL!!! Send one of each	$70.00		

Order 5 or more books: Only $20.00 each! Discount price available *only* on the *book*.

Prepaid Orders over $89: Subtract $4 from total.

International Orders: Shipping and handling cost: Actual Cost.

California Residents: Please add 7.75% sales tax.

SHIPPING CHARGES: (all orders mailed first class)
$ 0-15   Postage $2
$16-35   Postage $4
$36+   Postage $5

SUBTOTAL	
Less $4 for prepaid orders over $89	
Sales Tax (CA only) 7.75%	
Shipping	
TOTAL ENCLOSED	

Name _____

Address _____

City _____ State _____ Zip _____

Send to:
RUGG'S RECOMMENDATIONS
P.O. Box 417 • Fallbrook, CA 92088

For information on our 2001 COLLEGE ADMISSIONS SEMINARS, call us at 760-728-4558 or Fax 760-728-4467 OR visit our Website at http://www.thegrid.net/frugg